D0915905

⁄FEMICIDAL FEARS ⁄

Narratives of the Female Gothic Experience

Helene Meyers

State University of New York Press

Published by
State University of New York Press, Albany

Printed in the United States of America

For information, address State University of New York Press,
90 State Street, Suite 700, Albany, NY, 12207

Production by Christine L. Hamel
Marketing by Anne M. Valentine

Library of Congress Cataloging-in-Publication Data

Meyers, Helene.
    Femicidal fears: narratives of the female gothic experience /
by Helene Meyers.
        p. cm. — (SUNY series in feminist criticism and theory)
    Includes bibliographical references and index.
    ISBN 0-7914-5151-8 ISBN 0-7914-5152-6 (pbk)
    1. English fiction—20th century—History and criticism.
    2. Gothic revival (Literature)—Great Britain—History—20th
    century. 3. Feminism and literature—Great Britain—History—
    20th century. 4. Women and literature—Great Britain—
    History—20th century. 5. English fiction—Women authors—
    History and criticism. 6. American fiction—20th century—
    History and criticism. 7. Feminist fiction—History and
    criticism. 8. Horror tales—History and criticism. 9. Gothic
    revival (Literature). 10. Feminism and literature. 11. Women
    and literature. 12. Narration (Rhetoric). I. Title. II. Series.

PR888.T3 M49 2001
823'.0872093548—dc21   00-054734
                                                           CIP

10   9   8   7   6   5   4   3   2   1

Contents

Acknowledgments

This book and the debates that form its heart have been a part of my scholarly, teaching, and private life for many years now. It is a joy to acknowledge the support that I have received over the years.

I am profoundly grateful to the readers of my earliest work in feminist Gothic Studies: Pat Brantlinger, Don Gray, James Naremore, and especially Susan Gubar, a tough critic, a marvelous mentor, and an inspiring teacher. Walt Herbert also read early versions of this work; his comments and queries were enlightening and helpful. Both the English department and the women's studies program at Southwestern University have stimulated my Gothic imagination in a variety of ways. I especially want to acknowledge Jim Kilfoyle, Jan Dawson, and Shannon Winnubst for their fine minds and good hearts; conversations with these dear colleagues have sustained me in immeasurable ways. I am also grateful to Michael Rosenthal and Jim Hunt, administrators who have promoted the ideal of the scholar/teacher at Southwestern. Thanks also to the Brown Foundation and to the Cullen Faculty Development Fund for providing valuable time and research funds. The Clearinghouse on Femicide as well as the professional staff of the A. Frank Smith Jr. Library helped me to locate a variety of useful materials. My contemporary Gothic students over the years have affirmed that femicidal fictions are anything but deadly and that intellectual rigor and emotional engagement can co-exist in the academy. Their excitement and interest in the progress of this book have made me a happier and more productive professor and writer.

Readers for State University of New York Press provided insightful and encouraging commentary. I especially want to acknowledge Michelle Massé, whose attention to this manuscript was extraordinarily generous and helpful; Eugenia DeLamotte, whose careful reading made this a better book in a myriad of ways; and Anne Williams, whose support for my work has been unflagging. I also want to thank James Peltz for his careful shepherding of this project through the various stages of the evaluation and publication process; Katy Leonard and the numerous staff members at SUNY Press who have helped bring this volume to publication also have my sincere thanks.

Knowing the Gothic world as well as I do, I managed to project all my desires for protection onto Cessna, my Australian Shepherd. He has not disappointed. Lady, my lab mutt, is no watchdog, but I love her all the same. The love and laughter I share with my partner, Guy Raffa, have been wonderful counters to my Gothic preoccupations. Finally, I wish to remember my father, Alfred Meyers, whose independent spirit and passion for the law have become my own in unpredictable ways.

To Susan G. and Mary G.,
women who taught me to refuse to be a victim,
and in loving memory of my father, Alfred Meyers

Critical Femicide: A Polemical Preface

The polemics of this preface were born of some well-intentioned career advice offered by a senior colleague several years ago. As I was discussing my scholarly interests, which include both James Joyce and contemporary women writers, Professor Von X reminded me that Joyce is a big deal and that nobody really cares about Muriel Spark or Beryl Bainbridge. I should note that my Professor Von X, unlike Woolf's, is, in general, a sensitive male feminist critic, that he was giving me advice that he thought would promote me professionally, and that he responded respectfully and even positively to my spirited comeback that I had a responsibility to shape as well as be shaped by current trends in literary studies. With him, I outwardly performed the cockiness of a newly minted Ph.D.; inwardly, however, I experienced the retro tremble of Ann Radcliffe's Gothic heroines. This preface, as well as the main text of *Femicidal Fears*, constitutes continuing efforts to write through the Gothic, a literary site where fear of female annihilation is a plot convention. And it reflects my sense that, in 2000, writing about the difference women's literature makes requires some explanation, some rationalization, some justification or, perhaps more positively, simply some theoretical self-consciousness.

Susan Faludi has argued that backlash is most powerful and most destructive when it is internalized—"when it goes private, when it lodges inside a woman's mind and turns her vision inward, until she imagines the pressure is all in her head, until she begins to enforce the backlash, too—on herself" (xxii). Tania Modleski, in her *Feminism without Women*, argues that postfeminism is a particular form of backlash, in that "it has been carried out not *against* feminism but in its very name" (x). Here I want to explore a specific form of postfeminist backlash in literary studies—a discomfort with contemporary women writers who are not explicitly identified or who do not label themselves as feminists. This critical discomfort is perhaps not coincidentally occurring at a moment when feminist critics are still dancing around the minefield of essentialism. I would suggest that the flight from essentialism in literary studies paradoxically may endanger the continued charting of diversity in female literary traditions and return us to a phallic economy of sameness in more ways than one.

The category "woman" has been philosophically undermined with the best and the most sophisticated of feminist intentions. By reifying "Woman" or even "Women," feminist theory runs into the danger of reifying sexual difference itself, often the basis for diverse forms of patriarchal practice. The attack on the category "Woman" obviously has serious implications for the charting of female literary traditions, dependent as they are upon the woman writer. What Barbara Christian has termed "the race for theory," as well as the shift to gender studies,[1] has further eroded academic support for the study of women writers *qua* women writers—especially those not already canonized. Recovery work, seen as a crucial part of feminist literary studies in the '70s and '80s, has increasingly come to be considered passé and theoretically naive, not to mention professionally suicidal; indeed, many classic feminist works associated with Anglo-American gynocriticism, works that have enabled members of my generation to claim the identity of feminist literary critic, have been branded the product of essentialist and patriarchal epistemology by Toril Moi and company.

Jane Roland Martin has recently sketched a critical double standard in feminist theory, one that excoriates female feminist scholars who are suspected essentialists and one that "look[s] tolerantly upon the gravest mistakes and omissions of a Michel, a Jacques, a Jean-Francois" (I would add a Sigmund to her list). Indeed, Roland Martin argues that we "need to do some soul-searching . . . about the discrepancy between our cordial treatment of the men's theories and our punitive approach to the women's" (651). Such critical double standards seem to apply not only to theorists but also to creative writers. Given such scholarly developments, those of us who work in the field of contemporary fiction worry about how many women writing today will survive this postfeminist age. In *Changing the Story*, Gayle Greene asserts that her project is "motivated by a pragmatic concern—to draw attention to major women writers so that they have a better chance of surviving. For they are an endangered species" (25). The Modern Library's recent list of the one hundred "greatest" novels of the twentieth century, which includes eight women, provides further evidence for Greene's concern.

Yet those of us who have come of age in the age of theory think that it is crucial to interrogate our conservation strategies. Greene's strategy—brilliantly executed—is to chart the rise and fall of a self-consciously feminist metafictional tradition. By charting this tradition, Greene simultaneously inscribes select women writers as postmodernist writers *and* evades the charge of essentialism—after all, what brings these writers together is their politics and their aesthetic strategies, not their anatomy. Significantly, the act of saving the feminist writer who writes about feminist writing is also an act of self-preservation, for what is the feminist writer who writes about feminist writing if not a feminist critic?

However, despite the political and intellectual savvy of such maneuvers, significant problems of exclusion result from constructing a canon in the image of the feminist postmodernist. Those writers who do not conform to the metafictional standards Greene has set for this project are not included; similarly, she leaves out a host of notable women writers whom she designates as nonfeminist.

Theoretically, this return to a feminist literary economy of sameness is troubling. It becomes even more so when we consider the context of literary studies today: the rise of gender studies means that canonical male writers are once again a significant focus of feminist critics. Shakespearean gender bending, the negotiations of gender conflict in the works of Hawthorne, and the proffering of James Joyce as a prototypical feminist are par for the course these days at MLA. I want to be very clear here—I am not suggesting that such developments are necessarily bad or antifeminist. Indeed, feminist literary criticism has a long tradition of exploring the work of male writers, and I am by no means arguing that the field should be a women's room. However, I am troubled that as we embrace canonical male figures and argue the feminist potential of their work, we hesitate to do the same for noncanonized women writers. Given that Judith Butler and other poststructuralists have argued convincingly that there is no utopian elsewhere, we should not be too quick to foreclose potential sources of gender trouble, "the possibilities that emerge when the law turns against itself and spawns unexpected permutations of itself" (Butler, *Gender*, 93).

Femicidal Fears argues that contemporary female-authored femicidal plots—plots in which women are killed or fear for their lives—constitute possibilities for understanding and intervening in the vexed and sometimes acrimonious feminist debates about victimology, essentialism, female agency, and the female body that have proliferated in recent years. As Elaine Showalter notes, feminist critics have spent more time charting female Gothic traditions based on "narratives of maternity, madness, or the grotesque" and less on the strand of the contemporary female Gothic centered on violent crime in general and murder in particular (139). At first glance, such critical trends would seem to be the result of feminist common sense. Mad, maternal, and grotesque female bodies would seem to have subversive feminist potential that dead female bodies lack. Moreover, some of these femicidal texts are written by women whose feminist credentials are nonexistent or suspect (indeed, texts by three of the writers whom Greene explicitly identifies as "major" but "not feminist"—Muriel Spark, Beryl Bainbridge, and Joyce Carol Oates—provide key moments for this study).[2] However, *Femicidal Fears* argues that this strand of the contemporary female Gothic explores the difficulties of, and the necessity for, taking gender oppression seriously without positioning women as pure victims. The Gothic, with its aesthetic links to both realism and postmodernism and its thematic emphasis on violence against women, becomes a site to negotiate between the scripts of "male vice and female virtue" associated with cultural feminism and the "gender skepticism"[3] associated with much poststructuralist criticism.

Several chapters of this book are devoted to close readings of literary texts, not only because I value the words of women but also because I think these texts show how and why seemingly abstract and abstruse feminist debates matter. My students are always surprised to discover that these novels of death bring the nuances of feminist thought to life. I hope that my readers will find the Gothic narrative I have woven similarly enlivening.

Chapter 1

Introduction: Feminist Gothic/Gothic Feminism

In Edna O'Brien's *Casualties of Peace*, one chapter begins with this news report: "A dentist suspecting that his wife had left him . . . followed [her] to the airport and murdered her" (52). N., the protagonist of Diane Johnson's *The Shadow Knows*, reads in the morning newspaper, "Agriculture prof. kills wife, tots, self" (34). Reflecting upon her recent mastectomy, Rennie of Margaret Atwood's *Bodily Harm* decides that "she disliked the idea of being buried one piece at a time instead of all at once, it was too much like those women they were always finding strewn about ravines or scattered here and there in green garbage bags" (23). As these fictional appropriations of "news" demonstrate, femicide—the killing of women—is a cultural convention.[1] For feminist critics concerned about violence against women, the challenge is to analyze cultural formations that underwrite femicide without essentializing women as victims. "This above all, to refuse to be a victim. Unless I can do that I can do nothing. I have to recant, give up the old belief that I am powerless and because of it nothing I can do will ever hurt anyone." The protagonist of Margaret Atwood's *Surfacing* reaches this conclusion (229). Yet as Atwood points out in an interview with Jan Garden Castro, such refusal is not easily or automatically accomplished: "It's all very well to say I refuse to be a victim, but then you have to look at the context in which one is or isn't a victim. You can't simply refuse. You can refuse to define yourself that way, but it's not quite so simple as that" (219). Popular discourses about a chimerical "victim feminism" belie the difficulties of

1

such a refusal; indeed, the culture writ large suggests that women simply say no to violence *and* feminism. However, the often acrimonious debates about essentialism and agency that have consumed feminist theoreticians for the past decade and a half attest to Atwood's disavowal of simplicity.

Feminist debates on violence against women center on the sometimes vexed relationship between the literal, fear-inspiring violation of female bodies and the theoretical status and limits of the female subject. The Gothic—defined here at its most generalized level as encounters with otherness, often violent transgression of boundaries, and the excess of fear that such encounters and transgressions breed—offers a novel and novelistic lens for negotiating the minefield of contemporary discourses about female victimization. Ultimately, *Femicidal Fears: Narratives of the Female Gothic Experience* uses contemporary femicidal plots to weave a story of the necessity for, and the difficulties of, refusing to be a victim. The shifting relationship between feminism and Gothicism in popular, theoretical, and literary imaginations constitutes the skeleton of this story.

ざ   ざ   ざ

On December 6, 1989, Marc Lépine entered the Polytechnique, the University of Montreal's school of engineering, with a hunting rifle.[2] By the end of his rampage, fourteen women were dead. Both his behavior during the siege and the suicide note that he left make it clear that the gendering of his victims was intended. When he first entered the school, he divided the people he found into groups by sex, shouting that he wanted to kill all the "fucking feminists" and that he "wanted the women." One man who gestured for mercy was spared; a women who proclaimed that she was not a feminist was slain. In his suicide note, Lépine wrote, "Because I have decided to send the feminists, who have always ruined my life, to their Maker. For seven years life has brought me no joy and being totally blase, I have decided to put an end to those viragos." To the end of his suicide note, he added a "hit list": the names of nineteen prominent women.

The acts of Marc Lépine were horrifying enough; however, initial reactions to the event perpetuated the horror. Bourassa, then premier of Quebec, publicly stated that this was "not a matter of deliberate acts of violence." After deleting the names of policewomen from the hit list, the police released it to the press, who published the list as well as photos of these women, thus potentially endangering them if someone decided to finish Marc Lépine's work for him. Lépine's best friend noted that Lépine often performed acts of verbal misogyny; however, such behavior did not seem particularly noteworthy when it occurred. A poll conducted at the end of December 1989 revealed that a majority of Canadians saw Lépine's mass murder of women as the random, isolated act of a madman, one that had nothing to do with societal patterns of violence against women. Mordechai Richler, a Canadian novelist, argued the inexplicability of the tragedy: "I don't think it lends itself to any explanation. . . . it shows that we're all vulnerable to madmen." Quebec's minister of the Status of Women, Violette Trepanier, also argued against any structural analysis of the event, preferring the lone madman reading. Telephone hotlines were set up to deal with the collective trauma caused by the event; one group of callers were men who felt that Lépine's acts stimulated their own women-hating impulses. In a twelfth grade electronics class, Lépine's crimes were reenacted with a water pistol used against the one woman in the class. Women who organized vigils for those slain received threats. At one vigil organized at the University of Montreal, a male student leader vociferously argued against gendered interpretations of the massacre.

A significant segment of the population and the media replicated Lépine's hostility toward feminism. Charlene Nero, a feminist student activist interviewed by the media, was stopped by a man who recognized her from the interview. According to her, he said, "You're the ones who deserved it. It's too bad those fourteen girls got killed and not you." Talk radio programs were inundated with calls that justified Lépine's sentiments though not his actions. In an editorial entitled "Overreacting," Ontario's Thunder Bay *Chronicle-Journal* suggested that "the gunman's rage was directed not at women in general but at the feminist movement in particular, perhaps *at its most strident aspects*" (my emphasis). Marcel Adam, an editorialist for *Le Presse*, wrote, "Feminism has provoked many acts of violence against women, especially in the U.S." (qtd. in Dufresne 10). Feminists who argued for a gender analysis of the slayings were accused of exploiting the tragedy for their own movement and of endangering other women; officials assumed that feminist rhetoric would provoke copycat violence. A few days after the massacre, a New York talk show, *Nine Broadcast Plaza*, ran a segment entitled "Have Feminists Pushed Men over the Brink?" Indeed, for some, an affirmative answer to that question provided the key to this macabre event. Ross Virgin, leader of In Search of Justice, a men's rights group, argued that feminist antimale sentiment was to blame for the massacre. As he put it, "I'm very annoyed, angry, and frustrated with the anti-male hatred that abounds, and though we do not endorse the shooting, we can understand why it happens.... We are not pleased that this man expressed his frustration by shooting but the anti-male hatred creates that kind of rage." In a logical sleight of hand, feminism was to blame for the murder of fourteen women who were presumptuous enough to be engineering students. However, the Montreal massacre is not an isolated case; according to many popular and academic accounts, feminists do not report the Gothic experiences of women but rather create them.

This trend is aptly summarized by a George Will column entitled "Gothic Feminism Creates Victims." This column lauds Katie Roiphe's *The Morning After: Sex, Fear and Feminism on Campus*. Roiphe argues that the "image that emerges from feminist preoccupation with rape and sexual harassment is that of women as victims" (6). Given that Roiphe doesn't personally know that many rape victims, she doesn't believe in the so-called rape crisis; rather, she worries that young women walking on campuses with a blue light security system will "learn vulnerability and lurking dangers in the bushes" (28). Indeed, Roiphe, a doctoral student in English when she wrote the book and thus well-schooled in the power of discourse, rightly notes that naming problems such as date rape and sexual harassment is an act of "interpreting everyday experience" (109). However, interpretation and causation quickly become conflated: "To create awareness is sometimes to create a problem" (110). However, later in the book, such sophisticated perspectives on the power of discourse disappear in a fit of common sense: "Myself, I've never been able to understand how the 'backlash against women,' that mysterious force lumbering through our consciousness, can actually 'construct' anything" (122). Ultimately, for Roiphe, the gift that feminism has given her generation is a "new stock plot, a new identity spinning not around love, not marriage, not communes, not materialism this time, but passivity and victimhood" (172).

Indeed, this reading of feminism has become so familiar that it threatens to become a stock plot itself. Christina Hoff Sommers uses the title of her 1994 volume to ask the provocative question: "Who stole feminism?" The answer, contained in her subtitle and elaborated in her book, is clear: "How women have betrayed women." According to Sommers, "gender feminists" are those who believe that a patriarchal sex/gender system exists and that cultural institutions "perpetuate male dominance" (16); such beliefs betray the mighty and respectable legacy of liberal or equality feminism. These new feminists who belie the name of the movement they purportedly represent "see revelations of monstrosity in the most familiar and seemingly innocuous phenomena" (27). Sommers continues, "The 'gender war' requires a constant flow of horror stories showing women that male perfidy and female humiliation are everywhere" (28). Gender feminists betray the foremothers of the liberal feminist movement, those women of Seneca Falls whose "aims . . . were . . . finite." Moreover, Sommers accuses feminists of projecting their war onto men: "There is no radical militant wing of a masculinist movement. To the extent that one can speak at all of a gender war, it is the New Feminists themselves who are waging it" (45). Like Roiphe, Sommers is repelled by feminist commentary on rape: "To view rape as a crime of gender bias (encouraged by a patriarchy that looks with tolerance on the victimization of women) is perversely to miss its true nature" (225). For Sommers, perversity, excess, and violence mark gender feminists; as writers of Gothic fictions, they become Gothic villains and Gothic bodies who will not be contained.

Significantly, Sommers suggests that gender feminists are applied Foucaultians, an irony considering the often productive but omnipresent tensions that have marked the relationship between poststructuralism and feminism in general (I address these tensions in more detail in chapters 7 and 8), and Foucault and feminism in particular. Thus Sommers, like Roiphe, seems to have an agenda that is antipoststructuralist.[3]

According to Rene Denfeld and the title of her book, feminists are *The New Victorians* whose "antimale sentiment" (Denfeld and Ross Virgin have much in common) has promoted a "victim mythology," which keeps "the woman revered on the pedestal, charged with keeping society's moral order yet politically powerless—and perpetually martyred" (16–17). Denfeld's description suggests the classic position of the Gothic heroine, whose only means of "self defense," as Eugenia DeLamotte has noted, is that of "self-worth." Like many of the commentators on the Montreal massacre, Denfeld assumes that Gothic plots originate with feminists; according to her, victim mythology is "a feminist mythology in which a singular female subject is *created*: woman as a helpless, violated, and oppressed victim. Victim mythology says that men will always be predators and women will always be their prey" (61–62, my emphasis). The new Victorians' return to femininity "has turned the movement from inclusive equality" (217); however, Denfeld's claim that the feminist movement has overprioritized lesbians (40–41) suggests the limits of her inclusive and egalitarian impulses. Like Sommers, Denfeld emphasizes individuality and positions the New Victorians as the enemies of equality feminism: "In the end, it doesn't matter if inequality comes from Victorians who call themselves the religious right or Victorians who call themselves feminists" (277). Whether the analogue of Marc Lépine or Jerry Falwell, gender feminists are purported to be women's worst nightmare.

Joining in this chorus of liberal individualism and Gothic feminism, Daphne Patai and Noretta Koertge claim that academic feminists have gone wrong because they have not upheld "fundamental liberal ideas: tolerance, the cultivation of a distanced and disengaged analysis, and a degree of skepticism toward one's own positions" (212). According to Patai and Koertge, the current state of women's studies has the potential to open a "chamber of horrors" akin to atrocities of the past, including "the Aryan university of Nazi Germany" (214–15). Thus these writers legitimate Rush Limbaugh's tirades against feminazis. Uncontested, feminists will visit Gothic horrors upon our democratic culture as they encourage students to become "fundamentalists" who "use their small store of fixed ideas to build walls around their tiny enclaves, not realizing that within these walls they themselves must live as prisoners" (215). Thus feminists have become the architects of Gothic castles in which women are imprisoned.

Naomi Wolf, one of the more thoughtful popular critics of feminism, strives to distinguish between "power feminism" and "victim feminism." Wolf's insistence on, and reproduction of, the misnomer "victim feminism" is problematic, and at moments her self-confessed "highly subjective" rendering of this supposed phenomenon reads more like parody than serious cultural analysis (136–37). Nevertheless, Wolf evinces an appreciation for the complexity of feminist theory and the ways in which it has often been misinterpreted and/or oversimplified. Unlike the other critics cited here, she is not resistant to structural analysis of gender oppression, and she is appalled that "victim culture critics" retreat from material evidence of female victimization and claim that the victim complex is a figment of feminists' imaginations. Her concern, one that I share, is that discussions of female victimization not foreclose or diminish women's sense of their own power and agency. Significantly, however, she too associates feminist thought with a penchant for Gothic horror: "Much feminist discourse is unrelievedly grim; waking up to feminism includes a certain pride in being able to stare unflinchingly at the 'horror, the horror' of it all. Horrifying the world of sexism truly is, but this sometimes monolithic focus on the dire . . . leads straight to burnout" (213). Wolf's agenda then is not to deny the feminist Gothic but to assess its effects upon women's psyches and the movement as a whole.

Like Wolf, Wendy Kaminer is aware of "thoughtful feminist debates being conducted in academia"; nevertheless, she readily uses and accepts such terminology as "feminist victimism." According to Kaminer, feminist "orthodoxy about victimization" is unabated by a "sense of black humor" (68). Kaminer and Wolf may be so quick to adopt such Gothic-inflected readings of feminism because of, rather than despite, their knowledge of thoughtful academic debates. Indeed, academic scholarship often uncannily reflects the demonization of gender feminists, though in feminist theoretical circles, the subgenre of gender feminists most often vilified are those labeled "cultural feminists" or, even less precisely, "essentialists." Paradoxically, antagonism toward scholarly and political uses of gender as an analytic category often joins Sommers, Roiphe, and Denfeld to those feminist Foucauldian multicultural poststructuralists that they love to hate. In other words, poststructuralism and liberal individualism often meet at the intersection of Gothic feminism.[4]

The rise of what Susan Bordo has termed "gender skepticism" has a complex history and, as I have begun to chart here, serves a number of different interests. Poststructuralist thought, most often derived from the work of Jacques Derrida, Jacques Lacan, and Michel Foucault, has put into question the Enlightenment notion of the rational, essential, unified, autonomous liberal subject. In his place—and that subject was conceptually always a "he"—is the fragmented subject whose body is the site of competing cultural discourses; thus the fiction of unity becomes an exercise of power. Through this lens, gender—and more specifically the category "woman" and even "women"—becomes a fiction like any other; those who not only claim that "woman" exists and propose to work on her behalf but also posit a power system based on gender, namely, patriarchy, are power brokers like any other—phallogocentric power brokers, to boot, given that the promotion of such unitary fictions is consonant with the Western metaphysic that underwrites hierarchical models of domination. The resistance to such consolidations of power lies in destabilization; hence the emphasis on polyvocality, contradiction, and undecidability. Resistance, deconstruction, and critique become favored strategies because they oppose unifying fictions, while generalization is increasingly viewed as a suspect practice.

Given such intellectual developments, feminists paradoxically and perversely came to be seen as policewomen for patriarchy, the upholders of gender law rather than those who make gender trouble. By keeping "women" in play as privileged subjects, feminists were accused of reifying sexual difference, often read as sexual opposition, the basis for diverse forms of patriarchal practice and gender oppression. By describing the world in the binary terms *male* and *female, masculine* and *feminine,* feminists were sleeping with the enemy—binary oppositions—and were sure to replicate the oppressive structures of Western metaphysics.[5] Mounting evidence that feminist fictions tended to reproduce race and class exclusivity gave force to this critique.

The strand of feminist thought that most came under attack for its purported essentializing and reifying tendencies was cultural feminism, often dubbed "femininity feminism" (the *cultural* in cultural feminism refers to its emphasis on the primacy of women's culture, which can be understood as a product of nature, nurture, or some interplay of the two; thus the label should not be confused or conflated with social constructionism). According to Alice Echols, cultural feminism is a devolved form of radical feminism. Writes Echols, "Most fundamentally, radical feminism was a political movement dedicated to eliminating the sex-class system, whereas cultural feminism was a countercultural movement aimed at reversing the cultural valuation of the male and the devaluation of the female" (*Daring* 6). Expanding upon earlier work by Echols, Linda Alcoff defines cultural feminism as "the ideology of a female nature or female essence reappropriated by feminists themselves in an effort to revalidate undervalued female attributes" (408). Hester Eisenstein characterizes the cultural feminist position as one "which eschewed an explicit political or economic program altogether and concentrated on the development of a separate women's culture" (xx). Perhaps most simply and most succinctly, Lynn Segal asserts that cultural feminism "celebrates women's superior virtue and spirituality and decries 'male' violence and technology. . . . [It] take[s] for granted and celebrate[s] women's greater humanism, pacifism, nurturance and spiritual development" (3–4). Although Segal rightly points out that cultural feminism became the most popular, perhaps because the most accessible, face of feminism in the 1980s, Alice Echols convincingly argues that its roots lay in the political and theoretical snafus of radical feminism and that its basic tenets were being debated early in the second wave, that is, in the late '60s and early '70s. Most commentators suggest that cultural feminism has its intellectual and political roots in the social purity movements of the late nineteenth century, and the phrase "male vice, female virtue" used to summarize the ideology of those movements is also used to describe that of contemporary cultural feminists.[6] Writers whose works have been classified as cultural feminist include Andrea Dworkin, Mary Daly, Dale Spender, Robin Morgan, Adrienne Rich, and Susan Griffin.

Taylor and Rupp, whose project is to reassess the activist accomplishments of cultural feminism, rightly note that critical "denunciations of cultural feminism have become commonplace" (32). Among the villainies of cultural feminism is its alliance with essentialism—a critical term that is "persistently maligned, . . . little interrogated, and . . . predictably summoned as a term of infallible critique" (Fuss xi). For Judith Grant, "Woman and experience always lead to essentialist arguments" and thus must be avoided (127); Ann Snitow identifies essentialism as a "counterpart" to cultural feminism (16), and Carla Freccero reads cultural feminism as a form of difference feminism that often "collapses" female difference from men into "an essential identity" (310). Even Taylor and Rupp use the "e" word to describe cultural feminism. However, it is important to note that, contrary to some common understandings and usages of the word, essentialism is not necessarily *biological* essentialism, and many commentators note that cultural feminists include both biological determinists and social constructionists.[7] Following Gayatri Spivak, Fuss has argued compellingly that not all forms and deployments of essentialism are equal, nor equally problematic; rather, "the radicality or conservatism of essentialism depends, to a significant degree, on *who* is utilizing it, *how* it is deployed, and *where* its effects are concentrated" (20). Thus a fuller discussion of cultural feminism is warranted.

The cultural feminist revaluation of femininity and women counters the self-hatred that a misogynist and sexist culture fosters in women; moreover, by constituting maleness and masculinity (the two are often conflated, as are femaleness and femininity) as the Other, cultural feminism promotes female solidarity and strives to transcend differences of race, class, and sexual orientation.[8] In *Gyn/Ecology*, an exemplar of cultural feminism, Mary Daly cautions against what she terms "the false polarization" of women by patriarchy:

> Women who accept false inclusion among the fathers and sons are easily polarized against other women on the basis of ethnic, national, class, religious, and other male-defined differences, applauding the defeat of "enemy women." Haggard Journeyers have learned to see through this false enmity to the true identity of

androcracy's Enemy. When this point has been reached, Crones
know who we are. The time has come for rekindling the Fire of
Female Friendship. (365)[9]

Yet such rhetoric is as much a poison as a cure, since it constitutes a "we"
that glosses over significant differences among women, implicitly positing a universal or essential Woman. In "An Open Letter to Mary Daly,"
Audre Lorde critiques *Gyn/Ecology* for such an erasure of difference, and
Linda Alcoff has noted that the essential Woman and the Man as Other are
problematized or absent theoretical constructs in the "writings of feminists who are oppressed also by race and/or class" (412). Perhaps not
coincidentally, the cultural feminist valorization of Woman not only
builds female self-esteem, but also enables white, middle-class women to
abdicate responsibility for complying with, and profiting from, systemic
racism and classism, as well as gender hierarchy.

Significantly, Mary Daly uses the idiom of the Gothic to describe
women's journey out of patriarchy into the Otherworld:

> Within a culture possessed by the myth of feminine evil, the
> naming, describing, and theorizing about good and evil has con-
> stituted a maze/haze of deception. The journey of women becom-
> ing is breaking through this maze—springing into free space,
> which is an a-mazing process.
>
> Breaking through the Male Maze is both exorcism and ecstasy.
> It is spinning through and beyond the fathers' foreground which is
> the arena of games. This spinning involves encountering the
> demons who block the various thresholds as we move through
> gateway after gateway into the deepest chambers of our homeland,
> which is the Background of our Selves. (2)

This mythic journey is one of transcendence into supposedly "free space";
the female Gothic experience is Man-made, and the goal seems to be a re-
appropriation of the female Self and the female body ("the deepest
chambers of our homeland"). As Daly and other cultural feminists map
the female Gothic experience in lurid detail,[10] men become the repository
of evil, the demons; ironically, however, such a reversal of patriarchal
myth risks putting women right back into the Male Maze since anatomy
remains destiny, and women's capacity to "spin" and "spark"—these are
Daly's terms—seems woefully inadequate against male rapaciousness. In
the Gothic scripts of cultural feminism, moral superiority can constitute
a primary mode of female self-defense.

Paradoxically, while cultural feminism seeks to empower women, it often naturalizes them as victims. The penetrability of the female body as it is hypostasized in heterosexual intercourse seems destined to ensure female vulnerability and male predation. Indeed, for Dworkin, hetero-sexual sex *is* war; the penis, metonym for the man, is the invader, and the vagina, metonym for the woman, constitutes occupied territory. In *Intercourse*, Dworkin writes:

> There is never a real privacy of the body that can coexist with intercourse: with being entered. The vagina itself is muscled and the muscles have to be pushed apart. The thrusting is persistent invasion. She is opened up, split down the center. She is occu-pied—physically, internally, in her privacy.
> A human being has a body that is inviolate; and when it is violated, it is abused. (122)

For Dworkin, intercourse is a Gothic crime of transgression; hetero-sexual activity and rape become indistinguishable from one another, and women who willingly have sex are "collaborators" in their own occupa-tion.[11] Read as a symptom of historically specific anxiety about female vulnerability, female subjectivity, female independence, and heterosexu-ality as an institution, *Intercourse* is fascinating. However, as a theory of female victimization, it makes all women into Gothic heroines, virgins awaiting, fearing, and, perhaps, desiring their defilement.

The reversal of cultural values that Echols defines as the heart of cultural feminism is precisely what poststructuralism finds theoretically suspect, for such a reversal keeps the terms of the opposition in place and thus upholds the system it is designed to dismantle. As Luce Irigaray cautions in her early work, "[I]f [women's] aim were simply to reverse the order of things, even supposing this to be possible, history would repeat itself in the long run, would revert to sameness: to phallocratism" (33). Indeed, she insists that "it clearly cannot be a matter of substituting feminine power for masculine power. Because this reversal would still be caught up in the economy of the same, in the same economy" (129–30).[12]

Irigaray and other feminist thinkers who promote a concept of sexual difference that does not revert to sexual opposition desire the dismantling of hierarchical systems and are thus leery of simple reversals that ultimately keep systems in order. However, they also note the practical necessity of "getting the goods together," as Irigaray puts it, of making theoretical moves that compensate for a context of inequality, even when equality—sameness—is not the ultimate goal. Indeed, even Derrida, the reluctant father of deconstruction and an early critic of feminisms that champion the essential female subject,[13] theoretically acknowledges the dangers of too hasty a retreat from reversal. As he puts it in "Positions,"

> [w]e must traverse a phase of *overturning*. To do justice to this necessity is to recognize that in a classical philosophical opposition we are not dealing with the peaceful coexistence of a vis-à-vis, but rather with a violent hierarchy. One of the two terms governs the other. . . .or has the upper hand. To deconstruct the opposition, first of all, is to overturn the hierarchy at a given moment. To overlook this phase of overturning is to forget the conflictual and subordinating structure of opposition. Therefore one might proceed too quickly to a neutralization that in practice would leave the previous field untouched, leaving one no hold on the previous opposition, thereby preventing any means of intervening in the field effectively. We know what always have been the practical (particularly political) effects of immediately jumping beyond oppositions, and of protests in the simple form of neither this nor that. When I say that this phase is necessary, the word phase is perhaps not the most rigorous one. It is not a question of a chronological phase, a given moment, or a page that one day will simply be turned, in order to go on to other things. The necessity of this phase is structural; it is the necessity of an interminable analysis: the hierarchy of dual oppositions always reestablishes itself. (41–42)

Thus cultural feminism may be read as more than a simple reversal, and cultural reification, of the sex/gender system. While the problematics of cultural feminism merit serious discussion and reflection, it seems important to note that cultural feminism does some of the work of "interminable analysis," especially on such issues as violence against women and heterosexuality as an institution.[14] Taylor and Rupp have argued that rather than an essentialist retreat from the political engagement of radical feminism, cultural feminism should be regarded as a strategy of abeyance, "a holding process by which activists sustain protest in a hostile political climate and provide continuity from one stage of mobilization to another" (36). In their perspectival shift from "the ideology of cultural feminism to concrete social movement communities" (34), Taylor and Rapp suggest ways in which cultural feminism has in fact promoted oppositional consciousness and feminist activism.

As I have already indicated in my discussion of Daly and Dworkin, charting the unintended consequences of feminist narratives has both theoretical and political import. However, it seems equally important to consider what is produced and repressed by popular and academic discourses that equate feminism with "victimology," that demonize cultural feminism, that use the word *essentialism* as an epithet resulting in intellectual damnation. Jane Roland Martin has charted some of the problems that the fear of essentialism has wrought in academic circles. Her reading of the academic landscape suggests that essentialism has been conflated with generalization; thus particularist studies are de rigueur and "generalizing integrative research" is "dismissed out of hand" (655). As Susan Bordo has pointed out, such an allergy to generalization paradoxically brings us back to liberal individualism: "[W]hat remains is a universe composed entirely of counterexamples, in which the way men and women see the world is purely as *particular* individuals, shaped by the unique configurations that form that particularity" (239).

Moreover, Roland Martin worries that the flight from essentialism is destined to "reproduce white male knowledge/power and other varieties of white male power" (649). Bordo, Tania Modleski, and bell hooks have expressed similar concerns. Such concerns seem particularly justified as Roland Martin charts the critical double standard that has infiltrated the academy: "Right now we look tolerantly upon the gravest mistakes of a Michel, a Jacques, a Jean-Francois, even as we denounce works by women that contain far less egregious errors. . . . We need to do some soul-searching . . . about the discrepancy between our cordial treatment of the men's theories and our punitive approach to the women" (651). Lillian Robinson has suggested that in the current political and academic climate, it has become difficult if not impossible to talk about oppression. Cultural feminism and essentialism have become the academic equivalent of "victim feminism." How can one say anything about oppression without being heard as valorizing victimhood? Is it possible to make any generalizations about gender without being branded and dismissed as an essentialist? Is it possible to promote women as subjects without being accused of merely reversing, and therefore reifying and reproducing, gender hierarchy?[15]

Indeed, an unrelenting theoretically correct retreat from reversal and essentialism may neutralize feminisms and prevent effective cultural and political intervention. As Susan Bordo explains,

> While in theory all totalizing narratives may be equal, in the context of Western history and of the actual relations of power characteristic of that history, key differences distinguish the universalizations of gender theory from the meta-narratives arising

out of the propertied white, male, Western intellectual tradition. . . . Feminist theory—even the work of white, upper-class
heterosexual women—is not located at the *center* of cultural
power. (224)

The theoretical assumption of an equal playing field where none
exists poses significant dangers. Indeed, if cultural feminism tends to
underestimate women's power, agency, and complicity, poststructuralism,
with its often attendant "gender skepticism,"[16] may overestimate women's
and feminists' power, agency, and complicity. Ultimately, poststructuralism
may be as implicated in the female Gothic as cultural feminism. However,
implication and causation need to remain distinct concepts if academic
discourse is not to devolve into mass media soundbites.[17]

Contemporary feminist thought is a labyrinthine set of activist and
academic narratives, and by focusing here on cultural feminism and
poststructuralist gender skepticism, I do not mean to suggest that this
binary adequately represents the massive amount of cultural, intellectual,
and political work classified under the rubric "feminism." However, I
have chosen to highlight these two strands of feminist thought for several
reasons. Their respective faith in, and skepticism about, the explanatory
power of gender causes them to be cast as polar opposites. To the extent
that such oppositional representations are accurate, I would argue that
they *need* one another. However, it also seems important to trouble the
opposition between them—after all, some of their primary questions are
remarkably similar: that is, what is the status of the female subject? what
are the implications of otherness and difference? what is the relationship
between knowledge and power? Moreover, these strands of feminist
thought are particularly pertinent to this project because their critics tend
to cast them as the archetypal feminist villains: cultural feminists as
essentialist, male-bashing victim-mongers; poststructuralist gender skeptics as theory-heads whose intellectual disavowal of "woman" has robbed
feminism of its political and activist foundations.[18] Neither
poststructuralism nor cultural feminism constitutes the demon of *Femicidal
Fears*; rather, I argue that the Gothic is a useful vehicle for what de
Lauretis has termed "upping the anti," for troubling the polarization
between cultural feminism and poststructuralism so that those terms can
do feminist work rather than signify a feminist catfight.[19]

My desire to intervene in the feminist gothic debates outlined here has
much to do with my generational position. My view that contemporary
feminist thought has developed as a relational labyrinth rather than a

progressive, linear narrative encourages synchronic interpretive work. However, even that view of feminism's development may be related to the fact that, diachronically, I am part of a transitional generation, poised as I am between the second and third "waves" of feminist thought. Second-wave feminism grew out of the civil rights and new left movements; a somewhat arbitrary beginning point might be the publication of Betty Friedan's *Feminine Mystique* (1963); an equally arbitrary ending point might be the failure to ratify the Equal Rights Amendment in 1982. The second wave encompassed diverse agendas—for example, both Mary Daly's *Gyn/Ecology* and Audre Lorde's critique of that work (see chapter 5 for a fuller discussion of the dialogue between Lorde and Daly) are part of that wave. In the academy and especially in literary studies, the years of the second wave are marked by the development of women's studies programs, by the charting of female literary traditions, and by the intellectual and practical challenges posed by poststructuralist thought. The '80s, the period between the waves, is marked by backlash, postfeminism, and the conservative, retrogressive politics of Reagan and Thatcher. According to Heywood and Drake, third-wave feminists were born between 1963 and 1974 (4). Indeed, the idea of feminism as a relational labyrinth would seem to fit third wavers, who are

> young feminists who grew up with equity feminism, got gender feminism in college, along with poststructuralism, and are now hard at work on a feminism that strategically combines elements of these feminisms, along with black feminism, women-of-color feminism, working-class feminism, pro-sex feminism, and so on. A third wave goal that comes directly out of learning from these histories and working among these traditions is the development of modes of thinking that come to terms with the multiple, constantly shifting bases of oppression in relation to the multiple, interpenetrating axes of identity, and the creation of a coalition politics based on these understandings—understandings that acknowledge the existence of oppression, even though it is not fashionable to say so. (3)

Despite my accord with the strategically eclectic vision delineated above, I, born in 1962, find myself at odds with the third-wave assessment of cultural feminism. As Drake and Heywood put it, "for most women who are generationally third wave, the feminist-separatist, pro-woman 'gynocriticism' . . . of some feminisms, although they sometimes sounded nice, seemed all too wishful and frilly and arcane to make any sense of our lives" (13). As my sometimes trenchant critique of cultural feminism indicates, I think it's important to understand how scripts of "male vice and female virtue" may unwittingly contribute to the gothic fear associated with violence against women and detract feminist attention from complicity with oppressive systems. Neither the demonization nor the dismissal of cultural feminism can accomplish such critical work. However, for me, the feminist utility of elements of cultural feminism is as readily apparent as the feminist utility of elements of poststructuralism. Put another way, cultural feminism does not just serve as a monitory story here; rather, it also needs to be credited and even honored for its feminist contributions. As Taylor and Rupp point out, cultural feminism played a major part in keeping rape crisis and battered women's shelters operating during the retrograde '80s (38). Moreover, it continued to denaturalize heterosexuality as a woman-friendly institution despite the onslaught of "family values" rhetoric and initiatives. As both a happily partnered straight woman and a Gothic scholar, I am profoundly grateful to cultural feminism for the critical consciousness it provides on the heterosexual contract. In 1989, Nancy Miller, charting the effects of the essentialist debates and poststructuralist gender skepticism, claimed that "it has become a positive embarrassment to talk about women" (351). I wonder whether cultural feminism's revaluation of femininity, its emphasis on woman positivity and women centeredness, hasn't helped to give some of us the courage to continue to talk about and care about female bodies—albeit in revised ways—even when it had become embarrassingly unfashionable to do so.

In literary studies, the demonization of cultural feminism and essentialism has been accompanied by a persistent critique of realism. Like cultural feminism, realism is often read as a reification of social reality, the autonomous subject, and experience. As Catherine Belsey writes,

> classic realism offers the position of knowingness which is also a position of identification with the narrative voice. To the extent that the story first constructs, and then depends for its intelligibility, on a set of assumptions shared between narrator and reader, it confirms both the transcendent knowingness of the reader-as-subject and the "obviousness" of the shared truths in question. (664)

Thus realism—or perhaps a naive reading of realist texts—erases the process of producing "reality" and the transcendent subject even as it participates in that very same process. According to this dominant theoretical narrative, classic realism is positioned as the literary vehicle of liberal humanism and the emblem par excellence of unitary fictions.

As a literary genre, the Gothic has long been considered a bastard cousin of both Romanticism and psychological realism.[20] More recent feminist writings on the Gothic suggest that it also functions as a genre of social realism, that it "maps a plot of domestic victimization" (Heller 2), and that "the boundaries between Gothic and real clearly are not as fixed as we once thought" (Massé 19). Writing about the nineteenth-century Gothic, DeLamotte argues that the Gothic world is a reflective distortion of social reality:

> The terrifying events at the core of the Gothic romance take place in an alien world set apart from normal quotidian experience and from the logical and moral laws of everyday reality. . . . It is also separated from the usual social relations of life in its outward forms, although—and this fact has never been adequately recognized—these relations appear in this alien world in disguise and are in many ways its primary subject. (18)[21]

However, even as the Gothic is yoked to the realist tradition, it also has much in common with postmodern aesthetics. Epistemological uncertainty,[22] the rupture of narrative, and multiple points of view mark both the Gothic and the postmodernist text. Howard reads the Gothic novel as "a type in which the propensity for multiple discourse is highly developed and . . . *dialogic* because of its indeterminacy or its open structure" (16). Botting points out that the Gothic has, from its inception, been engaged with what we now term the crisis of representation, and that "[o]ne of the principle horrors lurking throughout Gothic fiction is the sense that there is no exit from the darkly illuminating labyrinth of language" (14). Doubling—an obvious staple of the Gothic—puts into question the autonomy and integrity of the subject, a paradigmatic issue of poststructuralist thought. Indeed, Eve Kosofsky Sedgwick suggests that it is in the "creation of characters that the Gothic novel looks most alien, has been most vulnerable to criticism, has strained its resources most, and may therefore be inferred to be acting on the most daring ambitions" (39).[23] As she later succinctly puts it, "[i]n the Gothic view . . . individual identity, including sexual identity, is social and relational rather than original and private" (142). Thus the Gothic is a literary site where the reifications of realism and cultural feminism and the radical disruptions of postmodernism and poststructuralism are negotiated and collide.

Moreover, from its inception, the Gothic romance has been preoccupied with women's economic, psychological, and physical vulnerability. Indeed, the script of male vice and female virtue that is oft used to describe cultural feminism is an apt description of the literary Gothic. Leslie Fiedler rightly notes that the Gothic heroine, as Ann Radcliffe constructed her, owes much to the Richardsonian Persecuted Maiden, the sentimental heroine who attends the rise of the novel. Yet, according to Fiedler, while the sentimental novel privileges the triumph of virtue, "the Gothic fable, . . . though it may . . . permit the happy ending, is committed to portraying the power of darkness" (108–9). Interestingly, Fiedler makes this distinction by pushing the Gothic heroine into the background: "[T]he fully developed Gothic centers not in the heroine (the persecuted principle of salvation) but in the villain (the persecuting principle of damnation). The villain hero is, indeed, an invention of the Gothic form, while his temptation and suffering, the beauty and terror of his bondage to evil are among its major themes" (109).

Although the latter statement may be true if one privileges Walpole's *Castle of Otranto* and Lewis' *The Monk*, it does little to illuminate the major themes of Radcliffe's *Mysteries of Udolpho*, or, for that matter, Wollstonecraft's *Maria, or The Wrongs of Woman*, Brontë's *Jane Eyre*, or du Maurier's *Rebecca*, texts that represent a female-centered Gothic romance tradition in which love, fear, and mystery are the constituent ingredients. Indeed, in these texts, "the power of darkness" lies not, or not solely, in the figure of the Gothic villain-hero (who is not always combined into one figure), but rather in the heroine's *relation* to him/them as well as in her connection to another, victimized woman. In this strand of the Gothic, the world is presented as a confusing and dangerous place for women. Villains and protectors are often at least temporarily indistinguishable from one another, and thus these narratives explore the fear that men represent a threat and women victims-to-be. As Tania Modleski puts it, "it is against assuming the victim role that the heroine desperately struggles" (72).[24] Ultimately, as I will show in the next chapter, from Radcliffe to du Maurier, women writers have used the Gothic romance to meditate upon the connection between gender norms and female victimization.

The contemporary female Gothics considered here—Edna O'Brien's

Casualties of Peace and *I Hardly Knew You*, Beryl Bainbridge's *The Bottle Factory Outing*, Angela Carter's *Honeybuzzard*, Muriel Spark's *Driver's Seat*, Diane Johnson's *The Shadow Knows*, Joyce Carol Oates' *Soul/Mate*, and Margaret Atwood's *Bodily Harm*—were written from the mid-'60s through the late '80s. Thus I argue that contemporary women writers adopted and adapted the tropes of an already gendered literary tradition to address the sexual politics of their own time. Whereas the nineteenth-century Gothic, according to Ferguson Ellis, explored the domestic violence that was officially repressed in order to maintain the ideology of the home as a safe haven, contemporary Gothics critically engage with feminist discourse on violence against women. Indeed, contemporary women writers meditate upon not only the relationship between femininity and Gothicism but also the relationship between feminism and Gothicism. Rita Felski argues that women's literature is a viable category of contemporary literature because it is during the second-wave movement that women define themselves as an oppressed group (1). Thus in a variety of ways and from a variety of perspectives, women writers reflect upon such gender consciousness. Here I particularize Felski's argument: given the extent to which feminists have argued that a continuum of violent acts[25]—both material and imagistic—maintains and reinforces gender oppression, it makes sense to identify a contemporary female Gothic tradition, a body of works that address the feminist Gothic.

Literature, like feminism, is a "technology of gender,"[26] and *Femicidal Fears* argues the imbrication of those two discourses. I particularly want to emphasize the use of these contemporary female Gothics for the development and critique of feminist thought on female victimization. De Lauretis has argued that "the critique of all discourses concerning gender, including those produced or promoted as feminist, continues to be as vital a part of feminism as is the ongoing effort to create new spaces of discourse, to rewrite cultural narratives, and to define the terms of another perspective—a view from 'elsewhere'" (25). I contend that, taken together, the femicidal plots under discussion here perform both the critical and creative functions of feminism.[27] Thus this project is in keeping with the critical trend of viewing the boundaries between fiction and theory as productively permeable.[28]

Although I consistently identify these femicidal plots as contemporary female Gothics, my goal in *Femicidal Fears* is not to define formal genre boundaries. As Todorov makes abundantly clear, the boundaries of the uncanny, a subgenre of the Gothic, are notoriously ambiguous:

In works that belong to this genre [the uncanny], events are related which may be readily accounted for by the laws of reason, but which are, in one way or another, incredible, extraordinary, shocking, singular, disturbing or unexpected . . . . The definition is, as we see, broad and vague but so is the genre it describes: the uncanny is not a clearly delimited genre, unlike the fantastic. More precisely, it is limited on just one side, that of the fantastic; on the other, it dissolves into the general field of literature. (20)

Derrida's musings on genre as a concept suggest that the fuzzy borders of the Gothic[29] may in fact reflect the law of genre: "A text would not belong to any genre. Every text participates in one or several genres, there is no genreless text, there is always a genre and genres, yet such participation never amounts to belonging" ("The Law of Genre" 230). What interests me is not that these texts adhere to a formal code that separates them from other texts, but rather that they participate in the Gothic experience, which involves an encounter with otherness (both within and without), the transgression of boundaries[30] (especially those of the body), and, perhaps most important, the fear that is born of such encounters and transgressions. Ultimately, I assume that the female Gothic experience is not foundational but rather is already a narrative in need of interpretation.[31]

Although the feminist politics of the authors represented here range from the committed (e.g., Angela Carter) to the skeptical (e.g., Beryl Bainbridge), all seem keenly aware of two related scripts highlighted by feminists: the prevalence of violence against women and the tendency to blame the victims of such violence. Indeed, in these novels, femicide borders on becoming a cultural norm.[32] The belief that women somehow desire and/or deserve such violent ends is articulated and textually refuted in these contemporary fictions. Herod, the most nefarious character in O'Brien's *Casualties of Peace,* says to Willa, "You do not go because you would rather have a man that punished you than one who did not, because you are a woman" (172). Willa's flight from Herod, which constitutes her—and, by extension, O'Brien's—refutation of essential female masochism, is seconded by Angela Carter, who counters Ghislaine, her own pathologically and pornographically masochistic creation, with Emily, a fully sexual woman who doesn't need to be tortured or mutilated in order to be recognized as a human being. When Brenda in Bainbridge's *The Bottle Factory Outing* thinks that her chosen protector, Patrick, has killed her friend Freda, she recoils from him. Unlike the unnamed narrator of du Maurier's *Rebecca,* Brenda understands that men who are dangerous to active, rebellious women are dangerous to all women. In Atwood's *Bodily*

Harm, Rennie responds to her lover's pornographic fantasies with discomfort and fear rather than desire. Violence is not eroticized in these texts, nor is the mutilated female body fetishized. Yet, although these works carefully avoid blaming female victims or heroizing male victimizers, they also collectively demonstrate the multiple dangers of subscribing to myths of pure, powerless women and essentially sadistic men.

Although the explicit feminist commitments of the fiction writers discussed here vary, these writers are a racially homogeneous group. My textual choices are a function of both the specific feminist debates highlighted here and a conscious strategy to avoid and even counter some troubling critical trends. In "The Highs and Lows of Black Feminist Criticism," Barbara Christian provocatively asks, "Do we know our own literatures? Why, for example, does it appear that white feminist critics have abandoned their contemporary novelists? Where is the palaver among them? Or are Freud, Lacan, Barthes, Foucault, Derrida inevitably more appealing?" (55). The work of Valerie Smith and Margaret Homans suggests that one answer to Christian's question might be that such critical tendencies associate white feminist critics with the high-mindedness of theory. Valerie Smith has pointed out that when Anglo-American feminists "rematerialize their theoretical discourse," they often do so by "invoking the specific experiences of black women and the writings of black women" (316). Building on Smith's work, Margaret Homans notes that white feminist critics tend to embody their theoretical ideas with examples drawn from the works of black female artists; thus white women become aligned with the mind of theory and black women with the body or matter of example. Thus I purposely use literary works by, and largely about, white women to reclaim female bodies that are neither pure nor powerless; it is also no coincidence that the theoretical underpinnings for this mediation between cultural feminism and gender skepticism derive in large part from the work of such feminist critics as Barbara Christian, Angela Davis, Audre Lorde, and bell hooks.

Indeed, the whiteness of this strand of the contemporary female Gothic is related to the racialization of both cultural feminism and gender skepticism. Cultural feminism tends to "reflect the historical conditions of white women in particular" (McCaughey 146). For women of color, phrases such as "male vice and female virtue" and even "violence against women" belie men and women as "comrades in struggle" in liberation movements (hooks, *Feminist Theory*, 67–81), the collusion of women in the violence of militarism and imperialism (hooks, *Feminist Theory*, 117–131), and the normalized vulnerability of male bodies in "the killing streets" (Lorde, "Man Child," 78). Similarly, women of color have met with skepticism a poststructuralist critique that theorizes difference based on the work of white male philosophers and de-authorizes raced and gendered voices emerging from the margins (Christian, "Race for Theory"; hooks, "Postmodern Blackness"; Alexander and Mohanty xvii). Thus it should come as no surprise that the fiction of contemporary white women should be a particular site of negotiation of white feminist debates and positions. As my discussion of *The Shadow Knows* and cultural feminism in chapter 5 makes clear, white women wrestling with the Gothic entails an exploration of their own complicity with oppressive racialized and racist systems.

More than any other Gothic trope, *Doppelgängers* obsessively appear in these texts, a fact that explains my own repetition compulsion for sustained character analysis. Indeed, anxieties about the ineluctability of female victimization are often worked out through externalized victim selves. However, in addition to this conventional psychological function, the practice of doubling suggests useful parameters for gender as a category of cultural analysis. When female doubles, and often double protagonists,[33] face femicide and/or the fear of it, the Gothic narrative becomes more than a story of one uniquely unlucky individual. Moreover, doubling patterns often illuminate the differences among women that cultural feminists tend to downplay and point to the relationship between privilege and survival. Some of these texts are marked by cross-gender doubling; such literary cross-dressing challenges biologically essentialist scripts even as it suggests gendered patterns of projection. Thus, for example, in Carter's *Honeybuzzard*, Morris works out his vulnerability on Ghislaine's mutilated body, and in Oates's *Soul/Mate*, Colin becomes the repository of Dorothea's aggression. Such culturally inflected forms of projection are shown to have deadly consequences.

Even as the violent events of these plots retain gendered dimensions, so do they remain arbitrary and unpredictable. N. of *The Shadow Knows* is raped in her garage when she least expects it; in *Casualties of Peace*, Willa is mistaken for another woman and is killed as she walks home happy and unafraid; Lise is raped when she only wants to be murdered in Spark's *Driver's Seat*; and Rennie, the protagonist of Atwood's *Bodily Harm*, unknowingly "escapes" to a Caribbean island on the verge of political upheaval. Such happenings are more than mere plot contrivances, more than contemporary Gothic claptrap; rather, they promote epistemological uncertainty, which breeds both fear and opportunities for critical interpretive work.[34] Like earlier Gothics, these contemporary femicidal plots set and keep the hermeneutic code in play. DeLamotte credits Radcliffe with introducing mystery to the sentimental novel; as the former wittily puts it, "In Richardson, the heroine and the reader know only too well who it is at the door—the same person it has been for hundreds of pages and will be for hundreds more. Radcliffe's heroines hear breathing, see something move, discern a shape indistinctly; they are not sure" (43). Significantly, the contemporary Gothic takes such uncertainty a step further by not always providing definitive resolutions. In *The Bottle Factory Outing*, the identity of Freda's murderer remains uncertain; in *The Shadow Knows*, we don't find out who raped N., and the text suggests but does not confirm the identity of Ev's assailant. Similarly, we don't know whether Rennie and Lora of *Bodily Harm* ever make it out of prison alive. Such ambiguity foregrounds—sometimes for the heroine, but almost always for the reader—the role that interpretation plays in the creation of knowledge. Relatedly, these texts are much more writerly than their predecessors. They tend to be achronological with an abundance of flashbacks and—sometimes—flashforwards. Thus the reader must reconstruct these stories as well as the (dis)connections among past, present, and future. Heroine and reader are detectives together as always[35]; however, the narrative structure invites the latter to retain that role beyond the limits of the text. Thus the postmodern features of these texts promote not only female fear but also female agency.

Although these contemporary femicidal plots demonstrate the Gothic potential of scripts of male vice and female virtue, they simultaneously sustain a profound critique of heterosexual romance and its seductions. Indeed, in the strand of the late-twentieth-century female Gothic charted here, the passively feminine woman who expects a man to save her is, most likely, a goner and hence functions as a monitory figure. Relatedly, the heroic capabilities of men are undercut or altogether destroyed. In these texts, Mr. Right is always a disappointment and sometimes the cause of death. However, the protagonists of these femicidal plots are endangered not only by an abundance of villains but also by their own belief in male saviors. These texts consistently demonstrate that romantic ideology—the belief that heterosexual romance constitutes the key to female identity and security—constructs women as victims.

Just as the femicidal plots under discussion here deconstruct husbandly saviors, so do they deny female characters the refuge of a safe if limiting space. Although the Gothic places of old are recalled in some of these texts—Lise looks for her murderer in Italy, Dorothea in *Soul/Mate* is abducted and taken to a "mock Swiss chalet"—the Gothic world tends to be coterminous with, or the same as, the "real" world. Contemporary femicidal plots bring the Gothic and the quotidian together; thus the housing project, familiar streets, a park, the home that is not a castle—all harbor potential danger. The Gothic and gender are revealed to be related (but not conflated) concepts, and neither can be transcended. However, the impossibility of transcendence does not become a dead end.[36] As Angela Carter puts it in her Afterword to *Fireworks*, "We live in Gothic times. Now, to understand and interpret is the main thing" (122).

Chapter 2

Gothic Traditions

Often denigrated for its reliance on plot, supernatural or providential contrivances, and conventions that border on formulas, the Gothic has gotten a bad rap and a bad rep, so much so that even critics who take the genre seriously have felt the need to apologize for or distance themselves from it. Robert Kiely entitled his study on the Gothic canon *The Romantic Novel*, thus rhetorically aligning such works as Walpole's *Castle of Otranto*, Ann Radcliffe's *Mysteries of Udolpho*, and Matthew Lewis' *The Monk* with a respectable, legitimate literary movement. Early on in *The Coherence of Gothic Conventions*, Eve Kosofsky Sedgwick provides the following disclaimer: "[M]ost Gothic novels are not worth reading, making it otiose to labor a definition for their sake" (3). At least in part, sexual politics has been responsible for the devaluation of the Gothic, a genre which has, from its inception, been seen as feminine and female: it privileges emotion and the domestic sphere, and middle-class women have obsessively written and read it. Significantly, some attempts to re-vision the Gothic novel as a genre of import have tended to masculinize it (DeLamotte 12). Thus in *Love and Death in the American Novel*, Leslie Fiedler sees the masters of the genre as male and the hero-villain as its central figure.[1] More recently, Camille Paglia has proclaimed, "The Gothic tradition was begun by Ann Radcliffe, a rare example of a woman creating an artistic style. The Gothic novel with the greatest impact on Romanticism, however, was Matthew G. Lewis' *The Monk*" (265). Paglia's "however," her subordination of the Gothic to Romanticism, and

Radcliffe to Lewis, exemplifies the gendered literary struggle that has attended the critical history of this genre.

Of course, Paglia notwithstanding, feminist literary critics have, within the past two decades, reengendered the Gothic as female, and such preeminent critics as Ellen Moers, Sandra Gilbert and Susan Gubar, Janice Radway, and Tania Modleski[2] have focused attention upon the myriad ways in which women writers and readers have used the female Gothic tradition to protest and accommodate themselves to women's lot. More recent feminist studies of the Gothic such as Kate Ferguson Ellis' *The Contested Castle* and Eugenia DeLamotte's *Perils of the Night* pointedly put female-authored texts at the center of the Gothic tradition; indeed, Ellis "treats the masculine Gothic as a reaction to the feminine" (xvi), and DeLamotte argues for the centrality of Ann Radcliffe in any consideration of the Gothic (10). Reading the early female Gothic tradition via the limited and problematic rhetoric of "victim feminism," Diane Long Hoeveler argues that female Gothic writers "have been complicit in constructing limiting roles and self-destructive poses of femininity for other women, their readers, to embrace" (244). Although Michelle Massé and Anne Williams do not read the Gothic as a specifically female literary tradition, they do view female subjectivity as a quintessentially Gothic issue. Ultimately, feminist attention has done much to move the Gothic from literary margin to center.[3] The critical renaissance that has attended Gothic studies in recent years demonstrates that the politics of the Gothic are not uniform, nor uniformly feminist; however, feminist work on such touchstone Gothic texts as *Mysteries of Udolpho*, *Maria*, *Jane Eyre*, and *Rebecca* clarifies that, from its inception, the Gothic romance has meditated upon the potential for female victimization.[4] In this chapter, I want to provide a brief overview of those early female Gothics that are the literary precursors of contemporary femicidal plots. At issue in these precursor texts is the extent to which women's fears are warranted and derive from normalized cultural arrangements. In other words, these texts debate the basic tenets of the feminist Gothic.

In *The Mysteries of Udolpho* (1794), Radcliffe created the prototype for the Gothic heroine, the Gothic villain, and the Gothic setting in Emily St. Aubert, Montoni, and Udolpho. Since meaning in *Udolpho* is mediated, in large part, through event, a brief summary of its entangled plot is necessary for readers who have not had the pleasure—and the pain—of experiencing this text for themselves. At La Vallée, the St. Aubert family home, Emily has led an idyllic life; however, the death of her mother and then of her father leaves her in a precarious position. When her guardian/aunt Madame Cheron marries Montoni, Emily comes under his control as well. Although Valancourt, Emily's desired suitor, distrusts Montoni and suggests that they elope, Emily's sense of propriety will not allow her to enter into a clandestine marriage. Thus she is taken to Udolpho, an Italian castle noted for the "Gothic greatness of its features" (226). Significantly, Emily views Udolpho as her "prison" (227), and it is here that she experiences both real and imaginary terrors under Montoni's lock and key. Emily believes that Montoni has murdered her aunt and Signora Laurentini, the former owner of Udolpho; moreover, the protagonist fears that she will be his next victim. Although Emily's suspicions are false, Montoni *is* implicated in Madame Montoni's (née Cheron's) death: determined to control his wife's fortune and erroneously believing that she attempted to murder him, Montoni locks Emily's aunt in the turret of the castle and "without pity or remorse, had suffered her to lie, forlorn and neglected, under a raging fever" (365).

Besieged by the continual overtures of Count Morano, one of Montoni's associates, and by Montoni's unjust claim on Emily's inheritance from her aunt, this prototypical Gothic heroine escapes Udolpho via the help of a benevolent protector, Monsieur Du Pont. She finds a surrogate family, the De Villeforts, and is eventually re-united with Valancourt, though this is delayed by exaggerated reports of his disreputable behavior. Furthermore, she discovers that a dead woman she resembles, the Marchioness de Villeroi, is actually another aunt who had been murdered by her husband and his mistress, Signora Laurentini (yes, the same Laurentini who formerly owned Udolpho). Thus Emily's father's attachment to a picture of the Marchioness is explained, and Emily is reassured about her matrilineage; prior to the identification of the Marchioness as her father's sister, Emily feared that her father had been unfaithful to her mother and that she was not really the daughter of the one "whom she had always considered and loved as a mother" (663). At the end of the novel, Emily has settled down to enjoy conjugal life with Valancourt in La Vallée. Her life has come full circle, and the innocence and security of her girlhood is replicated by replacing St. Aubert with Valancourt.

In the penultimate paragraph of this heavily plotted, sometimes contrived, and truly fantastic tale, Radcliffe asserts her belief in Providence and (feminine) virtue: "O! Useful may it be to have shewn, that, though the vicious can sometimes pour affliction upon the good, their power is transient and their punishment certain; and that innocence, though oppressed by injustice, shall, supported by patience, finally triumph over misfortune!" Significantly, this hopeful vision contradicts the "power of darkness" that Radcliffe has invoked. Even as Radcliffe depicts Emily's moral superiority, what Eugenia DeLamotte has termed "the self-defense" of "conscious worth" (34), this prototypical Gothic romance writer demonstrates the untenability of Emily's position. Bereft of male protectors, orphaned, outside of the family, Emily is extraordinarily vulnerable, and the stories of Madame Montoni and the Marchioness de Villeroi hardly suggest that marriage as an institution guarantees women safety.[5] Yet Radcliffe sets the murder of the innocent Marchioness in the past and thus distances Emily and the reader from this femicide.[6] Moreover, Radcliffe strives to relieve anxiety about Madame Montoni's death by encouraging the reader to blame the victim: Emily's aunt is presented as avaricious—she marries Montoni to augment her fortune and then resists unto death granting him control of her finances. Hence she functions as a monitory story, and the fact that her economic desires cannot be fulfilled through work but only through a marriage contract is an unprotested given of the text.

Significantly, Montoni, an embodiment of the male economic threat, is vanquished when he tries to take advantage of the morally unimpeachable Emily, a fact that supports Ann McMillan's reading of this novel as a work of "Gothic fantasy," a subgenre permeated by "the efficacy of woman's innocent victimhood" (53).[7] Ultimately, Radcliffe returns Emily to society and the status quo and presents her as protected because she has reconstituted the nuclear family. Radcliffe seeks to reassure her readers that male protectors *are* available and, therefore, that women's position is secure. Thus David Durant rightly dubs Radcliffe the mistress of the "conservative Gothic."[8] Although she does so unconvincingly,[9] Radcliffe makes the case that the social order protects good women and hence, that female fear is unnecessary and counterproductive.

While Radcliffe used the Gothic to assuage her readers' fears, Mary Wollstonecraft employed the tropes of that genre in *Maria, or the Wrongs of Woman* (1798) to foreclose any such reassurance and to produce a feminist tract. In her preface to *Maria*, Wollstonecraft describes her main object as an overtly political one: "the desire of exhibiting the misery and oppression, peculiar to women, that arise out of the partial laws and customs of society" (7). As Moers points out (133), the first paragraph of *Maria* suggests that this story constitutes a realistic Gothic tale, despite the seemingly oxymoronic nature of such a characterization; Wollstonecraft begins *Maria* thus:

> Abodes of horror have frequently been described, and castles, filled with spectres and chimeras, conjured up by the magic spell of genius to harrow the soul, and absorb the wondering mind. But, formed of such stuff as dreams are made of, what were they to the mansion of despair, in one corner of which Maria sat. (23)

This "mansion of despair" is an insane asylum to which Maria's profligate husband has committed her in order to gain control of her inheritance. So that her daughter will know her mother at least indirectly, Maria has inscribed the story of her life in a diary; through this documentary device, the reader learns of the events that led up to Maria's incarceration.

Eager to escape an unhappy home, Maria married George Venables, the son of a merchant. Unbeknownst to her, Maria's well-meaning uncle arranged this match: keenly aware of her unhappiness, he enticed Venables into a proposal with a settlement of five thousand pounds. Supposedly Maria's savior, Venables turns out to be a licentious villain. When he endeavors to get money from a friend by "selling" Maria's sexual favors, she declares their bond null and void. Significantly, he responds to this declaration of independence by locking her in her room, an act that foreshadows his committing her to the asylum. Although she escapes from Venables's house, she has difficulty securing and keeping lodging because her husband publicly brands her a criminal and threatens those who aid her. About to leave the country with her infant daughter, she is drugged by the maid she had hired and awakens to find herself "buried alive" (135)—a paradigmatic Gothic horror—in the asylum.

During her incarceration, Maria becomes involved with Henry Darnford, another inmate unfairly imprisoned, and gains the sympathy of Jemima, a woman who works for the institution and thus functions as her keeper. Thanks to the help of the latter, Maria escapes from the asylum and establishes a home with Darnford, whom her husband subsequently sues for adultery. Since Darnford must take care of financial affairs abroad, Maria prepares a statement for the court and eloquently argues for the amendment of the legal status of women. However, as one landlady puts it to Maria, "women have always the worst of it, when law is to decide" (128); thus, it comes as no surprise that the judge cares little for a woman's feelings and makes his esteemed pronouncement that "too many restrictions could not be thrown in the way of divorces, if we wished to maintain the sanctity of marriage; and though they might bear a little hard on a few, very few individuals, it was evidently for the good of the whole" (150). Unwittingly, this judge reveals the fragility of the marriage contract. His assumption that less restrictive divorce laws would necessarily imperil the "sanctity of marriage" suggests that this institution is neither inherently stable nor benevolent.

Although the judge explicitly trivializes the Gothic excess that might arise from the status quo—"[T]hey *might* bear a *little* hard on a *few, very few* individuals" (my emphasis), Maria's chronicle demonstrates that the hardships of women bereft of legal and economic rights are the rule rather than the exception. Moreover, the family—the institution supposedly protective of women—is often the site of their greatest victimization. According to Kate Ellis, the Gothic is founded upon this contradiction: "It is when the home becomes a 'separate sphere,' a refuge from violence, that a popular genre comes into being that assumes some violation of this cultural ideal" (3). In *Maria*, Wollstonecraft exposes that ideal as a patriarchal farce. The tyranny and irresponsibility of Maria's father encouraged her precipitous marriage. Moreover, the good intentions of her uncle caused him to sell her unwittingly to a wolf. In the world of *Maria*, the marriage contract becomes little more than a genteel form of prostitution.[10] The lack of economic alternatives for middle-class women only exacerbates their desperate situation as Wollstonecraft shows through the figure of Maria's sister, a governess who dies young, weakened, and dispirited, a woman who "had abilities sufficient to have shone in any profession, had there been any professions for women" (96). Significantly, although Maria writes for her daughter, she fears that her husband's neglect may have already caused the infant's demise; thus this cycle of familial victimization threatens to leave its fatal mark on the next generation.

In her graphic depiction of the Gothic nature of women's experience, Wollstonecraft strove for inclusiveness; thus in her preface to *Maria*, she declares her intention to "show the wrongs of different classes of women, equally oppressive, though, from the difference of education, necessarily various" (8). To this end, Wollstonecraft includes the history of Jemima, Maria's keeper, confidante, and rescuer.[11] In this narrative interpolation, we learn that Jemima's lower-class Gothic experiences included child labor, sexual assault, prostitution, and the workhouse. At one point, Jemima wryly notes, "I have since read in novels of the blandishments of seduction, but I had not even the pleasure of being enticed into vice" (59); Wollstonecraft thereby reminds her readers that the niceties and distancing strategies of the conservative Gothic disguise the horrors—including violations of the female body—that she seeks to foreground. Significantly, in Jemima's story, (economic) competition between women becomes an issue as Jemima ashamedly admits that desperation once led her to convince a man to turn his current mistress out of his home so that she could take that woman's place. Jemima similarly rues her role as Maria's keeper. Indeed, Jemima's part in Maria's escape functions as atonement for the former's past crimes, and Wollstonecraft may be the first practitioner of the Gothic to cast a woman in the role of Gothic hero.

The stories of other women in *Maria* further underscore the fact that female victimization inevitably arises from legal and social arrangements that assume women will be taken care of by men. When Peggy, the sister of Maria's childhood nurse, loses her husband, she is faced with eviction and the loss of her children. When Maria flees from Venables, one of her landladies reports that her husband not only didn't provide for her but also squandered her earnings and caused her to lose desperately needed jobs. Once, trying to retrieve belongings that her husband had pawned, she was informed, "It was all as one, my husband had a right to whatever I had" (127). Thus Wollstonecraft exposes the practical ramifications of the *femme covert*.

Wollstonecraft died shortly after giving birth to Mary Shelley and before she could finish *Maria*. Her notes indicate that at least one ending she imagined involved Darnford betraying Maria and the latter committing suicide. Thus it seems that Wollstonecraft, consistent with her political agenda, would not have reassured her readers that female patience is rewarded with a good, protective man. Yet even more significant than this lack of reassurance is the fact that the Gothic villain, Maria's husband, has the law and social mores on his side. While Radcliffe represents Montoni as a perverse figure doomed to fail, Wollstonecraft shows that George Venables represents the social order, a system that invites rather than prevents the exploitation and victimization of women by depriving them of economic and legal self-defense. In Wollstonecraft's world, unlike Radcliffe's, the moral superiority of the innocent victim is not compensatory nor a means of self-defense; rather, it serves as a guarantee that female victimization will continue unabated. Significantly, Wollstonecraft's depiction of the plight of women is less the product of imagination and more that of autobiography. Physically violent and economically irresponsible, her own father served as a model for the hero turned villain, as did the father of her best friend, Fanny Blood, and the husband of her sister Eliza.[12] Surrounded by the disastrous effects of women psychologically and economically dependent on unreliable men, Wollstonecraft demonstrated in her work—as well as in her difficult life—that the status quo was more likely to damn a woman than to save her. For Wollstonecraft, the patrilineal household is—or has the potential to be—an abode of horror. As Ellen Moers eloquently put it, "For Mary Wollstonecraft, the terrors, the restraints, the dangers of the Gothic novel were not the fantasies but the realities of a woman's life" (134).

While Ann Radcliffe ultimately affirms the status quo and strives to show women the ephemeral nature of Gothic horrors, Mary Wollstonecraft uses Gothic conventions to expose the physical, economic, and psychological hardships that women routinely endure. *Jane Eyre* brings together these two contradictory impulses by combining feminist tract with a revamping of heterosexual romance. In Brontë's hands, the Gothic heroine becomes not just adventurous and curious, but also defiant and independent—in other words, a prototypical feminist. Jane shares Emily St. Aubert's consciousness of self-worth; however, the former adds rebellion to her repertoire of self-defense. Just as Wollstonecraft's Maria proclaims the world "a vast prison" and women "slaves," Jane insists that women, like men, abhor stagnation and confinement. Similarly, Jane's famous proclamation of equality with Rochester stands as an emotive analogue to Maria's courtroom speech. Moreover, with Bertha as her double, Jane gains psychological depth missing in both Maria and Emily. Indeed, while Bertha as the other woman/wife suggests the female competition seemingly endemic to the Gothic romance, she is simultaneously, as Gilbert and Gubar have persuasively argued, the embodiment of Jane's rage at women's lot (*Madwoman* 359–62).

Just as Brontë enriches and emboldens the Gothic heroine, so does she merge the Gothic villain and the Gothic hero in the figure of Rochester. As DeLamotte puts it, "If women's Gothic romance before Charlotte Brontë suspected that the hero who offered rescue and marriage was in some way the same villain who threatened to trap the heroine in his house forever, Charlotte Brontë's representation of Rochester as both hero and villain, egress and entrapment, brings that hidden identity to the surface" (211). Rochester's recognition of plain Jane's value establishes him as her Gothic hero. However, the sadism he evinces by letting Jane think he is marrying Blanche Ingram, his attempts to turn her into an *objet d'art* before their marriage, and his willingness to transgress the laws of man by committing bigamy align him with villainous predecessors. Rochester's ambiguous status becomes most apparent when his heroic actions during the burning of Thornfield are narrated to Jane:

[H]e went up to the attics when all was burning above and below, and got the servants out of their beds, and helped them down himself—and went back to get his mad wife out of her cell. And then they called out to him that she was on the roof; where she was standing, waving her arms above the battlements, and shouting out till they could hear her a mile off. . . . I witnessed, and several more witnessed Mr. Rochester ascend through the skylight on to the roof: we heard him call "Bertha!" We saw him approach her; and, then, ma'am, she yelled, and gave a spring, and the next minute she lay smashed on the pavement. (547–48)

Of course, such action is literally heroic. Rochester takes his role as master of the house seriously and not only enjoys the power but also fulfills the responsibilities of his position. Moreover, Rochester has consciously strived not to become a Montoni and kill off Bertha through neglect: as he puts it, "to each villain his own vice; and mine is not a tendency to indirect assassination, even of what I most hate" (383). Yet, ironically, despite his—and perhaps Brontë's—best efforts, he *is* ultimately implicated in Bertha's death. It is as if Bertha, as she burns down the symbol of his patriarchal power, demonstrates that his role as a savior is a farce and thus jumps to her death upon his approach.

Of course, as numerous critics have demonstrated, with Bertha literally out of the way, and with the inequalities she represented ameliorated—Rochester is humbled, crippled, and bereft of his ancestral mansion; Jane has found a family and an inheritance of her own—these two spiritual equals are free to marry and enjoy conjugal bliss at Ferndean. Significantly, their marriage is predicated not upon Rochester's untarnished virtue but upon his reformation.[13] Moreover, while he was previously the hero-villain, circumstances have forced him to eschew both roles. As Jane puts it, "I love you better now, when I can really be useful to you, than I did in your state of proud independence, when you disdained every part but that of the *giver and protector*" (570—my emphasis). Rochester has not been transformed from a villain to a hero but rather to a partner.

Is the resolution of *Jane Eyre*—the retreat to Ferndean—a retreat into the Radcliffean conservative Gothic? In other words, is Ferndean any different from La Vallée? In a word, yes. Rather than confirm conservative sexual politics, Brontë imaginatively reforms the heterosexual couple but suggests that such a new and improved unit has, as yet, no place in society.[14] Moreover, the active role Jane played in this heterosexual romance should not be underestimated. In the conclusion to the novel,

Jane writes, "Reader, I married him," and, as Joyce Carol Oates rightly notes, "The tacit message is that *I* married *him*—not that *he* married *me*" ("*Jane Eyre*: An Intro." 137).[15] Thus Jane declares herself a desiring subject rather than a bartered object. Yet, even as contemporary feminist readers applaud the boldness of Brontë's vision in 1848, they can't help but wish that Jane had a larger field for her efforts and that her revamping of heterosexual romance were not predicated upon Bertha Mason's dead, colonized body.[16]

By rescripting the terms of heterosexual romance, Brontë sought not only to expose but also to resolve the contradictions inherent in the Radcliffean plot. Almost a century later, Daphne du Maurier returned to the outlines of Brontë's narrative and adopted/adapted her Victorian predecessor's contributions to the genre; indeed, the very existence of *Rebecca* indicates that repetition with a difference occurs not only within but also between Gothic texts. In du Maurier's revision, the mad wife becomes the dead bad wife, and she functions not only as a psychological projection of the heroine but also as a character with considerable power of her own. Yet, seemingly resistant to the feminist protest at the heart of *Jane Eyre*, du Maurier attempts to discredit this rebellious dead woman even as she gives her life. Fraught with more contradictions than even the Radcliffean plot, *Rebecca* simultaneously legitimizes and denies female fear as its plot—often bordering on absurdity—illuminates the ideological tensions of the genre as a whole.

The first-person narrator, who remains unnamed throughout the novel, is the second Mrs. de Winter; Rebecca was the first. Narrated retrospectively, *Rebecca* chronicles the marriage of the unnamed narrator and Maxim de Winter, owner of Manderley. An orphan, the narrator meets Maxim in Monte Carlo, where she is earning her keep as a paid companion to Mrs. Van Hopper, a snobbish and vulgar member of the *nouveau riche*. As Massé astutely notes, the narrator's dislike of Mrs. Van Hopper is emblematic of her dislike of almost all of the women in the novel (151); indeed, the narrator's gendered double standard becomes more pronounced as her story continues. Attracted to the narrator's girlish innocence, Maxim proposes marriage as an alternative to her staying in Mrs. Van Hopper's service. The narrator's initial response—"I'm not the sort of person men marry" (51)—provides a clue to the enormous popularity of this book: heterosexual female readers identify with this timid, childlike creature who fears that she is too unlike the heroines of romance novels to get a man.

Paradoxically, the narrator's new identity as mistress of Manderley exacerbates her feelings of inferiority. Often moody, condescending, and impatient, Maxim is more attentive to the running of his estate than he is to his new bride. A hero-villain in the mold of Rochester, he remains inscrutable and does not share with the second Mrs. de Winter memories of his former life. Hence the narrator constantly feels that he, like everyone else, must be unfavorably comparing her to Rebecca, who, according to public accounts, was beautiful, smart, and gracious. Living in the shadow of this seemingly perfect first wife who supposedly perished in a tragic boating accident, the plain, shy, and often clumsy second Mrs. de Winter comes to feel like an inferior replacement, a representation rather than an original and thus not of much value. Perhaps unwittingly, the text legitimizes the narrator's anxieties by rendering her nameless in stark contrast to Rebecca, who managed to retain an independent identity not only after marriage but also after death.

Despite evidence of Maxim's benign neglect, it becomes clear that the *real* threat to the narrator lies in Mrs. Danvers, the housekeeper who raised and revered Rebecca and who continues to function as her agent. Mrs. Danvers treats the second Mrs. de Winter as an interloper unworthy of the Manderley fashioned by the competent, classy, and indomitable Rebecca. Brags Mrs. Danvers, "She had all the courage and the spirit of a boy, had my Mrs. de Winter" (243), and it seems clear that this servant vicariously enjoyed the masculine authority and freedom of the woman to whom she lays claim—"*my* Mrs. de Winter." Almost guilty of the villainy that Rochester explicitly eschewed—that of "indirect assassin"—Mrs. Danvers preys upon the narrator when the latter is in a weakened emotional state and tries to convince her to commit suicide:

> "Don't be afraid," said Mrs. Danvers. "I won't push you. I won't stand by you. You can jump of your own accord. What's the use of your staying here at Manderley? You're not happy; Mr. de Winter doesn't love you. There's not much for you to live for, is there? Why don't you jump now and have done with it? Then you won't be unhappy any more." (246)

Mrs. Danvers uses the idiom of romance—without the love of your man, you have nothing to live for—as a powerful weapon against the second Mrs. de Winter. Thus even as *Rebecca* sells romantic ideology to its readers, the text demonstrates the destructiveness of this heterosexual plot and the need for a sustained critique of it.

Indeed, Mrs. Danvers knowingly manipulates romantic ideology here, and the narrator almost falls for—and from—it. Weary and desperate, the second Mrs. de Winter begins to interiorize the words of Rebecca's live agent and, in a trancelike state, contemplates her own destruction. However, the sound of an explosion signaling the grounding of a boat brings the narrator out of this state and away from the murderous Mrs. Danvers. Significantly, this boat accident leads to the discovery of Rebecca's boat and her corpse. Hence the text produces the uncanny sensation that the narrator's life depends upon Rebecca's dead body.

Once Rebecca's body is found, Maxim reveals the secret of Manderley in the form of a confession: "There never was an accident. Rebecca was not drowned at all. I killed her. I shot Rebecca in the cottage in the cove" (266). Femicide thus becomes a literal though past event,[17] and the hero-villain justifies the blood on his hands: Rebecca was "vicious, damnable, rotten through and through . . . Rebecca was incapable of love, of tenderness, of decency. She was not even normal" (271). Since Maxim asserts that Rebecca "told me things I shall never repeat to a living soul," it remains unclear whether he is accusing his first wife of nymphomania or lesbianism here; however, he readily reveals that one of the symptoms, if not the cause, of Rebecca's abnormality was that she viewed marriage as a negotiable contract rather than one with fixed terms. Immediately after their marriage, Rebecca gleefully announced her sordid past to Maxim; she agreed to play the grand lady of Manderley if he would not abridge her (sexual) freedom, and she counted upon his pride in Manderley and his reputation to keep them out of divorce court. As Maxim tells it, Rebecca took particular delight in the subversion inherent in her terms: "'And people will visit us, and envy us, and talk about us; they'll say we are the luckiest, happiest, handsomest couple in all of England. What a leg-pull, Max,' she said, 'what a God-damn triumph'" (273). For Rebecca, triumph equals defying convention even as she appears to uphold it. Although Maxim welcomed the thought of getting a woman with "beauty, brains, and breeding," he didn't count on this same woman knowing the rules and using them to her advantage.

Significantly, being a threat to legitimacy, the linchpin of patriarchy, constitutes Rebecca's cause of death. Maxim kills Rebecca when she tells him that she is pregnant—the child is not his, and she taunts him with the fact that her bastard son would bear the de Winter name and be the heir of Manderley. Although in *The Mysteries of Udolpho* Emily worries about her matrilineage, *Rebecca* demonstrates that patrilineage is truly a legal fiction, one that depends upon the control of the female body. *Rebecca* links women's sexual freedom with the demise of the social order and suggests that men will kill to keep the status quo.

However, as the plot thickens, it becomes clear that Rebecca's identity as a victim of murderous patriarchal rage is not the whole story. Unbeknownst to Maxim, Rebecca was not pregnant but rather dying of cancer; thus she purposefully and gleefully manipulated him into killing her, knowing that he would be haunted—and possibly hunted—for his actions. And, indeed, we find out from Mrs. Danvers that after Rebecca died, Maxim closeted himself in the library and walked "backwards and forwards, like an animal in a cage" (244). In *Rebecca*, the hero-villain takes on the attributes of Bertha Mason Rochester, and the bad wife demonstrates the knowledge/power nexus. Ultimately, Maxim is not jailed for Rebecca's murder: when her cancer becomes public knowledge, the law rules her death a suicide. As Horner and Zlosnik astutely note, this legal ruling "enacts, in miniature, a discursive sanitizing of the violence at the heart of the patriarchal order" (105). However, Maxim does lose Manderley. The final scene of the novel is the burning down of the patriarchal house, a further paean to *Jane Eyre*. All evidence points to Mrs. Danvers as the firebug, the implication being that Rebecca's rebellion lives on through another woman.[18]

The story of Maxim and Rebecca might be read as a feminist fairy tale, a sign that it really is winter, the season of death, for the maxims of patriarchal rule. However, the other heterosexual relationship in the novel, that of Maxim and the narrator, considerably complicates such a reading. Significantly, when Bertha's existence is exposed, that knowledge separates Jane and Rochester, albeit temporarily. However, the revelation that Maxim is a murderer brings him and the narrator closer together.[19] The insuperable impediment between them was the fact that there was a secret; the content of the mystery matters little to the second Mrs. de Winter. In fact, Maxim's assertion that he hated and killed Rebecca makes him less of a villain and more of a hero in her eyes. Indeed, the narrator's reaction to the news that her husband has killed his former wife is truly a Gothic experience for the feminist reader: "None of the things that he had told me mattered to me at all. I clung to one thing only, and repeated it to myself, over and over again. Maxim did not love Rebecca. He had never loved her, never, never" (273). Ironically, Maxim's confession enables his second wife to disidentify with Rebecca and to embrace wholeheartedly her new identity as Mrs. de Winter: "It would not be I, I, I, any longer, it would be we, it would be us" (285).

Significantly, in order to sustain "we," the narrator must become Maxim's accomplice. When Rebecca's body is found, Maxim assumes that his crime will be discovered as well. However, the narrator convinces him that this need not be so: "Rebecca is dead. She can't speak, she can't bear witness. She can't harm you anymore" (282). The latter statement is singular in the reversal it evokes: Maxim as victim; Rebecca as victimizer? Given the fact that the securing of her identity as Mrs. de Winter and Maxim's confession are coterminous, the narrator can only vindicate his crime and protect him from Rebecca, who has become not a rival but a common enemy. By constituting the sexual, rebellious, "abnormal" Rebecca as an alien Other, Maxim and his second wife seem finally joined in holy matrimony.[20]

Written between the first- and second-wave feminist movements and just prior to the cataclysm of World War II, *Rebecca* inscribes rather than resolves the sexual tensions of the age. Indeed, it often reads like a conservative Gothic gone awry. As the title suggests, the heroine remains overshadowed by the first wife, and her erotic object is a murderer. Moreover, even the happy ending is lackluster. The narrator describes her post-Manderley life in exile with Maxim in less than idyllic terms:

> We have no secrets now from one another. All things are shared. Granted that our little hotel is dull, and the food indifferent, and that day after day dawns very much the same, yet we would not have it otherwise. We should meet too many of the people he knows in any of the big hotels. We both appreciate simplicity, and if we are sometimes bored—well, boredom is a pleasing antidote to fear. (6)

Significantly, the fear the narrator has experienced revolves around two issues: (1) that Maxim loves Rebecca and not her; (2) that Maxim will be imprisoned for killing Rebecca. Remarkably, it has not occurred to the narrator to fear Maxim. The novel is predicated on the assumption that Maxim could only have killed a woman like Rebecca. Thus good women, chaste women, monogamous women, "normal" women need not be afraid—real men only kill women who deserve to die. Informed by contemporary feminist thought, the femicidal fictions that form the core of this study begin by putting such assumptions into question.

Chapter 3

Love Kills

According to initial reports, Charles Stuart, his wife Carol, and their unborn child were casualties of random yet racialized street violence on October 23, 1989.[1] As Charles narrated the story, an African American man jumped into the Stuarts' car shortly after the white couple left a birthing class at Boston's Brigham and Women's Hospital; the abductor forced them to drive into a deserted ghetto area, robbed them, and then shot both of them, leaving Carol dead and Charles seriously injured. Several months later, as the ghetto-driven, gun-toting black man was being revealed as the figment of a white husband's Gothic imagination, Charles Stuart committed suicide. Matthew Stuart, Charles' brother, revealed to police that on that fatal October night, Charles had given him a Gucci handbag, a handgun, ten thousand dollars, and instructions to get rid of the first two items. Believing—or so he claimed—that he was helping his brother to commit insurance fraud, Matthew enlisted his friend, John McMahon, to dispose of the gun. Matthew denied knowing that Charles murdered his wife; however, he waited until January 3, 1990, to share his knowledge with the police. Matthew apparently confided in another brother, Michael. Michael's wife as well as sister Shelley also were aware of these incriminating details; they, too, chose to keep silent about their brother's crime. Charles's motive for uxoricide was financial: he wanted the insurance money from Carol's death to open a restaurant. Before involving Matthew, Charles had apparently elicited help from an old friend, David MacLean. Although MacLean refused to help with the murder, he did nothing to prevent it. Thus a network of family members and friends aided and abetted Charles' femicidal villainy.[2]

As the last chapter demonstrates, while the female Gothic has traditionally explored issues of female vulnerability and victimization, it has also provided male protectors and refuge for its heroines. When Emily St. Aubert, the protagonist of Ann Radcliffe's *Mysteries of Udolpho*, is threatened by Montoni's schemes and Count Morano's unrequited and unrelenting love, Du Pont, the De Villefort family, and most notably her beloved Valancourt ultimately help her to establish domestic tranquillity. Similarly, the second Mrs. de Winter in Daphne du Maurier's *Rebecca* finally feels secure in her relationship with Maxim once he confesses that he despised and killed his first wife. The Gothic plot traditionally has been resolved by joining the heroine to a family and a male lover. Indeed, Anne Williams argues that the female Gothic "demands a happy ending, the conventional marriage of Western comedy. This plot is affirmative. . . . The Female Gothic heroine . . . is awakened to a world in which love is not only possible but available; she acquires in marriage a new name and, most important, a new identity" (103).[3]

However, contemporary female-authored Gothics follow and develop the narrative line of Wollstonecraft's *Maria* and true crime stories such as the Stuart case.[4] The protagonists of more recent female Gothics are denied any assurances of security. Protectors are unrecognizable or nonexistent; rather than a shelter for women, heterosexuality and the nuclear family become explicitly and unrelentingly the site and origin of female victimization. Indeed, according to Edna O'Brien's *Casualties of Peace* (1966) and Beryl Bainbridge's *Bottle Factory Outing* (1974), women's trust in men is misplaced and deadly, since lovers and father figures are the most likely agents of female destruction. Thus these texts by O'Brien and Bainbridge (as well as those by Carter and Spark that I discuss in the next chapter) use the conventions of the Gothic to fictionally represent a set of gender generalizations proferred by cultural feminists— namely, that normalized familial and romantic relations are a form of violence against women.

In "Compulsory Heterosexuality and Lesbian Existence," a classic and much-debated essay for feminist and queer theorists alike, Adrienne Rich argues that "male power . . . enforc[es] heterosexuality on women"; indeed, a "pervasive cluster of forces, ranging from physical brutality to control of consciousness" is used to make women's submission within/to the institution of heterosexuality seem normal, natural, and desirable (185). Some cultural feminists suggest that male intimates *necessarily* pose a threat to women. In *Intercourse*, Andrea Dworkin argues that female subordination and vulnerability are inherent in the sexual act and that penetration is ultimately synonymous with violation and the erosion of female integrity. Clearly, Dworkin's argument verges on *biological* essentialism and is thus problematic; nevertheless, the vehemence with which she argues this position reflects the degree of victimization some women associate with heterosexuality. Significantly, Edna O'Brien, a writer born Irish-Catholic and known for her sexually explicit prose, shares Dworkin's violent images of intercourse. In an interview with Nell Dunn published in 1965, O'Brien posits that during intercourse a woman is "to some extent . . . being violated or invaded because when the maidenhead is first broken it is a rupture. Each time and for evermore she must carry the memory of that first rupture no matter how she desired it" (95). For O'Brien, the specter of unwanted pregnancy further complicates relations between men and women and causes sex antagonism: "To a great extent a man is a woman's enemy. Even if in the centre of her being she loves him, he is still her enemy much more than she is his enemy because he can abandon her and get on with his hunting but she cannot abandon him if she's impregnated" (96).

In 1984, nineteen years after the Nell Dunn interview, O'Brien persisted in returning to biology to explain dissatisfactions and inequities in male-female relationships. Although she acknowledges women's social advancement, she dismisses the idea that reforms have affected actual sexual relations:

> In the mating area things have not changed. Attraction and sexual love are spurred not by consciousness but by instinct and passion, and in this men and women are radically different. The man still has the greater authority and the greater autonomy. It's biological. The woman's fate is to receive the sperm and to retain it, but the man's is to give it and in the giving he spends himself more and then subsequently withdraws. Closeness is therefore always only relative. A man may help with the dishes and so forth but his commitment is more ambiguous and he has a roving eye. (Roth interview 40)

O'Brien ultimately believes that the "only real security would be to turn away from men, to detach, but that would be a little death—at least, for me it would" (40).

Thus heterosexual women, caught between the Scylla of men's desire and the Charybdis of their own, seem fated to suffer. For if detachment from men involves "a little death," attachment often poses even greater risks. In the Nell Dunn interview, Edna O'Brien asserts that she had refrained from an extramarital affair not out of "niceness," but out of "deep-rooted fear"; as O'Brien puts it, "he [O'Brien's husband] might kill me or something if he found out" (87). Significantly, such "deep-rooted fear" dominates O'Brien's fictional relationships as well. In her imaginative universe, violence between men and women becomes the rule rather than the exception. *Casualties of Peace* (1966), O'Brien's fifth novel, typifies the gender roles inherent in much of her work: men are the destroyers, and women are the destroyed. Via the intersected stories of two female protagonists, Willa and Patsy, this novel relentlessly links love to death and sex to violence; thus *Casualties of Peace* does the cultural feminist work of demonstrating that heterosexual romance is no protection racket for women.

Willa McCord is a fragile artist; she creates figures out of glass and uses her craft to protect herself from breakage. Frigidity, fear, and vulnerability characterize her. Patsy, Willa's companion/housekeeper/ double, aptly describes her as "pale and wrung. . . . All ready for the business of suffering!" (30). Willa's susceptibility to victimization is established at the outset of the novel as she struggles to wrest herself from a dream in which murderous males pursue her. This nightmare, which constitutes the first five pages of the book, not only draws the reader into Willa's fearful consciousness but also foreshadows the protagonist's violent end while simultaneously hinting at her terror-ridden past.

Throughout this intensely psychological novel, Willa alludes to a past, emotionally maiming relationship. Thus the origin of Willa's frigidity, the reason she has determined that "no one would ever catch her again" (40), constitutes the secret of Willa and of the novel. At the end of the novel, after Willa's death, the details of this mysterious relationship are revealed through a series of letters Willa had written but not mailed to her lover Auro. Via these letters, we discover how Willa's involvement with the sadistic Herod, a man who chose to rename himself after the biblical figure responsible for the Slaughter of the Innocents, has crippled her adult life.

Shortly after meeting Herod, Willa visits his decaying Swiss chalet. Significantly, this Gothic setting includes an "abandoned sanatorium" (162). Such a place is, paradoxically, associated with disease and cures, and the ambiguity of such scenic symbols reflects Willa's attraction to, and eventual repulsion from, the chalet and Herod himself. Herod offers Willa a retreat from the world, responsibility, the pain of insecurity, the necessity for self-motivated action. Writes Willa, "'Judge to what degree I love you,' he said as he drew the bolt of the door, and like a fool I smiled, thankfully" (171). Initially, Willa is drawn to Herod because she views him as he represents himself: as her much-needed protector.

However, Willa soon learns that a fine line exists between retreat and imprisonment, protector and tormentor. As their relationship evolves, Willa virtually becomes Herod's prisoner: he relieves her of her return ticket as well as her passport and thus, literally and symbolically, limits her mobility. Willa comes to realize the hazards inherent in a self-created savior. In one letter to Auro, Willa reports that "Herod said he felt he had been sent to save me from falling over a cliff" (161). Yet in the next letter, Willa writes, "Herod supplied the cliff" (161). This last statement is literally true—Herod has Willa walk on dangerously steep precipices; each time she loses her balance, he saves her. Moreover, on a figurative level, Willa's observation exposes the paradox of chivalrous relation- ships: the man saves the woman from the dangerous conditions that he creates and encourages. To cast himself in the role of savior, Herod must have someone to save. Thus he maintains Willa's dependency at all costs. Herod is simultaneously Gothic hero and Gothic villain; as such, he demonstrates the interdependency of those roles.

Herod's sadism is appropriately matched with a belief in female masochism. As he says to Willa, "You do not go because you would rather have a man that punished you than one who did not, because you are a woman" (172). Implicitly refuting this essentialist view of female psy- chology, Willa does escape from Herod's enclosed Gothic world. After she becomes accustomed to the dark forest surrounding the chalet, she makes a run for it and thus becomes her own rescuer. However, in her last letter to Auro, Willa differentiates between physical and psychological escape. Ironically, she quotes her former jailor to make this point: "But as Herod himself might say, 'Entries in the heart are not like entries in ledgers, they cannot be crossed out.' The more you try the more unsightly the inner page becomes, which is why I always say that memory is the bugger" (185). Willa has internalized Herod's villainy; in particular, he has left his mark on her sexual life. Herod's idea of lovemaking is manually to bring Willa to the brink of orgasm, stop all further stimula- tion, and then shame her for getting "carried away on a little solitary flood hearing nothing but the echo of his laughter" (166). Under Herod's tutelage, Willa learns to associate sexual desire with physical and emo- tional vulnerability; her body becomes an agent of betrayal. For Willa, the Gothic nightmare world has become reality.

To protect herself from further victimization, Willa hires Tom and Patsy as live-in servants/companions. Indeed, it seems that Willa has reconstituted a nuclear family with Tom and Patsy positioned as the parents and Willa as the child. Since she has developed badly with Herod, she strives to return to an asexual childhood, to be protected by a peaceful family unit. Simultaneously, she views Patsy as her alter ego and thus lives an adult female life through her. Whereas Willa is mousy and frigid, Patsy is assertive and passionate. Much of Willa's security is derived from Patsy's relationship with Tom, and the emptiness of Willa's life is mitigated by Patsy's stories, Patsy's vitality, Patsy's adventures. "To forage through Patsy's letters was another way of escaping into Patsy's world. To live a little of her bleak life through Patsy. To find comfort there" (57). Ultimately, Tom and Patsy's relationship not only allows Willa to retreat into childhood but also enables her to participate vicariously and thus safely in heterosexual romance.

However, as Willa soon finds out, Tom and Patsy's relationship is not a source of satisfaction and security for Patsy; rather, the latter is involved in an extramarital affair with Ron and is plotting her escape from Tom. Significantly, Willa convinces Patsy not to run away but to confront Tom. This naive and self-interested advice turns Willa's peaceful reconstituted home into a war zone: it puts Patsy into grave danger and ultimately causes Willa's death.

Initially, Willa characterizes Tom, her surrogate father/lover, as kind and considerate. She discounts the violence inherent in his profession— he is a demolitions expert—as well as his perennial boasting that there are forty ways of killing a man. Yet after Patsy tells her husband about Ron, Willa is forced to recognize Tom's capacity for violence. Although Willa (unlike the reader) does not directly witness Tom beating and raping Patsy, she recognizes the effects of such brutalization. Thus Willa realizes that Tom is "another of the ones that put love on a leash" (101–2). Like Herod, Tom starts out as a savior and ends up as an antagonist.

Just as Tom becomes "a poor man's Herod" (Eckley 49), so does Patsy begin to look like Willa's reflection. While Patsy is being beaten and raped, Willa is having dinner with Auro, a married suitor to whom Willa is attracted but with whom she finds herself unable to have sex. When Willa checks up on Patsy the next day, she finds her "in bed, her cheeks as mauve as the nightdress she wore. One of Willa's. One worn in one of her failures with Auro and promptly given away to reduce shaming memories" (100). This shared clothing suggests a common plight. The garment that symbolizes Willa's frigidity and thus recalls past terrors with Herod also comes to stand for a break in Patsy's spirit, her failed and violent marriage, *her* vulnerability. Memory cannot be escaped, and the collective memory of women in this novel seems to be a torturous one.

As Tom and Patsy move toward separation, Willa and Auro move toward intimacy.[5] The rift in relations between Tom and Patsy threatens the peaceful domestic sphere that Willa has tried to establish. When Willa first finds out that Patsy is involved with Ron, she thinks, "Who now will protect me from Herod, who now will I turn to when that knock on the door, that ring, that tap on the shoulder catches up with me" (60). Willa seems to find the answer to her question in Auro. While Patsy informs Tom of the imminent end of their marriage, Willa welcomes Auro and happily accepts a fur coat that his wife has refused. Similarly, when Willa feels threatened by Tom, she sends Auro a telegram saying that she wants to go away with him and try bed one more time. Willa seems most drawn to Auro and his sexual advances when she feels in need of protection. Fear keeps Willa desirous of male protectors, even as experience—her own and Patsy's—blurs the boundaries between tormentor and rescuer.

At first glance, Willa's relationship with Auro seems like a healthy corrective to her connection with Herod. While Herod's name recalls scenes of slaughter, Auro's suggests a precious and rare material, a new age of hope. As a light-skinned Black man abandoned at an early age, Auro seems to understand vulnerability.[6] In addition, Auro seems capable of deep affection; he remains gentle with Willa, despite their failed attempts at intercourse. Ultimately, he appears to offer an alternative sexuality to Willa—one of satisfaction and mutuality rather than denial and shame. Yet Auro is a married man who claims to love his wife but nonetheless cannot be satisfied with her. Hence Auro, as good as he is, is still a prototypical male, defined by O'Brien as one whose commitments are "ambiguous" and who "has a roving eye." Despite his affection, he is capable of betraying Willa (as he has betrayed his wife, Beryl) and rendering her more vulnerable than she is already.

Furthermore, even Willa's most pleasurable moments with Auro are subtly associated with Herod. In one of her unmailed letters to Auro, Willa discusses her marriage to Herod: "The marriage ceremony was grim. It was held in a Roman Catholic church, because he said the old mythology dies hard in all of us" (169). To be sure, the moment when Willa's desire for Auro overcomes her fear is anything but grim; rather it is a triumph, a figurative and literal climax in Willa's life:

[Auro's] fingers going faster and faster and her head and neck and arms tossing back and forth vehemently with animal tosses and he smiling through it all not at his expertise but at her unimpeachable deceit at the resisting head, neck and voice, all devoted to the utterance of no, and her limbs begging no, and all of her being saying no except for one soft little central screech of skin and this saying yes louder and stronger and fiercer than all the other orchestras of nos and his fingers giving the totality of their love, their hostility, their stretch, their fury, their patience, their cruelty, their softness, their nimbleness, their kneading and their love to that most secret and central cause in her. And her voice was intermittent as her panting increased and finally when his body covered hers the panting replaced the words they might have said. (153–54)

Such lurid, lyrical prose not only suggests O'Brien's debt to Joyce but also explains why many of O'Brien's novels, *Casualties of Peace* included, have been banned in Ireland.[7] However, even the profound pleasures of intimacy with Auro are tinged with his "hostility," "fury," and "cruelty." Moreover, the place in which Willa and Auro successfully consummate their relationship is a refurbished stone abbey. Thus even this seemingly healthy relationship, even "good" sex, lies in the shadow of "the old mythology," a mythology in which woman is sinful and is destined to suffer.[8]

As if to underscore that this "old mythology" is still operant, Willa dies almost immediately after she and Auro consummate their relationship. The circumstances of her death make it clear that Auro is necessarily contaminated by the role he plays in Willa's life, that of savior and lover. After they have intercourse, Willa clearly identifies Auro as the antidote to Herod: "She would weigh him against Herod hour by hour, day by day. . . . Down the Herod road she need not go" (155). However, in O'Brien's world, men inevitably damn the women they are supposed to save. Hence the fur coat Auro gives to Willa ultimately leads to her death. Tom, intending to kill Patsy, kills Willa instead; he mistakes her for his wife because he thinks that Willa has given Patsy the coat (actually, Willa *had* given Patsy the coat; however, Tom doesn't know that they swapped again later). While Auro is, of course, not literally responsible for Willa's death, his offering to his lover at least tangentially enables her sacrifice. Ironically, it is the chronicle of another love that incites Tom's murderous rage: he conceives of his plan to kill Patsy after he reads her and Ron's love letters.[9] In *Casualties of Peace*, love and death seem causally related.

A further irony is that Tom kills Willa at a moment when she feels fearless and invulnerable. After her rendezvous with Auro, she walks home "without any nervousness. On dark nights in the city of London women were raped but she was not going to think about that. . . . Something had been accomplished. She felt that she could even confront Herod" (159). A few moments later Tom strangles her. Up until this point, the reader is led to believe that Willa needs to exorcise fear from her consciousness. However, her murder and the subsequent disclosure of her relationship with Herod serve to legitimize her fear. *Casualties of Peace* ultimately suggests that Herod and Willa are the archetypal heterosexual couple and that the vulnerable position of women in the Gothic is women's position. Thus O'Brien provides us with a literary version of cultural feminist Gothic.

ಳೆ ಳೆ ಳೆ

While in interviews Edna O'Brien virtually dismisses the effects of social change upon women's personal lives, Beryl Bainbridge expresses ambivalence about such change: "I disapprove, in a way, of men becoming too domesticated, doing the washing-up or looking after the children. I disapprove of it sexually: if people get too friendly and the roles too intermixed, we shall all end up with brothers and sisters, mums and dads. I think men are superior, or you have to think they are" (May interview 49). In another interview, Bainbridge asserts, "I'd like to have lived in Victorian times. Women knew where they were then" (Bannon interview 11). Such statements obviously reflect profound anxiety about gender bending and the loss of a specifically female space.

Yet, when read in the context of Bainbridge's fifth novel, *The Bottle Factory Outing*, such statements seem less reactionary than cautionary. At one point in that work, Brenda, the passive survivor of this Gothic murder mystery, dreams that she and her dead friend Freda share the memory of a nursery rhyme:

> A little woman with a great big hat
> Went to the pictures and there she sat
> Man behind couldn't see a bit
> Finally got tired of it
> Turned to woman sitting there
> See that mouse beneath that chair
> Little woman, great big hat

> Couldn't stand the thought of that
> Up she got and left the house
> Man made happy, saw no mouse. (199, 215)

This rhyme, with its disturbing message that men quickly and cleverly rid themselves of female nuisances who presume to add to their stature, can serve as a gloss on the novel from which it comes. Indeed, *The Bottle Factory Outing*, a nominee for the Booker Prize and the 1974 winner of the Guardian Fiction Award, reverberates with the fear that while women who act like "born victims" survive the onslaughts of men, formidable females are endangered by their relations with the "other" sex. Although the crime at the heart of this text is not definitively solved, *The Bottle Factory Outing* suggests that Freda's romantic aspirations may be linked to her macabre death. Thus Bainbridge's work, like O'Brien's, betrays considerable anxiety about the security of women in heterosexual romance.

The germ of Bainbridge's novel is autobiographical, and the author has loosely cast herself as Brenda. Indeed, in the sketch that adorns the British edition of *The Bottle Factory Outing*, Bainbridge *is* Brenda.[10] Like the latter, Bainbridge worked in a wine bottling factory with mostly Italian co-workers. An outing did take place, and many details of the novel's main event are derived from that experience. As Bainbridge tells it, the outing occurred

> [m]ore or less exactly as I describe it. The van was cancelled and most workers had to go home. The rest went off in two cars. The driver of mine tried to lose the other one because he had designs on me. He still visits me bearing bottles of wine. Freda is based on a friend I used to work with. (May interview 51)

Even more than *Casualties of Peace*, *The Bottle Factory Outing* relies on the juxtaposition of two female protagonists, one brazen and brawny, the other mousy and fearful. Although Brenda has recently summoned enough courage to leave her husband, she is still one of the most pathologically passive characters in literary history. In one comic scene after another, she displays the effects of an upbringing that taught her that "it was rude to say no, unless she didn't mean it" (29). Predictably, such lessons make her prey to all sorts of harassment, especially those of a sexual nature. A man fondles her on a bus, and she apologizes when she reaches her stop and thus has to disturb his probings. A janitor at the bottle factory where she works grabs her and asks, "You want to give me a little kiss?" "Smiling politely and shaking her head," she replies, "No, not really" (41). Less humorous is Brenda's memory of being raped:

> She thought of the commercial traveler who had stopped to give her a lift when she was going into Ramsbottom to buy groceries. In vain she said she was married, that her husband was big as an ox. He inveigled her out of his car and bundled her down beneath the bridge, his big feet snapping the stems of foxgloves, and panted above her. (117)

Significantly, Brenda is grammatically and otherwise the object of this man's actions. To protect herself, she can only imagine calling upon the strength of another male; she does not perceive herself as a subject capable of struggle and sustained resistance.

Brenda's passivity is particularly pronounced in her relations with Rossi, the manager of the bottle factory. Although she abhors his persistent sexual advances, her attempts to discourage him are futile because they lack any degree of force and self-assertiveness. At one point, she thinks, "If his happiness depended on her, who was *she* to offend him" (105). Indeed, when Rossi paws her, she can only hope that circumstances protect her. "[Rossi] wanted his Outing, his escape. If the missing mini caught up with them, disgorging its quota of fellow-countrymen, then she would not be to blame if he was thwarted. 'It's not my fault,' she thought. 'I can't be expected to take any blame'" (105). Brenda is a parody of feminine selflessness; her way of being in the world invites victimization at the same time that it denies her direct means of self-defense. Yet, such selflessness with its ensuing victimization also enables her to be free of blame, to evade responsibility for her own actions and her own wishes.

Freda, the novel's coprotagonist, is what Brenda fears she would turn into if she began to assert herself. Indeed, Freda is presented almost as a grotesque figure: allusions to her five-foot-ten, 224 pound body abound. Unlike shrinking Brenda, Freda is a formidable woman who knows what she wants and aggressively acts to achieve her goals. She does not hesitate to ask for better working conditions at the bottle factory, and she gladly tyrannizes Brenda.

Despite Freda's looks, her situation is that of the traditional Gothic heroine: an orphan, she is bereft of family ties except for a distant aunt. Although Brenda's community is of questionable value—it consists of a vulgar ex-husband, a mother-in-law who tries to kill her,[11] and a stiflingly conventional family—Freda envies it. Indeed, her goal is to gain familial and thus cultural legitimacy: "All her life she had cherished the hope that one day she would become part of a community, a family. She wanted to be adored and protected, she wanted to be called 'little one'" (13). Such a wish exposes not only the conventionality of Freda's desires but also the subtlety of Bainbridge's humor. At an aggressive five foot ten, 224 pounds, Freda needs little protection, nor does the epithet "little one" seem appropriate. Yet Freda is willing to deny her corporeal reality in order to achieve the security traditionally accorded a Gothic heroine. Freda seeks not to subvert the status quo but rather to join it.

Every Gothic heroine needs a Gothic hero (or so the plot goes), and thus Freda casts Vittorio, the nephew of Mr. Paganotti, the Italian owner of the wine-bottling factory, into that role. Freda views Vittorio as a suave, sophisticated foreigner who will carry her away to an edenic Mediterranean home and provide her with the family and the traditionally feminine life she has always craved. Her hopes are encouraged not only by Vittorio but also by Maria, a co-worker at the factory and a fortune-teller. In Freda's future, Maria sees horses, men in uniform, "a journey by land and sea," and a white dress (35). To minds intoxicated by romance, this could only be a prediction of Freda's marriage to Vittorio.

Like Brenda, Freda understands her subjectivity in terms of objectification. However, the latter perceives and manipulates the forms of power that such terms accord to her. Indeed, there's a touch of the Rebecca about Freda. "Beyond the romantic dreams, the little girl waiting to be cuddled, it was power of a kind she was after. It is not so much that I want [Vittorio], she thought, but that I would like him to want me" (49). Freda, outside of a nuclear family, apprehends its latent power structure. She perceives that women are not powerless; rather, their agency derives from being the object of men's desire. Freda aggressively deploys such agency; she thus strives to ensure the progress of her romance. To these ends, Freda plans a company outing; her fantasy is that in the wilds of nature, Vittorio will profess his love and seduce her.

Yet, from the first, the material world opposes her fantasy, and this outing seems doomed to failure. As in Bainbridge's outing, the van that was ordered to take the workers into the country never materializes. Hence, two cars must serve as transportation, and most of the workers are necessarily excluded from the adventure. To Freda's disappointment, Vittorio is reluctant to go and only does so at Rossi's insistence. When Patrick, the factory's Irish driver who is enamored of Brenda and strives to be her protector, tries to cram into the car that already contains Rossi, Brenda, Freda, and Vittorio, Freda's romantic dream verges on slapstick comedy:

[Patrick] tugged at the handle of the door, the henspeckled face beneath the peak of his cloth cap distorted with urgency. The door swung open and he tried to squeeze inside. Freda struck him repeatedly in the face with the french loaf and he fell backwards onto the pavement in a sprinkle of breadcrumbs. (92)

By fending off Patrick with a loaf of bread, Freda reminds the reader—and Vittorio—that she is a far cry from the shy, retiring, "little one" she aspires to be.

Significantly, the next altercation with Patrick not only puts into relief Freda's brutally indelicate behavior but also calls into question Vittorio's heroic capabilities. Patrick, determined to save Brenda from Rossi's lust and Freda's manipulation, shows up at Windsor Castle, one of the first stops on the outing. While Freda and Vittorio roam through a chapel, Patrick appears, demanding to know Brenda's whereabouts. Freda looks to Vittorio for protection; however, he retreats from the scene, and she must take on Patrick herself:

> Freda, seeing how [Vittorio] deserted her, was filled with hatred for Patrick. She wished the loaf of bread had been a broken bottle. Spitting, they faced each other, and Patrick held her by the shoulders.
>
> "Help me," she cried and twisted round to appeal to Vittorio, but he was no longer there.
>
> "Swine," she shouted, "beater of women." And she struggled with the Irishman, pinning him with her knee in his groin against the surface of the wall. (115)

Ironically, Freda proclaims the role of the helpless woman at the very moment she becomes a "spitting" streetfighter. Indeed, she proves herself capable not only of beating a "beater of women" but also of humiliating and intimidating Vittorio. When Freda reproaches Vittorio for not interfering in this altercation, she blatantly asks, "What sort of man are you?" Vittorio's answer is silent but shameful: "He turned and made for the exit, conscious he was a coward but terrorized by her loud voice and the strength of her arm" (115).

Designed to inspire love, the outing serves only to provoke further violence. Interpersonal disputes continue throughout the day. Freda walks in the woods and is pelted with pebbles; she responds by throwing a rock at her unseen assailant. Brenda, weary of Rossi's advances, uses Freda against him: she claims that if Rossi does not stop pawing her, Freda will report him to Mr. Paganotti. This threat prompts Rossi to ask Vittorio to seduce Freda so that she, too, would be guilty and could not go to Mr. Paganotti. Rossi's request infuriates Vittorio, and they argue. At the root of all this tension is formidable Freda; yet by the end of this picnic, she is formidable no longer, since she lies dead in the woods, with a broken neck.

From this point on, the novel becomes a Gothic murder mystery and the elaborate details of the plot become crucial to an understanding of the work.[12] The key question, of course, is "who killed Freda and why?" Writing about anonymous stalkers, Melley suggests that "there might be a theoretical advantage to being *unable* to pin one's persecution on an individual—since the problem may stem not from a single, deviant individual, but from a larger set of social institutions, narratives and conditions" (83). This theoretical advantage is obtained as narrative details accumulate to engender distrust of all the key male figures in the novel. Vittorio immediately suspects Patrick, who appears at the picnic grounds shortly after the discovery of Freda's body. Although Patrick repeatedly declares his innocence, considerable evidence mounts against him. Like Tom in *Casualties of Peace*, Patrick seems stereotypically violent by nature. A fighting, drinking Irishman, Patrick often comes to work with cuts and bruises from brawls. That day, he has had two violent encounters with Freda, and he clearly feels that Freda takes advantage of his beloved Brenda. In addition, a fresh gash on his forehead suggests that he is the one who stalked Freda in the woods. Although Brenda initially sympathizes with Patrick and his fears that the Italians will stick together and blame him for the murder, she does begin to doubt him: "She longed for him to take hold of her. She wanted to be protected. She wanted her hand held, but she couldn't be sure that it wasn't he that frightened her" (166). In this contemporary Gothic world, the threatened dissolution of the boundary between protector and murderer amplifies female fear.

While Vittorio seeks to blame Patrick, the latter insists that all the meaningful evidence points to Rossi's guilt. Rossi had been seen in the woods shortly before Freda was found; in fact, he seems to have been the one to discover her body. Rossi, too, clearly has a motive: his fear that Freda will tell Mr. Paganotti about his harassment of Brenda. Material evidence incriminates Rossi even further—the glass on Rossi's watch is shattered, and fragments of glass are found on the back of Freda's sweater. Thus the reader is forced to consider whether this man, known to be guilty of sexual harassment, is also guilty of femicide.

Initially, Rossi, too, proclaims his innocence. Shortly after Freda is found, Rossi talks to Brenda about events leading up to the outing and

Freda's demise. He explains that Vittorio did not want to participate in the outing; in fact, Vittorio made him secretly cancel the van so that the outing could not take place. Rossi refers to the argument he and Vittorio had about Freda and explains that Vittorio, too, feared the tales that Freda might tell to Mr. Paganotti. When Rossi saw Freda go into the woods, he decided that he would talk to her and intervene on his own and his friend's behalf. However, Freda and Vittorio were talking, so Rossi left. When Rossi returned to the woods, he found Freda dead. However, later, Rossi changes his account of events and "confesses" that he has inadvertently caused Freda's death. According to this version, Rossi saw Freda in the bushes; she was hot and had pushed her dress up around her stomach. Inflamed with drink and lust, Rossi tried to grab her. Freda took a step back, fell, and broke her neck. Rossi fell on top of her, bruising her and breaking his watch. This story accounts for all the evidence against Rossi. It also explains the bruises that Maria, who attends Freda's body, discovers on her stomach and legs.

At first, Brenda believes Rossi's revision. Patrick is cleared, and Brenda thinks that Rossi's confession "sounds reasonable. . . . It was the sort of thing that could happen to anyone, if they were tall and they were grabbed in the bushes by a small man. It certainly wasn't anything you could hang someone for" (214). Thus Brenda passively accepts the story told to her and watches as the men in the factory prepare to dump Freda's body, encased in a wine barrel, into the sea. Yet, despite this initial acceptance, Brenda is haunted by doubts. At one point during the outing, she had taken a nap. She vaguely remembers Vittorio taking something from Rossi's wrist (a watch?) and then later putting it back on. In addition, she thinks back to Rossi's confession and finds it significant that he says "I have forgotten nothing" as he looks at Vittorio. The implication is that Rossi has been primed to tell this second, self-incriminating story to protect Vittorio and the reputation of the Paganotti family.

Brenda's reaction to such doubts is to ignore them. "She shook her head and wished she could stop thinking about it. Rossi was such a loyal little man. He would do anything to protect the name of Paganotti. It doesn't matter, she thought, it is no longer of the slightest importance" (216). Thus Brenda denies memory and the possibility of knowledge. Just as she is unwilling to assume blame, so she avoids ascribing it. Rather than find out the truth of Freda's death, she retreats into the nuclear family that has constructed her as a victim and from which she has so recently escaped. At first, she tries to return to her husband; when she finds that he is otherwise engaged, she decides to go back to her parents. On some level,

Brenda now apprehends that a woman outside a legitimate (i.e., male-dominated) community risks a broken neck.

Although Bainbridge's text relegates Brenda to intellectual and actional inertia, it challenges the reader to construct another, grimmer story. By the end of the novel, we know that Maria's vision of Freda's marriage to Vittorio is actually a foreshadowing of Freda's death: the white dress is not a wedding gown, but a shroud; the "journey by land and sea" refers not to a honeymoon but to the disposal of Freda's bulky body. Similarly, the text leads us to believe that the groom-to-be is actually the murderer, that Rossi's second story is a cover for Vittorio. Massé has coined the term "marital Gothic" to describe narratives in which a recently married woman discovers with horror that the husband who was supposed to shore up her subjectivity is, instead, actively engaged in denying it. *The Bottle Factory Outing* might usefully be considered a premarital Gothic.

Brenda's groggy memory of the watch exchange prompts the reader to consider seriously Vittorio's guilt. The strongest evidence against Rossi—the glass from the watch—now seems to indict Vittorio, since it appears that the latter possessed the watch at the time of Freda's death. Rossi's original story increases suspicion. In that version, Vittorio's rearrangement of the transportation plans demonstrates that he is not only capable of scheming to get what he wants, but also deft at covering his tracks. Rossi's first story also suggests that Vittorio was the last to see Freda alive. Additionally, it is Vittorio who initially tries to blame Patrick; Vittorio comes up with the plan for disposing of Freda; Vittorio prompts Rossi and nods encouragingly during the latter's confession.

Intentionally or not, Freda has continually undermined Vittorio's masculinity; this constitutes a compelling motive for murder. When Freda and Patrick fight in the Windsor Castle chapel, Vittorio perceives himself as a coward. Also, he feels that Freda's forwardness threatens his family honor and his professional position: he is engaged to Rossi's niece and thus worries that Mr. Paganotti would balk at his flirtation with Freda. At one point, Vittorio tries to explain to Freda that he is committed to another woman; however, she misunderstands him and thinks he is declaring his love for her. She responds with forceful amorousness, and once again Vittorio exhibits anxiety about her power: "Was it possible she knew him better than he knew himself? Did she think she could take him by force?" (114). Vittorio is used to knowing and controlling himself and others; hence his relations with Freda jeopardize the security he derives from dominance.

As if to underscore the connection between Vittorio's anxiety about his manhood and Freda's death, Vittorio fingers his collar during Rossi's "confession." This seemingly trivial gesture recalls an earlier scene in which Freda tries to seduce Vittorio and, as part of her aggressive foreplay, chews the collar of his sweater. Freda's seduction fails because Vittorio is impotent (he excuses himself by saying that he needed to use the bathroom but was unable to gain access to it). Thus at the moment that Rossi gives his "reasonable" explanation of Freda's death, the reader is reminded of Vittorio's sexual failure. Ultimately, Freda poses a psychological, social, and physical threat to Vittorio's manhood. "You do not let me be the man" (111), he baldly tells her, and the text implies that this may be Freda's real cause of death.

On one level, then, *The Bottle Factory Outing* is an extremely pessimistic book. While Freda, the text's repository of female energy and power, is disposed of, Brenda, the "born victim," survives. Of course, Brenda's bleak future, like Patsy's in *Casualties of Peace*, undercuts the value attributed to this survival; nevertheless, the plot of this book suggests that women who let "men be men" and who accept the ensuing forms of victimization are safer than those who strive to subvert the privileges associated with hegemonic masculinity. Hence complicity in one's own and other women's victimization becomes the only viable survival strategy. Significantly, however, the structure of this novel, with its Gothic mystery, circumstantial evidence, but no definitive solution, proposes an alternative to Brenda's passivity though not necessarily a way out of the seemingly ceaseless cycle of female victimization it presents. Like Brenda, the reader must decide what to do with evidence that contradicts a "reasonable" story. By challenging the reader to question and rewrite the story of Freda's death, Bainbridge implicitly argues against Brenda's passive acceptance of the tales men tell her. Although both Freda and Brenda share the fate of the little woman with the great big hat—they are both effectively dispensed with—Bainbridge invites her readers to do feminist interpretive work, to look under their chairs and construct their own Gothic narratives, painful, scary, and uncertain as those may be.

Out of Freda's death comes macabre comedy; out of Willa's, ironic tragedy. Yet, despite tonal differences, both these tales frustrate the conservative Gothic plot and show that female fears about sexual violence and male domination are justified. While more conventional Gothics insure the safety of the protagonist, O'Brien and Bainbridge resolve their plots with femicidal violence. Although Patsy and Brenda return to traditional family structures, they do so out of resignation rather than desire. In these two novels, heroes do not defeat villains; rather, the former become aligned with the latter. The traditional Gothic plot promises that Mr. Right can and will be found. These contemporary works seem convinced that every man is Mr. Wrong. Ultimately, while most earlier Gothic texts posit that heterosexual romance is the norm that provides women with happiness and security, these works intimate that heterosexuality is a sexual orientation and political institution responsible for female destruction.[13]

Much of this destructive energy revolves around men's control of heterosexual relations. Throughout these two novels, we see the pernicious effects of attempts at such control. Herod perversely tries to stimulate and then restrain Willa's sexuality. Auro is presented as an antidote to Herod, the implication being that only another man can end Herod's domination of Willa. Tom tries to control Patsy's extramarital sexuality through rape; when that fails, he determines that the fit punishment for adultery is murder. While the sexual harassment of Brenda is relentless, Freda seems to have incurred the death penalty for trying to wrest romantic control from Vittorio. The message seems to be that in heterosexuality men control women. Under such domination, women are vulnerable; yet they become even more vulnerable if men feel themselves losing their power.

One must remember, however, that for straight-identifying women, such a critique of heterosexuality is immensely threatening, for it potentially leaves them in a no-win situation. As Simone de Beauvoir explains early on in *The Second Sex*, women "live dispersed among the males, attached through residence, economic condition and social standing to certain men—fathers or husbands—more firmly than they are to other women. . . . The bond that unites her to her oppressor is not comparable to any other" (xxii–xxiii). In heterosexuality, women desire and depend upon those systemically positioned to dominate; thus the stage is set for female ambivalence toward male love objects.

Perhaps that ambivalence combined with the omnipresent propaganda for heterosexuality accounts for the extremity of O'Brien's and Bainbridge's plots and even for the excessiveness of Dworkin's rhetoric.[14] Ultimately, O'Brien and Bainbridge counter not only the conventional Gothic formula but also the romantic relationships and ideologies firmly entrenched in that formula. In order to refute the idea that men and heterosexual relations protect women, these authors have envisioned femicide as the result of heterosexual romance. Thus they perform some of the important ideological work of cultural feminism. Antiromantic narratives such as *Casualties of Peace* and *The Bottle Factory Outing* can serve as a strategic part of the necessary process of destroying dangerous illusions about heterosexual love and the nuclear family.

However, such demythologizing and gothicizing of heterosexual romance also risk the unintended consequence of leaving women in another dead-end position; both *Casualties of Peace* and *The Bottle Factory Outing* crystallize these risks. In these novels, no safe place exists for women; indeed, Willa and Freda die when they least expect violence. Fear has been inextricably connected to heterosexual desire, but no alternative to, or rewriting of, male/female relations has been proposed.[15] By naturalizing heterosexuality as a Gothic gender system,[16] O'Brien, Bainbridge, and cultural feminist discourse potentially leave us suspended in a seemingly permanent state of victimization and paralyzing paranoia.[17] Acknowledging such risks and finding strategies to either diminish or productively reconfigure them is also important feminist work. However, as we do this work, we need to avoid blaming cultural feminism for the violence of heterosexuality as an institution; put another way, we need to avoid conflating cultural feminism with the female Gothic conditions it strives to diagnose.

Chapter 4

The Construction of the Sadomasochistic Couple

$\mathbf{M}$y overarching argument concerns the ways in which the strand of the contemporary female Gothic I'm charting here stages and intervenes in debates between cultural feminism and gender skepticism. In this chapter, I take the risk of being charged with critical masochism and return to the scene where cultural feminists purportedly committed one of their most heinous "crimes": pornography. A great deal of feminist ink and bad blood has been spilled on the "sex wars"[1]; however, my primary concern here is that cultural feminists find in pornographic scripts the crystallization and reproduction of culture's desire for female victims. When Susan Griffin argues that "pornographic culture annihilates the female sex" and that "a woman inherits from culture a continual experience of fear" (217), she is reading culture as a femicidal plot. In *Pornography: Men Possessing Women*, Andrea Dworkin describes a pornographic photograph entitled "Beaver Hunters" that depicts a woman tied to the hood of a black jeep: the bound woman, whose genitals are exposed and foregrounded, is the "beaver," and two men who sit inside the jeep are clearly the hunters. According to Dworkin,

> Terror is finally the content of the photograph, and it is also its effect on the female observer. That men have the power and desire to make, publish and profit from the photograph engenders fear. That millions more men enjoy the photograph makes the fear palpable. That men who in general champion civil rights defend the photograph without experiencing it as an assault on women

> intensifies the fear, because if the horror of the photograph does not resonate with these men, that horror is not validated as horror in male culture, and women are left without apparent recourse. (27)

Dworkin's prose, her emphasis on female fear and female horror, suggests that the production, consumption, and cultural acceptance of pornography is a paradigmatic narrative of the female Gothic.[2]

Indeed, Ellen Moers's offhand comment that "the Marquis de Sade . . . is known to have admired Mrs. Radcliffe's works" (137) embeds a connection between the Gothic and the pornographic from the start.[3] However, whether or not one makes an argument about direct influence, it seems clear that these two genres overlap. Pornography, predicated as it is upon violations of the female body, acts out the worst fears of the Gothic heroine. Male villains and the young, attractive females whom they often cause to suffer are muted versions of sadists and masochists. As Edmundson quips, "S & M is where Gothic, in a certain sense, wants to go" (131).[4] From the point of view of feminist critics, such sadomasochistic tendencies of the Gothic point to the "cultural, psychoanalytic, and fictional expectation that [women] *should* be masochistic if they are 'normal' women" (Massé 2). Thus, hints of female masochism in the Gothic appear inextricably related to social conformity. For example, in *The Mysteries of Udolpho*, where protectors still exist, Emily could have saved herself a lot of trouble by eloping with Valancourt rather than traveling to Italy with Montoni and her aunt. However, since elopements aren't ladylike, she eschews Valancourt's protective and loving offer, hence becoming Montoni's dependent and prey.

Angela Carter's *Honeybuzzard* (1966) and Muriel Spark's *Driver's Seat* (1970) explore these inchoate connections among pornography, female Gothicism, and gender norms. In these two novels, the female Gothic experience is situated in the primary pornographic relationship, the sadomasochistic couple, and both authors use this couple to suggest that perversion and femicide are the logical outcome of hegemonic definitions of masculinity and femininity. Thus, like cultural feminist discourse, they use sadomasochism to make generalizations about gender.[5] However, by portraying masochistic female victims and men who struggle against their own sadistic tendencies, Carter and Spark considerably complicate the gendered roles of victim and victimizer that seem clearly defined and inevitable in O'Brien's *Casualties of Peace* and Bainbridge's *Bottle Factory Outing*. Ultimately, both Spark and Carter represent sadism and masochism as gendered strategies that assuage contemporary anxieties about identity and vulnerability. By reading sadism and masochism as perverse, culturally encouraged, and gendered forms of agency, Spark and Carter counter determinist, normalizing trends in psychoanalytic and cultural feminist thought. Significantly, however, Carter and Spark do not represent the cultural playing field for sadists and masochists as an equal one. Rather, the ready-made scripts for male sadists and female masochists make it doubly difficult, though not impossible, for women to simply refuse to be victims.

Of course, the spectre of female masochism has long haunted psychoanalysis and feminist thought. Freud recognized that masochism could exist in men; in fact, in his 1924 paper "The Economic Problem in Masochism," he concerned himself with feminine masochism only as it is found in men. Clearly, he linked masochism with femininity and passivity; even Juliet Mitchell, who defends Freud against feminist "misreadings," acknowledges this (115). However, for Freud, sex and gender often became problematically entangled. Thus even when Freud discussed male masochists, his remarks tended to associate this perversion with his perception of normal, biologically female bodies:

> But if one has an opportunity of studying cases [of male masochists] in which the masochistic phantasies have undergone specially rich elaboration, one easily discovers that in them the subject is placed in a situation characteristic of *womanhood*, i.e. they mean he is being castrated, is playing the passive part in coitus, or is *giving birth*. (258—my emphasis).

The suggestion here and elsewhere is that masochism is part of both the female and the feminine personality. As Luce Irigaray puts it in her essay "Psychoanalytic Theory: Another Look," "As for *masochism*, is it to be considered a factor in 'normal' femininity? Some of Freud's assertions tend in this direction" (44).

Two of Freud's disciples, Helene Deutsch and Marie Bonaparte, intuited such tendencies and essentialized them.[6] Deutsch, who embraced Freud's idea of the castration complex, infamously believed that female masochism and biology are intertwined. According to Deutsch, "the absence of an active organ [penis] brought the turn toward passivity and masochism in its train" (251). Although Deutsch recognized that masochistic tendencies pose dangers to the ego, she asserted that female masochism is a necessary and natural means to prepare women for the pain of defloration and childbirth. As Deutsch put it in her reactionary 1944 study *The Psychology of Women*, "In one of her functions woman must have a certain amount of masochism if she is to be adjusted to reality. This is the reproductive function" (276).

Marie Bonaparte, in whose "enormously interesting" company Muriel Spark spent many hours during World War II, also believed that masochism is inherently female.[7] In *Female Sexuality* (1953), Bonaparte, too, pointed to the pain involved in menstruation, defloration, and childbirth as evidence of the need for female masochism. Yet her argument went even further; since the ova awaits the penetrating spermatozoa, she deemed that

> fecundation of the female cell is initiated by a kind of wound; in its way, the female cell is primordially masochistic. Now it would appear that these prototypal cellular reactions pass unchanged into the psychical apparatus of those who bear the same cells and, indeed, our psycho-sexual responses, whether male or female, seem thoroughly permeated with them. (78)

Bonaparte, like Deutsch, wholeheartedly accepted the castration complex in women and asserted the primacy of the penis and thus the inferiority of the clitoris. As the following quotation illustrates, the activation of female masochism was inextricably related to this theoretical castration complex:

> The girl . . . discovers the difference between the sexes and then must submit to the castration complex with all its disappointments as regards the too-small clitoris. This, the executive organ, properly speaking of the infantile phallic sadism, soon therefore becomes depreciated and the envied penis, that big paternal penis with which the clitoris could never compare, must, in the little girl's eyes, take its place as the true representative of sadism. A sort of surrender of the clitoris to the greater and mightier power of the penis would occur, as it were. This is when the primary, passive masochistic drives dormant in the female are no doubt mobilized. The active clitoridal sadistic attitude, which now must be abandoned, is reversed, and the little girl desires the father's assaults and the blows of his big penis. (82)

Psychoanalytically, Bonaparte imagined the penis as a great, mighty weapon capable of delivering blows; as women become masochistic, so does the penis become "the true representative of sadism." Thus reproduction, compulsory heterosexuality, female masochism, and male sadism become mutually constituting and reinforcing discourses, and psychoanalysis plays its part in normalizing the female Gothic by reading sadomasochism as *the* script of sexual difference.[8]

Significantly, while most cultural feminist thought has refuted such determinist and normalizing explanations for female masochism, the tendency to associate penises and penetration with violence has retained traces of an essentialized male sadism. Alice Echols highlights the contradictory problematic of such arguments: "Although some [cultural feminists] seem to attribute women's masochistic fantasies to their masochism, most argue that they are a patriarchal invention or that they reveal women's powerlessness and socialization rather than their masochism. Of course, men's sadistic fantasies are still seen as confirmation of their fundamentally murderous nature" ("New Feminism" 448). Clearly this cultural feminist double standard is contaminated by the same reactionary essentialism of the hyperFreudian Deutsch and Bonaparte. I purposefully modify the term *essentialism* here. My assumption is that not all forms of essentialism are equal, nor equally bad. However, a belief in the essence of male sadism invites a belief in the inevitability of female victimization, a self-defeating stance for a feminist vision of social change. Given that the charge of essentialism during the past decade has both served the forces of backlash *and* fueled productive and progressive feminist self-consciousness, it seems necessary to use the word with care.

In the work of Karen Horney lies a social constructionist response to such essentialist trends in Freudian psychoanalysis and, by extension, cultural feminism. In her paper "The Problem of Feminine Masochism" (1935), Horney suggested a cultural culpability in the formation of female masochists. Horney astutely pointed out that the female castration complex or "penis envy" is "an hypothesis, not a fact" (216). Hence she undermined arguments based on the assumption that the castration complex forces women to turn their aggressive drives inward and thus become masochistic. Even more importantly, Horney argued that large numbers of masochistic women do not automatically support theories of biologically essential female masochism; cultural as well as biological factors have to be considered, and Horney chided psychoanalysis for its denial tendencies:

> Whenever the question of frequency enters into the picture, sociological implications are involved, and the refusal to be concerned with them from the psychoanalytic angle does not shut out their existence. Omission of these considerations may lead to a false valuation of anatomical differences and their personal elaboration as causative factors for phenomena actually partially or wholly the result of social conditioning. Only a synthesis of both series of conditions can lead to a complete understanding. (224)

Although Horney did not discount biology, her interest lay in determining the cultural conditions that may cause the development of female masochism. The conditions she cited include the "blocking of outlets for expansiveness and sexuality," the "estimation of women as beings who are, on the whole, inferior to men," the "economic dependence of women on men or on family," and the "restriction of women to spheres of life that are built chiefly upon emotional bonds, such as family life, religion, or charity work" (230). Obviously, such conditions are coterminous with traditional ideals of femininity, a fact that caused Horney to assert that "in our culture it is hard to see how any woman can escape becoming masochistic to some degree, from the effects of the culture alone, without any appeal to contributory factors in the anatomical-physiological characteristics of woman, and their psychic effects" (231). Thus Horney recognized female masochism as a phenomenon but viewed it as culturally constructed. Horney also shrewdly exposed the ideological power of psychoanalysis by noting that biologically deterministic theories of female masochism bolster androcentric cultures. Moreover, Horney strove to disrupt the seamlessness between sadomasochism and heterosexuality, even as she recognized their cultural entanglements. Horney included "biological differences in intercourse" as a factor that may "serve" but not cause the formation of female masochism. As if prescient of the cultural feminist critique of intercourse, Horney clearly stated, "Sadism and masochism have fundamentally nothing whatsoever to do with intercourse, but the female role in intercourse (being penetrated) *lends* itself more readily to a personal misinterpretation (when needed) of masochistic performance; and the male role, to one of sadistic activity" (232).

In their fictions, Angela Carter and Muriel Spark expose both the pervasiveness and the perversity of the gendering of masochism and sadism. Like Horney, they privilege the social implications of such sadomasochistic plots and reveal their characters' misinterpretations to be cultural ideology. Taken together, *Honeybuzzard* and *The Driver's*

Seat suggest that hegemonic definitions of femininity and masculinity tend to construct female masochists and male sadists. Carter and Spark share cultural feminism's reading of the pornographic sadomasochistic couple as a cultural norm constituting Gothic horror.

Angela Carter's first novel *Shadow Dance* (1966; released in the United States as *Honeybuzzard*)[9] explores the connections among pornography, the female Gothic, and gender norms through the figure of the male sadist. However, by highlighting the process and the struggle of endorsing sadistic feeling and action, Carter reads sadomasochism as a Gothic gendered script but does not naturalize it as such. Indeed, in that early novel, Carter plays the role of the moral pornographer, an idea that she develops in *The Sadeian Woman and the Ideology of Pornography* (1978). In that work, Carter proposes that pornography might not only constitute the female Gothic but also have the potential to produce feminist effects. She imagines a "moral pornographer" who "might use pornography as a critique of current relations between the sexes" (19).

In *Shadow Dance*, Carter explores "a dimension of pure horror" as she depicts the violence of Honeybuzzard, a stereotypical sadist and part owner of a junk shop. Honeybuzzard chooses Ghislaine, his masochistic ex-girlfriend, as the main object of his violence. Early in the novel, we learn that Honeybuzzard has slashed Ghislaine's face and has permanently disfigured her. Despite such abuse—or perhaps because of it—Ghislaine craves Honeybuzzard's mastery over her and begs him to become her lover once more. Ghislaine is what Herod from *Casualties of Peace* erroneously assumed Willa and all women to be. Meanwhile, Honeybuzzard has begun a romantic relationship with another woman, Emily; the latter, who is initially unaware of Honeybuzzard's sadistic tendencies, is young, sexy, and emotionally self-sufficient. Honeybuzzard ultimately responds to Ghislaine's pleas by strangling her. Upon discovering her lover's capacity for violence, Emily betrays Honeybuzzard to the police and excises him from her heart, despite the fact that she is pregnant with his child.

Although the plot of this novel depends heavily on Honeybuzzard and Ghislaine's perversions, we are denied access to their consciousness. Occasionally, we derive information from Emily's point of view; however, the bulk of the narrative is limited to the consciousness of Morris Gray, Honeybuzzard's business partner and best friend. Morris is simultaneously attracted and repelled by Honeybuzzard's perversity, and the climax of the novel revolves around Morris's response to Honeybuzzard's murder of Ghislaine. Indeed, the meaning of this work lies in understanding and interpreting Morris's psyche. Carter uses Honeybuzzard's murderous perversity to expose the Gothic elements in Morris's more mainstream male imagination.

Angela Carter explicitly identified herself as a feminist in her life and work. In "Notes from the Front Line," Carter writes, "The Women's Movement has been of immense importance to me personally and I would regard myself as a feminist writer, because I'm a feminist in everything else and one can't compartmentalise these things in one's life" (69). For Carter, the study of philosophy and the social unrest of 1968 merged to form her feminist consciousness: "I can date . . . to that sense of heightened awareness of the society around me in 1968, my own questioning of the nature of my reality as a woman. How that social fiction of my 'femininity' was created, by means outside my control, and palmed off on me as the real thing" ("Notes" 70). Despite such self-identification and feminist self-consciousness, feminist controversy has sometimes surrounded her work. While Dworkin dubbed *The Sadeian Woman* "a pseudofeminist literary essay,"[10] Keenan reads that work—rightly, I think—as evidence of "Carter's extraordinary capacity to tap into crucial critical debates relevant to feminism and cultural politics, long before those debates had been fully staged" (132).[11] Significantly, the brutal violation of female bodies in Carter's fiction has made some critics question the efficacy of her feminist politics. As Gamble summarizes one strand of critical opinion, Carter's views on pornography along with "her graphic depictions of violence against women in her writing . . . have led some critics to conclude that . . . she actually only furthers reactionary portrayals of women as nothing more than the objects of male desire" (4).

Unlike a lot of other women's fiction written in the 1960s and the 1970s, *Honeybuzzard* is technically male-centered—as noted above, much of the narrative is from Morris's point of view—and this fact lends credence to another critical view that Carter's *early* work is male-identified. Indeed, responding to Carter's own comments about "patriarchal bias" in her work, Gamble writes, "It is in *Shadow Dance* that this bias is most disturbingly obvious, for this is a text in which women are resolutely denied the privilege of a narrative voice. By excluding them from the formation of discourse, they are rendered figments of a fevered male imagination, and become the targets of a disturbing blend of violence and eroticism" (54).

Certainly, Carter distinguishes between her pre- and post-'68 performances. As she puts it, "I was, as a girl, suffering a degree of colonialisation of the mind. Especially in the journalism I was writing then, I'd—quite unconsciously—posit a male point of view as a general one. So there was an element of the male impersonator about this young person as she was finding herself" ("Notes" 71). Thus Elaine Jordan, a critic who astutely notes the feminist pleasures and dangers that Carter provides, accepts such remarks as immutable fact: "[I]t's true that she started writing as a kind of male-impersonator, with a strong streak of misogyny" (119).[12] However, Carter's own accounting of her feminist consciousness suggests that male identification[13] and male mimicry need not be equated: "I realise, now, I must always have sensed that something was badly wrong with the versions of reality I was offered that took certain aspects of my being as a woman for granted. I smelled the rat in D. H. Lawrence pretty damn quick" ("Notes" 70). Lee comments that "it is useful to speculate whether Carter saw her own novels as fulfilling the demands of a moral pornography" (10); as I advance a reading of *Honeybuzzard* in the related terms of a female Gothic that does feminist work and a work of moral pornography, we might remember that Carter herself argued that sexual relations are symptomatic of social relations, and thus if the latter are "described explicitly [they] will form a critique of those relations, *even if that is not and never has been the intention of the pornographer*" (22— my emphasis).

Honeybuzzard is the prototype of the lupine masculine principle that pervades "The Company of Wolves," Carter's version of "Little Red Ridinghood." However, unlike the male beast whose murderous desires are harnessed by an aggressive female sexuality, Honeybuzzard seems untamable.[14] Even his physical appearance underscores his violent nature: "It was impossible to look at the full, rich lines of his dark red mouth without thinking: 'This man eats meat.' It was an inexpressibly carnivorous mouth; a mouth that suggested snapping, tearing, biting. . . . How beautiful he was and how indefinably sinister" (57). Thus Honeybuzzard is the repository of evil, and much of the plot revolves around his malevolent acts. Seemingly devoid of feeling, Honeybuzzard coolly slashes Ghislaine's face, unthinkingly humiliates Morris by creating a cardboard jumping jack in his image, and responds to the suicide of a pregnant woman (who mistakenly believed that her husband had slashed Ghislaine) with a practical joke.

Together, Honeybuzzard and Ghislaine represent the classic sadomasochistic couple, and their depiction exposes the co-implication of pornographic, psychoanalytic, and Gothic scripts. Feminist commentators on sadomasochism such as Susan Griffin and Jessica Benjamin have noted that the sadist and the masochist are complements, that the couple becomes the projection of a divided self.[15] In this case, that self is Morris, for the tension between Honey and Ghislaine represents the tension within Morris himself. Ultimately, Honey and Ghislaine are little more than cardboard figures; the real power of this novel lies in Morris's relationship with the two members of this couple and his eventual decision to side with and protect the sadistic Honey.

Morris is the contemporary antihero *par excellence*. A failed artist, he occupies himself by scavenging through abandoned buildings with Honey and selling found objects in a jointly owned junk shop. Predictably, this business venture is less than profitable, and Morris relies on his wife, Edna, for economic stability. Morris self-consciously meditates on his own uselessness and impotence; he often alludes to his childless marriage, his disastrous sexual exploits with Ghislaine, and his dependence upon Honeybuzzard. Ultimately, Morris recognizes that the junk he gathers and sells is a metonym for his life.

Significantly, Morris's personal history prepares him for a life among the rubble. During World War II, a building in which he and his mother were staying was bombed. His mother, who was copulating outside the door of this building, was presumably killed; he was buried under debris for a time. Thus Morris's primal scene is set for profound ambivalence toward Mom, whom Morris loves but also hates for abandoning him in the act of loving another.

The specifics of Morris's childhood trauma inevitably connect sexuality with death, desire with abandonment and lack. Such connections inhere in the pornographic imagination, and thus Honeybuzzard's battle against Ghislaine's sexualized flesh becomes aligned with Morris's battle against his own vulnerability. Significantly, however, Morris's fear is also linked to Western cultural traditions of misogyny not readily identified as pornographic. In the opening scene of the novel, Ghislaine has just gotten out of the hospital—she was recovering from the wound Honeybuzzard inflicted on her—and Morris meets her in a bar. When Morris first sees her, he utters, "'Oh, God in Heaven,' as if invoking protection against her" (1). Repeatedly, Morris compares her to infamous female monsters. Thus Ghislaine reminds him of the Bride of Frankenstein, a Fury, a witch-woman, and Medusa. Threatened by her voracious desire, Morris thinks of her as a "candle flame for moths, a fire that burned those around her but was not itself consumed" (3). Morris also associates the phrase "memento mori" with Ghislaine; his consciousness is emblematic of a culture that links women with death, the womb with the tomb. Following such great traditions, Morris translates such fear of mortality and vulnerability into aggression.

Clearly, Morris receives vicarious pleasure from Honeybuzzard's violence against Ghislaine. We find out that only hours before Ghislaine was mutilated, Morris, frustrated by his own impotence with Ghislaine, had told Honey to "take her and teach her a lesson" (34). After the opening scene in the bar, Morris returns home and surveys several pornographic photographs of Ghislaine; he, Honey, and Ghislaine had spent an afternoon together taking these pictures. Although Honey posed with Ghislaine for some of these photos, Morris's attention is fixated on the latter; indeed, he soon finds himself engaged in an act of imagistic mutilation:

> Yet, once he had the pen in his hand, he found he was finely, carefully, striping each image of her with a long scar from eyebrow to navel. All the time, he wondered why he was doing it; it seemed a vindictive thing to do and he had never thought of himself as a vindictive man. But he did not stop until he had finished marking them all in. (17–8)

Thus Morris has essentially done to Ghislaine's image what Honeybuzzard has done to her body.

Yet, unlike Honeybuzzard, Morris has flashes of guilt about and identification with Ghislaine, and thus his response to Honeybuzzard's brutality and his own sadistic feelings is complex and ambivalent. When Morris runs away from Ghislaine at the bar, someone throws a bottle at him but misses. Yet he imagines that he has been struck, and this vision reveals much about his relation to Ghislaine:

> He felt the bottle shattering against his face and, raising his hand, was bemusedly surprised to find no traces of blood from a gashed forehead on his fingertips. Why not? In a metaphysical hinterland between intention and execution, someone had thrown a bottle in his face, a casual piece of violence; there was a dimension, surely, in the outer nebulae, maybe, where intentions were always executed, where even now he stumbled, bleeding, blinded. . . . He walked on in a trance, *scarred like her*. (11—my emphasis)

Since Morris's own violent intentions toward Ghislaine have been executed by the sadistic Honeybuzzard, Morris imagines that he must be punished. Significantly, however, the envisioned punishment merely confirms that Morris shares Ghislaine's wounded status—he is "scarred like her." Morris's figurative wound surfaces again in a dream during which he cut Ghislaine's face with "a jagged shard of broken glass and blood was running on her breast not only from her but also from himself, from his cut head" (18). Here Morris figures himself as both victim and victimizer; in his psychic melodrama, Ghislaine, the female masochist, plays his wounded, needy self, and Honeybuzzard, the male sadist, is presented as an impenetrable and therefore invulnerable alter ego.[16]

Although Ghislaine and Honey are presented as parts of Morris, the latter attempts to strengthen his ties with the seemingly unassailable Honey and to sever his association with Ghislaine's vulnerable flesh. At one point, Morris thinks, "I am a second hand man; and [Ghislaine], now, is a second hand woman." Morris momentarily recognizes that Ghislaine's physical mutilation parallels his own psychic wounding. However, rather than sustaining this identification, Morris seeks to realign himself with Honey and to deny his own feelings of worthlessness and vulnerability. Hence Morris's next thought is that he and his sadistic business partner could display Ghislaine in their storefront window: "They would put her in the window arranged on a rug or a sofa, with a label Sellotaped to her navel: 'Hardly used'" (19). However, it is precisely Ghislaine's use that is underscored here. By dehumanizing Ghislaine and establishing her as an object of exchange, Morris strives to reassert his connection to Honey and thus his own value.

However, Morris's identification with Honey is not yet secure. On one of their junk-finding excursions in an abandoned building, Morris and Honey happen upon the living space of a waitress whom Morris has dubbed a "Struldbrug," a Swiftian allusion to those who are decrepit but immortal. Given that structures in the Gothic often represent the maternal body[17] and that Morris regards this waitress as a mother figure, it seems clear that the scene in this abandoned building is inextricably related to the rubble of Morris's youth, the abandonment and ambivalence he felt upon his mother's demise. As an equal opportunity sadist who does not distinguish between nurturing women and sexual women, Honey decides to have his fun. Thus when the waitress arrives home, Honey purposefully frightens her; as a result of this fright and her inebriation, she falls into a stupor. Fearing for her life, Morris wants to seek medical aid, but Honeybuzzard forbids such action. In a rare act of rebellion, Morris thwarts Honey's will and tries to run away to get help. Honey responds to such opposition with violence: he catches Morris, they wrestle, and Honey finally threatens to kill his partner with the same knife that he used to mutilate Ghislaine. Beaten into submission, Morris is forced to abandon the Struldbrug and is taken by Honey back to the junkshop.

Like Ghislaine, Morris has become the victim of Honey's sadism; thus Morris has not been freed from association with the female embodiment of his victim self. Moreover, Morris's inability to aid the Struldbrug provokes guilt about violent impulses that precede the events of this overdetermined evening. Indeed, during the delirium that results from his injuries, Morris moans that he has killed his mother. By refusing to make distinctions between sexualized flesh and maternal bodies, distinctions that Morris and the cultural psyche he represents have deployed to manage embodied vulnerability and matricidal impulses, Honey alienates Morris.[18]

Significantly, Emily, Honey's current girlfriend, represents the possibility of Morris sustaining this alienation and finding an alternative resolution to the ambivalence that causes him to identify with Honey. On the night that Honey and Morris fight about the Struldbrug, Emily comforts Morris by making love to him. Such use of sexuality clearly muddies the division between nurturance and carnality that Morris has internalized and that Honey has violated that very night. The fact that sexualized Emily, "a new-style matriarch" (Sage, *Angela Carter* 14) is also an expectant mother—Morris later finds out that she is carrying Honey's child—could further disrupt Morris's dichotomizing of women.[19] Thus in the figure of Emily, Morris is offered an alternative to Honey, a revision of the terms that originated Morris's interest in Honey's sadistic acts.

However, Morris's investment in Honeybuzzard is stronger than his identification with bodies capable of being scarred, buried, or terrified into oblivion. At the end of the narrative, as the threat of Honeybuzzard's violence against Ghislaine escalates, Morris bonds anew with his sadistic alter ego. When Emily, Honey's girlfriend, informs Morris that Ghislaine has returned and that Honey has gone with her, Morris experiences "a premonition of horror" (167). Although he suspects that Ghislaine is in grave danger, his chiding of Emily shows that his real concern is for Honeybuzzard:

> "You shouldn't have let him go alone!"
> "What?"
> "There's something wrong with him, *he* needs help. He oughtn't

to go with Ghislaine, I know it. He—"
    "He's not a kid. What he does is his own business and if he
wants to go off with that mad bitch, then it's up to him, isn't it."
    "But I don't know what he might do with her. Oh, God, if only
I knew. . . . He's always seemed so essential to me, like a limb. You
can't call your hand a friend, it's just there. And you don't bother
to ask why it does things—picks things up, puts them down. And
he was like *my* hand that belonged to me but I never understood
how it functioned." (172—my emphasis)

Thus Morris acknowledges that Honeybuzzard is figuratively a part of
himself, whom he seeks to protect rather than interrogate.

The climax of the novel underscores Morris's empathy with
Honeybuzzard. Fearing the worst, Morris takes Emily to the abandoned
building he and Honey visited on the previous night. Once inside, Morris
and Emily discover the body of Ghislaine and understand that Honey has
strangled her. Now that Ghislaine is dead, Morris's ambivalence toward
her is nonexistent; since he no longer needs to fear her, he can feel "pity
and tenderness, for the first time unmixed with any other feeling" (180).
However, he still reserves most of his concern for Honey, who has acted
out Morris's desire by "doing what Morris had always wanted but never
defined . . . filling up her voracity once and for all by cramming with death
the hungry mouth between her thighs" (180–81). Gamble aptly notes that
"[a]s a statement of murderous misogyny, this could hardly be bettered"
(55).[20] Clearly, Morris has projected his own neediness onto Ghislaine
and labeled it her "voracity"; to his mind, male vulnerability and the lack
associated with female genitalia are inextricably connected.[21] Since
Honeybuzzard has destroyed the emblematic cause of Morris's own
hungry, childish mouth, Morris feels indebted to, and protective of, his
murderous double: "But I wanted it. I am to blame, too, I should have
guessed, I should have protected *him*" (181—my emphasis).

The details that surround Ghislaine's death clearly suggest that such
hatred of sexualized flesh originates not in Morris, nor even in Honey, but
rather in a dominant mythology of Western culture. Susan Griffin has
argued that the underlying ideology of Christianity and pornography is
the same—the hatred and flagellation of the flesh.[22] Carter fictionally
makes the same point by repeatedly associating pornographic and Christian iconography. Ghislaine is the daughter of a minister; her obsession
with the mortification of her flesh (at one point, she reopens her facial
scar; even after Honeybuzzard has slashed her, she returns to him and
proclaims him her master) seems ordained by family history. Signifi-

cantly, Honeybuzzard murders Ghislaine in the room where he had previously shared with Morris his fantasy of raping Ghislaine on a plaster Christ. Indeed, Morris and Emily find Ghislaine's body on a table surrounded by candles; thus Ghislaine's death scene resembles a black mass. In addition, in the last glimpse we have of Honeybuzzard, he is cradling that plaster Christ. As Lee astutely notes, "Honeybuzzard finds religious images powerful; they incite his increasing perversity because they seem to sanction his treatment of women" (27).[23] Clearly images of sadistic violence and sacred sacrifice merge in this final scene, and thus Carter once again links mainstream culture with the pornographic imagination.

Unlike the narrator in *Rebecca* and Brenda in *The Bottle Factory Outing*, Emily refuses to be complicit in the death of another woman. Despite her involvement with Honey, she has managed to reject not only the dualities of the sadomasochistic script but also its violence; thus she flees the building to call the police. Morris, following her, is thrown into another psychic crisis. Appalled by Emily's betrayal of the father of her child, Morris wants to aid a clearly maddened Honey; yet Morris fears the consequences of such an action. To his mind, protecting Honey is a heroic act; hence he sees his dilemma as one of courage versus cowardice. Significantly, Morris looks to the mythological realm for guidance and nerve. At one point, he questions his responsibility to Honey and utters the legendary question: "Am I my brother's keeper?" Thus he sees his loyalty to Honey as an avoidance of Cain-like behavior. He also casts himself as Orpheus and his journey back into the abandoned building as a journey into the underworld. Interestingly enough, earlier in the novel when Morris is presented with the Orpheus/Eurydice myth, his response is to think "Orpheus was a fool, in the first place, to want to go and retrieve the silly bitch" (24). However, when Eurydice takes on a male form, this journey "to rescue or destroy a dear companion" makes sense to him.

Via such androcentric mythological visions, Morris finds the strength to align himself with Honey, and he returns to the literal and figurative shadows of the abandoned building. At this point, Morris knows that Emily has already contacted the police and that Honey will be caught. Nevertheless, Morris turns his back on Emily, who is overcome by the nausea of pregnancy, and embraces the Gothic underworld where he will excuse femicide and do battle against male vulnerability. Symbolically, Morris eschews sexualized maternity and instead chooses the ruins of a paternalistic culture where body and soul cannot meet. Carter's 1974 commentary—"We live in Gothic times. Now to understand is the main thing"[24]—reads like a metacommentary on her first novel. However, even as she represents the Gothic, she avoids naturalizing it. Indeed, by envisioning Morris's ultimate identification with, and defense of, the male sadist as a struggle and a choice (albeit a culturally overdetermined one), Carter refutes the essentialist tendencies of both psychoanalytic and cultural feminist discourses. About Carter's works, Peach generalizes: she "complicated the familiar villain/victim . . . binarisms while not eschewing the way in which pain and suffering are employed to dominate women" (167). That generalization is particularly apt for *Honeybuzzard*. Thus I would argue the feminist potential of her early Gothic work, too often dismissed as the misogynist product of male impersonation.

Significantly, Carter does not imagine that Emily has any trouble rejecting Ghislaine's masochism; indeed, although *Honeybuzzard* makes use of the sadomasochistic couple, it ultimately privileges the first member of that pornographic dyad. Hence Carter's text is complemented well by Muriel Spark's *Driver's Seat* (1970), a novel that focuses upon the other half of that couple, the female masochist, as it cautions against using victimization to establish one's identity.

❦   ❦   ❦

The Driver's Seat, Spark's tenth novel, is the story of Lise, a thirty four-year-old woman who has worked most of her adult life in an accountant's office. At the beginning of the novel, Lise is preparing for a vacation in southern Italy; the novel follows her movements the day before and the day of her flight from Copenhagen to Rome. Early on in the novel, we find out that Lise will be murdered. Thus the reader is led to believe that only two questions remain: who has committed this femicide and why? By the end of the novel, these two questions are answered: we know that Richard, a fellow traveler on Lise's flight and a supposedly reformed victimizer of women, has committed the crime and that, ostensibly, he has only obeyed orders, since the climax of the novel reveals that Lise has suicidally planned her own femicide. This revelation indicates that the needs served by her masochistic performance constitute the real mystery of this novel.

Such concerns may seem unduly macabre and worldly for an author often characterized by her Catholicism and her vision of a transcendent realm. In an interview with Sara Frankel, Spark clearly identifies her unswerving religious faith as her life's compass:

> It's very important for me to have a point of departure, because in the modern world nobody has any fixed belief or fixed idea of anything, and in a world like that a fixed point is very important. And it's not that I took it on for convenience—it's that I can't *not* believe that there is this norm. What other norm could there be, for someone brought up in the Western world, really wanting something. Whether we like it or not, the Christian-Judaic tradition that grew up around the Mediterranean dictates what we think is good or evil, and defines all of the absolutes that we hold to be important. The idea of Christ as an example, for instance, was terribly important to the whole development of the West—sociologically, morally, even politically. (445)

Possibly Spark cannot imagine herself living without this "fixed point" because she can and does imagine the despair of characters who lack it. Indeed, Lise seems like a casualty of the modern world, a traveler without a literal or figurative compass. It is perhaps not incidental that Spark, suffering from "nervous exhaustion," finished *The Driver's Seat* in a hospital (Whittaker 36) and that Lise has appropriated the Christian strategy of martyrdom while neglecting the redemptive purpose of that act.

Significantly, Lise's search for her destroyer reflects her creator's belief that violence is both a fact of life and a novelistic necessity:

> I'm quite fascinated by violence. I read policiers, detective stories, all that sort of thing, and I think a lot of life is violent. A lot of my novels don't have violence, but sometimes it's necessary: you can't have novels without violence. For instance, in a lot of romantic novels—take Daphne du Maurier's—there's violence all over the place. But she weeps a lot over it, it's very romantically presented. And generally speaking you find more violence in love story novelists, taking extreme cases. I don't know if you've ever read Barbara Cartland, but her books are full of violence, men whipping brides and oh my God, this is the romantic thing carried to its absurdity. (Frankel interview 452)[25]

Clearly, Spark is familiar with the conventions of the Gothic romance and the ways in which this genre overlaps with pornography. *The Driver's Seat* seems indebted to, and a refinement of, such conventions, since in that novel Spark removes any trace of "weeping" and carries the connection between romance and violence to an even more absurd extreme than Barbara Cartland: Lise spends the last day of her life looking for Mr.

Right, the man who will murder her. Thus the heterosexual horror that O'Brien's Willa and Bainbridge's Freda find when they least expect it is exactly what Lise actively seeks.[26]

In *The Driver's Seat*, Spark, unlike Angela Carter, has eschewed the conventions of the modernist psychological novel and has instead appropriated some of the strategies of the *nouveau roman*. Lise's story is told almost wholly in the present tense; as Bold and Whittaker note, this device promotes narrative tension and the illusion of immediacy. Yet the occasional flash-forward,[27] with its requisite use of the future tense, disrupts that illusion and irrevocably alters the hermeneutic code. The most dramatic use of this flash-forward technique occurs early in the novel when the narrator informs us that Lise will shortly become a murder victim: "She will be found tomorrow morning dead from multiple stab-wounds, her wrists bound with a silk scarf and her ankles bound with a man's necktie, in the grounds of an empty villa, in a park of the foreign city to which she is travelling on the flight now boarding at Gate 14" (25). At this point, we do not yet know that Lise actively seeks this fate, that she is purposefully traveling to achieve this end, that a cause-effect relationship exists between the willful boarding of this plane and the pornographic pose of her dead body. Nevertheless, we do know what will happen to the protagonist as well as how it will happen ("multiple stab-wounds"). By structuring the novel in this achronological manner, Spark assures her readers of the inevitability of Lise's victimization, but she does not use that victimization as the climax of the novel. While psychoanalysts, journalists, and Lise herself might fetishize a wounded female body, Spark's narrative does not.

Although the third-person narrator of *The Driver's Seat* knows and tells about Lise's imminent death, his/her knowledge of causality and psychological motivation is nonexistent. Early on, the narrator objectively describes Lise: "Lise is thin. Her height is about five-foot-six. Her hair is pale brown, probably tinted" (16). Note the last qualifying phrase. Although the narrator can report the objective data of color, the source of this color (from genes or a bottle) remains unknown. Similarly, the narrator finds it impossible to ascertain the state of Lise's psyche. At one point, s/he reports Lise's actions but adds, "Who knows her thoughts? Who can tell?" (53).

Since *The Driver's Seat* is not a psychological novel and we do not have access to Lise's mental processes, it remains unclear why Lise plots her own murder. Unlike Carter, Spark does not provide us with a detailed personal history, with family background, with past pain that results in present pathology. However, the narrative does suggest that Lise has experienced mental illness in the past. During the first pages of the novel, she breaks down at work, and the reactions of her co-workers "conveyed to her that she had done again what she had not done for five years" (6). In addition, a conversation with Richard, her soon-to-be murderer who has only recently been released from a psychiatric hospital, reveals that she is familiar with the decor of such places as well as the habits of its inmates:

> "Were the walls of the clinics pale green in all the rooms? Was there a great big tough man in the dormitory at night, patrolling up and down every so often, just in case?"
> "Yes," he says.
> "Stop trembling," she says. "It's the madhouse tremble."

Thus Lise and her murderer have a shared experience, and Spark, like Carter, links the pathology of the sadist to the self-destructiveness of the masochist. Yet Spark's narrator cannot explicitly identify the forces that have driven these two characters to assume such perverse roles.

However, we are provided with information that may be construed as both symptoms and causes of Lise's desperation. We know that Lise has worked in an accountant's office for over sixteen years, a period that constitutes much of her adult life. "She has five girls under her and two men. Over her are two women and five men" (6). Lise has her place in a fairly strict hierarchy where gender plays a role, though not an absolute one. Such facts perhaps sketch Lise as an alienated, stultified middle manager. Even more telling is the description of her apartment:

> She has added very little to the room; very little is needed, for the furniture is all fixed, adaptable to various uses, and stackable. . . . The writing desk extends to a dining table, and when the desk is not in use it, too, disappears into the pinewood wall, its bracket-lamp hingeing outward and upward to form a wall-lamp. The bed is by day a narrow seat with overhanging bookcases; by night it swivels out to accommodate the sleeper.. . . A small pantry-kitchen adjoins this room. Here, too, everything is contrived to fold away into the dignity of unvarnished pinewood. . . . Lise keeps her flat as clean-lined and clean to return to after her work as if it were uninhabited. The swaying tall pines among the litter of cones on the forest floor have been subdued into silence and into obedient bulks. (12)

Clearly, Lise's living quarters are functional but sterile. Pinewood, a wood often used for coffins, dominates; thus the text suggests that in this cold, clean, impersonal space, Lise experiences death in life. If one's physical space reflects one's identity, then Lise doesn't seem to have one. She has a room of her own but precious little to add to it. The final image of this description intimates that the movement of nature has been processed into stasis. Like the pinewood of her apartment, Lise seems to have been "subdued into silence" and obedience. Apparently, she can only imagine breaking out of such an empty and superficially ordered life by actively seeking her death.

The encounters Lise has during the last day of her life demonstrate that bleakness and superficiality are the marks of contemporary existence as well as Lise's life. In an airport concession stand, Lise briefly talks with a woman who is dutifully searching for paperback novels with pastel-colored covers: she wants this reading matter to conform to the decor of her South African beach house.[28] Apparently, in the world in which Lise lives, books are literally judged by their covers, and one's facade renders one's interior moot.

Lise's experience with Mrs. Fiedke, Richard's aunt who fatefully ends up staying in the same *pensione* as the protagonist, also underscores the transitory and disconnected nature of human relationships.[29] Lise and Mrs. Fiedke meet, share a taxi, lunch together, shop together. And yet, when Mrs. Fiedke fails to emerge from a bathroom stall in a department store, Lise deserts her. A few pages later, Mrs. Fiedke reappears and finds Lise attentively watching a woman dancing in the music department:

> Mrs. Fiedke comes up behind Lise and touches her arm. Lise says, turning to smile at her, "Look at this idiot girl. She can't stop dancing."
> "I think I fell asleep for a moment," Mrs. Fiedke says. (65–66)

Lise is not surprised to see Mrs. Fiedke and does not ask what happened to her; Mrs. Fiedke is not angered by Lise's desertion and offers an unasked-for explanation. As Ian Rankin has noted, there is a Beckett-like quality to the conversations between Lise and Mrs. Fiedke (151). In this world, conversations are collections of utterances rather than dialogues dependent upon understanding and response. Shortly after this scene, Mrs. Fiedke and Lise are separated during a student demonstration, and they do not meet again. Although Mrs. Fiedke contributes to the success of Lise's plan—she purchases the murder weapon (a letter opener) and gives Lise valuable information about Richard's past—she remains unaware of Lise's search for death in the form of a man. Ultimately, Lise's relationship with Mrs. Fiedke demonstrates that human contact does not ensure communication, continuity, or connection.

Significantly, sexual intercourse is presented as an especially alienating, mechanistic, and impersonal form of communication. Spark satirically dramatizes this point through her depiction of Bill, a macrobiotic enthusiast who meets Lise on the plane to Italy and decides that she is his "type." Subscribing faithfully to an Eastern doctrine that divides the world into yin and yang, negative and positive, passive and active, feminine and masculine, Bill decides that Lise will be the one to provide him with his orgasm (a yang experience) that night. Bill is a comic character; he obviously represents an alternative lifestyle—one that ascribes significance to everything. In order to counter the chaos and nothingness of modernity, Bill follows a regime that neatly divides the world into complementary opposites.

About Bill and his macrobiotic system, Rankin writes, "It is as if Spark were offering Lise a way out, another, radically different, life to which she might attach herself. It is a lifestyle which Lise cannot accept" (150). Thus Lise is presented as perversely refusing heterosexual romance as a life preserver.[30] However, it seems important to note why this purportedly "radically different life" is not a viable alternative for Lise. Although the Eastern doctrine of yin and yang is predicated upon complementarity, Bill's division of experience looks suspiciously like the traditional Western gender hierarchy. According to Bill's view of the world, pleasurable experiences such as orgasm are yang, and toxic foods such as salami and coffee are yin. In addition, Bill humorously manifests his belief in strict sexual difference by insisting that men are supposed to urinate three times a day and women twice. When Bill tries to force Lise to help him achieve his daily orgasm, it becomes obvious that this revolutionary lifestyle caters to male desire and exploits women:

> the tussle that ensues between Bill and Lise, she proclaiming that she doesn't like sex and he explaining that if he misses his daily orgasm he has to fit in two the next day. "And it gives me indigestion," he says, getting her down on the gravel behind the hedge and out of sight, "two in one day. And it's got to be a girl." (106)

Although Bill's macrobiotic way of life privileges bodily experience, it also propagates a false sense of intimacy and thus only adds to the disconnection that seems rampant in modern life. Lise underscores the disillusionment caused by sex when she tells Richard, "Most of the time, afterwards is pretty sad" (113). Thus Lise experiences postcoitus as a time of pain and loneliness; for her, the body is the site of vulnerability. Margaret Moan Rowe asserts that in *The Driver's Seat*, "one sees Spark's most extreme dismissal of sexuality. . . . [T]here in the most extreme form sex is without any meaning whatsoever" (174). However, the episode with Bill suggests that the problem might lie with what sex is revealed to mean here: the satisfaction of men's needs and the psychological and physical vulnerability of women. Ultimately, Spark implies that the sexual revolution may not be quite so revolutionary for women.

Paradoxically, although the objective, external style of this narrative precludes our knowing Lise's full story, it may well symbolize the source of her despair and pathology. Spark asserts that narrational choices are inevitably tied to the theme of each individual work.[31] In *The Driver's Seat*, the narrator seems capable only of observing and reporting, not of making or finding significant relationships. That narrative stance seems to mirror the plight of the characters in this novel. Indirectly, we are given to understand that Lise is invisible and vulnerable in this world; she lacks a "fixed point" and thus cannot find meaning in life. Hence she chooses death. Michelle Massé has argued that "masochism can work to create and preserve a coherent self" (45). By contriving her own murder, Lise will use the mutilated remains of her body to gain posthumous attention. In short, Lise will create an identity by becoming a victim.

Significantly, Lise's masochistic plan makes abundant use of the rites of traditional womanhood. First and foremost, Lise uses the romantic paradigm as the model for the search for her murderer. Whenever she meets a man, she tries to determine if he is her "type"; indeed, Mrs. Fiedke believes that Lise is looking for a boyfriend and tries to help her find her match. Although Lise wants to be in "the driver's seat," to be in control of her fate,[32] she can only imagine gaining that control through Mr. Right. The script that Lise writes for herself is ultimately an extreme and perverse form of the conventional romantic script. In that script, when you find your man, you find a respite from the dangers of the world; in Lise's script, when you find your man, you die and thus are rendered invulnerable and publicly visible. In both cases, compulsory heterosexuality mediates female fate and female identity. The very extremity of Spark's narrative exposes as it echoes the perverse underpinnings of Deutsch and Bonaparte's plot.

Lise's preparation for her death mainly revolves around shopping. In the first scene of the novel, Lise searches for the dress in which she will meet her man; this outfit will be her analogue of a wedding dress, and she desires something that will draw attention. Initially, she is offered a stain-resistant dress, which she immediately and somewhat hysterically rejects—she can only be a spectacle in her death if the stains of her stigmata show.[33] She finally finds the brash outfit for which she has been looking: the dress consists of a "lemon-yellow top with a skirt patterned in bright V's of orange, mauve, and blue"; over this, she wears a "coat with narrow stripes, red and white, with a white collar" (6–7). Dressed in this way, Lise can ensure that people will notice her and thus that witnesses will be able to reconstruct the story of her death. Similarly, she assiduously shops for the accessories necessary for her murder. These include a scarf and neckties with which she expects to be bound at the moment of her death. Ultimately, Lise constructs her identity as a victim from the world of women's fashion[34] and gives new meaning to "shop 'til you drop"; like Freda in *The Bottle Factory Outing*, her desire involves using the status quo rather than changing it. Clearly, Spark is more interested in charting the effects rather than the origins of female masochism. However, by yoking the details of Lise's plan to heterosexual romance and conspicuous consumption, Spark, like Horney, intimates that female masochists are made, not born.

Indeed, Lise is a case study of a woman who has wholly internalized stereotypical assumptions of female masochism. The only way she can imagine taking control of her life is through self-destruction, and she extends her strategy into a general and familiar theory of female victimization. When Richard laconically tells Lise as she drives through a park that "a lot of women get killed" in such locations, Lise readily agrees: "Yes, of course. It's because they want to be. . . . Yes, I know, they look for it" (113–14). For Lise, blaming the victim equals the assumption of agency.[35] However, Richard's response to Lise's self-serving pronouncements on female masochism testify to the inadequacy and inaccuracy of such views: "No, they don't want to be killed. They struggle. I know that" (114). As a man who has formerly stabbed but not killed a woman, Richard knows all about imposing violence on others and the resistance that results from such imposition. Here the male sadist provides the best evidence against the omnipresence of female masochism.

Just as Spark refuses to blame the victim, so does she challenge a simplistic victim-victimizer dichotomy. Indeed, Lise's plan to be mistress of her own murder blurs that dichotomy considerably, and the linguistic level of the novel underscores that point. Early in the novel, the narrator states that "the combination of colours [in her outfit] . . . *drags* attention" to Lise (53—my emphasis). The verb "drags" seems like an odd choice here and certainly calls attention to itself. However, later, this word reappears in a context that illuminates its initial use. Lise gets a lesson on hunting from a man whom she temporarily mistakes for her "type." According to this man, the predatory habits of big game enable their own slaughter: "You've got to wait for the drag. They call it the drag, you see. It kills its prey and drags it into the bush then you follow the drag and when you know where it's left its prey you're all right. The poor bloody beast comes out the next day to eat its prey, they like it high" (95–96). A synchronic cycle of victimization is described here—at one moment, the same being is both predator and prey. Thus Lise's implication in such a cycle is subtly suggested by the first use of "drags."

Indeed, Lise's predatory instincts constitute her use of masochism to "regulate others as well as the self" (Massé 45). Richard, Mrs. Fiedke's nephew and Lise's murderer, had been Lise's right-hand seat companion on the plane to Italy. She had initially identified him as her "type." Discomforted by Lise and the flirtatiousness of Bill (who sits on Lise's left), Richard changes his seat.[36] When he arrives at the *pensione* where his aunt is staying and sees Lise, he immediately leaves in an attempt to elude her. Richard has just emerged from a six-year stint in a psychiatric hospital; treatment there served in lieu of a jail sentence for his assault on a young woman. This reformed slasher apparently senses that Lise can incite the sadism that is still within him but that he is determined to control. Nevertheless, when Lise encounters Richard later that night as he returns to the *pensione*, she is determined that he will put her plan into action. Despite his "fear" and "resistance," Lise pursues him. She commands him to follow her, "leads" him to the door, drives him to the spot she has selected for her murder, and instructs him in great detail how to murder her. Lise counts on her active masochism to provoke an act of passive sadism. She wants to control not only her murder but also her murderer.

Yet Richard's sadism becomes anything but passive. Lise gives Richard explicit directions: she tells him to first tie her hands together, next to tie her ankles together, and then to strike her with the letter opener. However, Richard does not follow instructions exactly, and thus comes the final, subtle twist to this macabre plot:

He ties her hands, and she tells him in a sharp, quick voice to take off his necktie and bind her ankles.

"No," he says, kneeling over her, "not your ankles."

"I don't want any sex," she shouts. "You can have it afterwards. Tie my feet and kill, that's all. They will come and sweep it up in the morning."

All the same, he plunges into her, with the knife poised high. (116–17)

The use of the phrase "all the same" indicates that Richard has violated Lise's instructions and her body. What initially plunges into her is "he," not the knife, although the subtle rendering of this scene momentarily confuses the weapon with the male sex organ.[37] Although this confusion is not sustained, male sexual sadism is presented as a powerful weapon of control. By raping Lise, Richard asserts his authority in this script and thus figuratively replaces Lise in the driver's seat. In her final moments, Lise learns the hard way that not all women ask for what they get. Her desire to control her life by controlling her own victimization ultimately fails since Richard (a.k.a. "Dick") thrusts sexual violence into Lise's final act.

Not all critics agree that Lise has been victimized and thus has forfeited her place in the driver's seat; indeed, some ignore or render insignificant the sexual violence that occurs against Lise's will. Sproxton comments, "He performs the murder precisely to her instructions" (142). Rankin comments that Lise "is, in the end, not to be pitied too much, for her plan has worked. Her victim is more in need of sympathy" (154). And Rowe asserts that "at the end, Lise's plot has unfolded completely, and she remains in the driver's seat." However, in Muriel Spark's universe, no one takes the driver's seat for long. Richard, like Lise, is quickly ousted from that position: the ending of the novel indicates that the police will arrest him for murder, and although substantial evidence will corroborate his statement that "she told me to kill her and I killed her" (117), it is unlikely that he will lead a normal life hereafter. The novel ends with "pity and fear, fear and pity," and it seems clear that both parties involved in this sensational crime merit both reactions. The chiastic structure of the phrase "pity and fear, fear and pity" rhetorically represents an object and its reflected image and is perhaps meant to suggest the doubled and tragic nature of the sadomasochistic couple.

Spark's interviews underscore Ruth Whittaker's observation that "[t]he novels of Muriel Spark are written from a Roman Catholic standpoint, whether or not her religion is specifically mentioned" (37). Hence the theological implications of Lise's and Richard's story deserve note. For the feminist concerned about gendered patterns of violence against women, the female masochist commits a crime against herself, and the male sadist commits a crime against women; however, for Spark, the sadomasochistic couple also sins against God by not recognizing that divinity rather than humanity is in the driver's seat. By taking control of life and death, Lise and Richard attempt to usurp the power of God. Thus Spark thrusts them both from their illusion of mastery: Lise's death scene does not go as planned, and the power Richard derives from rape is transitory. Ultimately, from both a theological and feminist perspective, Lise and Richard are cautionary figures who seek agency and identity in all the wrong places.

Muriel Spark's *Driver's Seat* extends our understanding of the cultural work that scripts of female masochism do. For Deutsch and Bonaparte, masochism "naturally" produces a heterosexual, reproducing female subject. Horney, more schooled in a hermeneutics of suspicion, astutely notes that the naturalizing of female masochism reproduces patriarchy. Spark particularizes Horney's insights by depicting the forms of social control and social recognition that masochism offers. In a world where death is certain and violent crimes against women an increasing possibility, masochism becomes a perverse form of agency: if one can't avoid sadists, then one might be able to control how and when they strike. Similarly, in a world where the role of victim is an all-too-viable one for women, life in death produces a more glamorous identity than death in life. As Massé astutely notes, "Masochism . . . can be a psychic strategy that makes the best of a bad business, that insists on wresting identity and self-affirmation from the biased social contract that traumatizes women" (42). Although Spark explores the productive use of masochism, she certainly doesn't endorse it. Indeed, the story of Lise suggests that women who choose this strategy are fucked by both God and men.

Lise looks for death in the form of a man and finds it; Morris fears death, projects it onto Ghislaine's sexualized flesh, and thus supports her destruction. Such plots suggest that, within contemporary sexual politics, both men and women view death as inextricably connected with the other gender. However, as Chancer rightly emphasizes, *"the organization of patriarchy itself necessitates that a group positioned masochistically, or women, cannot be truly equal to the one positioned sadistically, or men"* (139). Indeed, as Carter's and Spark's texts show, cultural forces which align female identity with masochistic performance and male identity with sadistic activity ensure an abundance of dead female bodies. Ultimately, both Carter and Spark recognize that women's bodies constitute the objects of male sadistic violence, and thus they refuse to disassociate masochism and sadism from biological sex. They refuse to be gender skeptics. Yet they also stop short of seeing these perversions as inherent or desirable expressions of sexual difference, and hence they avoid falling into the traps associated with cultural feminism and hyper-Freudian psychoanalysis that might make such gender relations seem inevitable. Like Horney, Spark and Carter link cultural norms and gendered perversions.

By situating the sadomasochistic couple within a larger cultural context, Spark and Carter suggest that the primary pornographic relationship is embedded in our cultural consciousness; thus their texts implicate men and women in femicidal scripts. Such a move is risky feminist business: a serious consideration of female masochism perilously borders on blaming the victim, and empathy with male sadists raises the fear that those figures will be exonerated. Since our culture already tends toward such blame and exoneration, many feminists rightly approach with caution any strategies that might reinforce such positions. Yet Carter and Spark adroitly negotiate such potentially antifeminist minefields. In *Honeybuzzard*, Carter focuses on the man who protects and identifies with the sadist, not the man who actually commits the heinous crime. Hence she distances her readers from sadistic action and focuses instead on sadistic feeling. Further, she offers Emily as a counter to Ghislaine.[38] In *The Driver's Seat*, Spark presents Lise's sickness as a societal symptom, and she emphasizes that Richard's sadism is incited by, but does not originate with, Lise's masochism. Spark and Carter carefully avoid indicting the dead; however, they also refrain from presenting femicide as a simple story of unrelenting and essential male aggression. These texts distance us from the resignation to the female Gothic represented in Willa's and Brenda's story. Taken together, *The Driver's Seat* and *Honeybuzzard* short-circuit scripts of male vice and female virtue. Indeed, these texts use stock characters from cultural feminism and the Gothic to offer a promising scenario: if culture and not nature constructs female masochists and male sadists, then the mutability of these Gothic beings perhaps becomes easier to imagine. Thus the understanding that there *are* ready-made Gothic plots but they need not be followed becomes a crucial part of refusing victimization.

Chapter 5

Paranoia Will Destroy You, or Will It?

The gendering of the sadomasochistic couple is a crucial part of the strand of the contemporary female Gothic highlighted here. However, representing it as the whole story, even from a social constructionist perspective, risks perpetuating Gothic horror, albeit unwittingly. Positioning women as victims of cultural scripts can veer into a form of cultural essentialism that forecloses female agency and resistance. As Judith Butler notes, presuming "an inexorable cultural law" can make it seem that "gender is as determined and fixed as it was under the biology-is-destiny formulation. In such a case, not biology, but culture, becomes destiny" (8). Moreover, narratives of male predation and female victimization, if not supplemented with other stories, can produce accounts of female subjectivity that preclude aggression as well as implication in structural forms of one's own oppression and that of others. Tania Modleski argues that the popular Gothic appeals to female readers because it enables them to experience aggression while simultaneously identifying with a blameless, virtuous, besieged protagonist. In Edna O'Brien's *I Hardly Knew You* (1978) and Diane Johnson's *The Shadow Knows* (1974), such patterns of identification are explicitly thematized and critiqued. Indeed, these texts suggest that such psychic maneuverings work against exposing psychic and social contradictions; thus these patterns of identification tend to reproduce rather than revise Gothic scripts. O'Brien and Johnson do not deny that women are besieged; in other words, they are not skeptical about gender oppression or a female

Gothic predicated on normative heterosexual relations. However, these texts demonstrate that understanding female victimization through a lens of mythic female virtue deprives women of valuable though often discomforting knowledge. In this chapter, I want to argue that O'Brien's and Johnson's texts help feminists to work through and with paranoia; such work can mobilize the agency women have to refuse not only their own individual victimization but also that of others.

According to Modleski, the paranoid process, the popular Gothic, and patriarchy revolve around a particular family constellation—a powerful parent (usually the father), a victimized parent (usually the mother), and a child whose psyche becomes the parental battlefield. In order to assuage the pain of this internal warfare, one of the internalized combatants, usually the victimizing father, gets projected outward. Thus the paranoiac, the Gothic heroine, and the feminized child can identify with the purity of the victim as any aggression that is felt is justified and/or displaced into fear.

Like the popular Gothic and the "normal" patriarchal family, cultural feminism participates in this paranoid process. Such a statement is not intended to pathologize or even merely psychologize cultural feminism. Rather, I want to show the political imperatives for such participation as well as the strategic losses that ensue.

A femicidal culture promotes and even demands paranoia as a necessary, even healthy strategy of self-defense. As Judith Halberstam comments, "The women who are not worried about being watched within the horror film very often die; the alternative to paranoia very often is nothing more than a gullibility and a kind of stupid naivete." Halberstam's commentary seems valid both on and off screen; indeed, she argues for "a notion of productive fear which marks the female within the Gothic as a subject who watches as well as a subject who is watched" (126–27).

Indeed, cultural feminism understands that a paranoid orientation to the world is justified and is a necessary part of feminist consciousness-raising. At one point in *Intercourse*, Andrea Dworkin graphically relates the crimes of a necrophiliac male murderer and a Nebraska court that found nothing particularly heinous about his behavior. Addressing her readers, Dworkin writes, "Are you afraid now?" (129). The obvious answer to this rhetorical question is "Yes, and with good reason." Dworkin's goal is to collectivize, legitimize, and politicize female fear.

Significantly, this Gothic dimension of cultural feminism is, I think, inextricably related to its revaluation of that which is associated with women and the feminine. Women's bodies matter, despite a culture that often takes violations of those bodies for granted.

However, the necrophiliac nature of the case Dworkin cites suggests that this example is doing more cultural work than simply organizing women around their fear. A dead woman who becomes sexual prey is a pure victim; since a corpse is definitionally deprived of physical activity or emotional desire, there can be no question that she asked for it. Thus the evocation of female fear here functions as a counternarrative to the scripts of provocation that are firmly embedded in the law and the cultural imagination. Moreover, just as the female victim is relieved of responsibility for her victimization, so is the male victimizer held fully accountable, a useful counter to cultural patterns of evasion. The blamelessness of the pure victim and the sadistic villainy of the male victimizer also neatly reverse the storylines of female monstrosity and evil that descend from Pandora and Eve to La Belle Dame Sans Merci to Glenn Close in *Fatal Attraction*.

However, even as the paranoid plot *usefully* reverses cultural narratives that excuse and perpetuate violence against women, it upholds dominant forms of cultural logic. Establishing clear and inviolable boundaries between victim and victimizer is in keeping with the binary, oppositional structures of thinking that mark the West. Moreover, such firm identities uphold the model of a subject who is coherent and unified. As Bersani suggests, "We must therefore begin to suspect the paranoid structure itself as a device by which consciousness maintains the polarity of self and nonself, thus preserving the concept of identity" (109). Thus narratives of complicity, the production of a particular fragmented subject, are difficult to produce.

To be sure, to speak of female complicity in gender oppression is a dangerous game, since it hovers perilously close to the discourses that invoke provocation, that blame the victim, that in one way or another suggest she had it coming. The fact that these discourses have become ever more subtle in response to feminist discourse increases the danger.[1] Moreover, some fear that taking seriously feminist and/or female complicity in a whole range of oppressive relationships based on gender, class, sexuality, race, and nationality might feed into backlash discourses. However, both feminist critiques by women of color and poststructuralist questionings of transcendence or utopian alterity have made it more politically, ethically and intellectually dangerous to avoid discussions of a wide range of feminist and female complicity than to engage in them. Ultimately, neither myths of female or feminist virtue will serve us well. Of course, feminist complicity should not be collapsed into identity with patriarchal compliance. As Teresa de Lauretis astutely notes, complicity must be distinguished from "full adherence, for it is obvious that feminism and a full adherence to the ideology of gender, in male-centered societies are mutually exclusive. . . . To what extent this newer or emerging consciousness of complicity acts with or against the consciousness of oppression is a question central to the understanding of ideology" (11).[2]

Johnny, I Hardly Knew You and *The Shadow Knows* use their besieged, paranoid protagonists as testing grounds for the meeting of these forms of consciousness. The paranoid process, with its emphasis on purification of the self through projection, foregrounds the consciousness of oppression and seemingly forecloses the consciousness of complicity. However, taken together, these two novels from the '70s suggest that the female paranoid subject who staves off such a foreclosure is better equipped for survival than she who knows herself only as a victim. Significantly, these texts do not agree with Bersani that the cure for paranoia is "to renounce the comforting (if also dangerous) faith in locatable identities" (109) and that such a loss is necessary "if we are also to disappear as targets" (112). O'Brien and Johnson are keenly aware that not all are equally targeted nor equally empowered to disappear as targets; thus even as they problematize patterns of projection, they justify a specifically female form of paranoid anxiety.

❦   ❦   ❦

At first glance, *I Hardly Knew You* seems like an anomaly in Edna O'Brien's *oeuvre*. While murderous male characters logically extend from O'Brien's pessimistic view of sexual relations, murderous females do not; yet *I Hardly Knew You* is the first-person prison monologue of Nora, a woman about to be tried for killing her young lover, a man whom she calls "Hart." Henrik Ibsen's Nora lurks behind O'Brien's: while Ibsen ends his heroine's story with the dramatic slamming of a door, O'Brien envisions postmarriage life. Joyce's Nora Barnacle and her fictional counterpart Molly Bloom also haunt the pages of *I Hardly Knew You*. Indeed, this O'Brien novel stylistically resembles the coda of *Ulysses*, Molly's soliloquy.[3] Nora's life, like Molly's, is revealed through a night's worth of stream of consciousness; lovers and sexual adventures structure both their personal histories, while Nora's prison cell substitutes for Molly's bed.

That Nora killed Hart (clearly, a pun on "heart") is never in doubt; however, *why* she did it is a mystery to both the reader and herself. At the outset of the novel, Nora (whose name we do not know for the first 85 pages) proclaims her own lack of clarity: "Tomorrow I shall have to tell them. I shall have to stand in that court and tell them why I did it. But how can I tell them when I do not know why. . . . So I will try to tell them as best as I can and perhaps ask them to fathom it, to piece it together" (1). Nora's subsequent narrative reads like a case history of a paranoiac. Nora's father clearly serves as the prototype for the villainous males that abound in her story. A drunkard, her father is marked by irresponsibility and brutal sexuality. Although the narrator only hints at her own sexual molestation, she readily acknowledges, and desires retaliation for, the crimes her father has committed against her mother: "Have I not lived day and night wanting to kill the father who sired me the father the scion of all fathers who soiled my mother's bed, tore her apart, crushed her and made her vassal" (78). Clearly, the phrase "scion of all fathers" underscores that this figure has taken on archetypal dimensions in the narrator's imagination.

The complement of the brutal father is, of course, the long-suffering mother, and Nora cultivates the appropriate empathy for this fellow victim. Significantly, however, this empathy is riddled with unexpressed rage at her mother's complicity and hypocrisy: "I have never really tackled her and my mind bends under the weight of accusations that I have not voiced. She went to him, her butcher husband, she went on command. She who objected to intimacy" (73). Fearing that her maternal inheritance is "crippledom" and that the mother is forever "interred" in the daughter's body, Nora reluctantly admits that she has fantasized about killing her mother as well as her father. Such aggression coupled with such identification ensures that the victim-victimizer dialectic, the organizing structure of the paranoid process, will mark Nora's life.

Nora is justifiably enraged by the sadomasochistic ritual that is family life. However, the narrator's attempt to disengage herself from this oppressive family system merely replicates its structure. Raised on the romantic claptrap that perpetuates the unbalanced patriarchal family, the narrator imagines that a male suitor will effect her escape: "I thought of our juvenile dream when we thought of nothing but weddings and trousers, when we thought we would be carried along on the pinion of man's valour" (126). Thus Nora complies with the romantic script and elopes, only to find that the violence of her home has literally and figuratively followed her. On her wedding night, her father and other "male family members" (40) try to intervene, ostensibly because she is underage. Their assault on her new-found protector includes blows to the groin, and her husband eventually responds in terms they understand: he raises a rifle. After the intruders leave, the husband verbally vents his anger on her: "I was hardly able to look at him. His diatribe had commenced, blaming me for them, combining me with them. I kept saying sorry, sorry and our roles were cast" (40). Thus marriage thrusts Nora back into a family romance that is the breeding ground of the Gothic.

Bereft of useful work, Nora wanders "the lonely moorland," a reminder of "one's romantic incarceration" (42). Like the second Mrs. de Winter in *Rebecca*, Nora lives in the shadow of a former wife: an old servant—the analogue of du Maurier's Mrs. Danvers—stresses the beauty of Nora's predecessor, and Nora even wears some of the former wife's clothing. The past of her paternalistic husband is ultimately as contaminating as her own, and even the birth of her son resonates with "the previous child by a previous marriage" (43). Significantly, disagreements over the rearing of this boy confirm that the husband who was to serve as a rescuer is really a persecutor in disguise, a character in the mold of Herod and Tom in *Casualties of Peace*. At one point, her husband uses binoculars to spy on her and decides that she has improperly supervised his son. He reacts by ordering her to a room, locking the door, and threatening her with commitment to an insane asylum.[4] Such domination and coercion serve as uncanny reminders of life in her father's house: "I had heard those words before, in fact heard them when I was poised to elope with him. Too ridiculous" (45). Once again on the run from the nuclear family, Nora declares, "There was nothing for it but to go away, to go out the gate and down the street, to become another woman and I did. No longer a wife not yet penitent and not yet whore. A bit of all three" (49). Although the narrator recognizes that she must remake herself, her impoverished imagination, her inability to conceive something other than these conventionalized and limited possibilities, forebodes disaster.

For Nora, becoming "another woman" entails taking on the role of the "other woman." Her relationships with married men provide further evidence of male villainy. The narrator falls passionately, obsessively in love with Jude, a married man who vows to leave his wife and love Nora forever. However, when he becomes disillusioned with the affair, he reneges on his promises and sadistically implies that he can easily replace her with one of the many women "zealous to serve" (120). On the rebound from Jude, Nora begins an affair with Dee, another married man destined to disappoint her, both sexually and emotionally. Dee manifests his brutal masculinity by relating his desire to catch and kill with his bare hands a mouse that kept him awake one night; this recitation occurs as he and the narrator are beginning to make love. Given such postmarital encounters, it seems fitting that Nora's description of love matches that of a Gothic castle, with all its attendant mysteries:

> I liken love to a great house, a mansion, that once you go in, the big doors shut behind you and you have no idea, no premonition where it will all lead to. Chambers, vaults, confounded mazes, ladders, scaffolding, into darkness, out of darkness—anything. (18)

Like all the women in this strand of the contemporary female Gothic, Nora's history suggests that Gothic romance may be the only type available. Patterns of male predation extend beyond her lovers' discourse to reinforce the narrator's sense of being under siege. Nora earns her living by restoring paintings. When she flies to Tuscany at the behest of an eccentric millionaire, she finds herself engaged in a power struggle with an employer who spends his leisure time collecting and training predatory birds. Although this falconer has invited Nora to work on his art collection, he puts off seeing her. When she strives to exercise some control over her professional life by sending him a note to arrange a meeting, he replies by chastising her for addressing him as "sir" rather than "duke." Thus the condescension and the humiliating imperiousness of her former husband is echoed by her employer. Even simple excursions turn into perilous journeys. On an errand in the outskirts of Florence, Nora must contend with the violence of a lustful taxi driver; although she thwarts his rape attempt, her flight from the taxi entails abandoning her luggage and roaming unfamiliar countryside. Thus we have a portrait of the female paranoid as one who has come to know the truth value of the cultural feminist Gothic.[5] Clearly, Nora resents her role as female prey; however, the victim-victimizer binary is so embedded in her consciousness that she, like Morris in *Honeybuzzard*, can only imagine disidentifying from the victim position through identification with the opposite term. At one point, feeling that love is more trouble than it is worth, she vows to avoid romantic attachments altogether. However, when she sights a "strange woman" who shows the negative effects of such isolation, Nora rescinds this vow and decides instead to look for a female lover. A retreat from victimization apparently equals a retreat from heterosexual relations. Yet Nora projects the terms of the heterosexual contract, as she has come to know them, onto this new relationship and acts like any "male-philanderer" (28): she controls the sex act and then inveigles her way out of any further commitment. Even in a relationship with another woman, she cannot revalue or remake the feminine; rather, she replicates the patriarchal masculine. Massé writes, "Reflective sadism simply means that the once-beaten become beaters in turn" (241); Nora exemplifies this troubling cycle. Her explanation for this behavior—"I must have been far removed from myself at the time" (28) suggests that this momentary reversal of position is a desperate attempt at alienation from her victim self.

Yet this very desire for alienation from, rather than a complex understanding of, her victim self prohibits knowledge that might ultimately save the narrator and Hart from unnecessary suffering. Just as Nora has difficulty admitting that her mother's complicity enrages her, so does she evade the recognition that in subtle ways, she, too, aids and abets her own victimization. At a point when Nora is becoming emotionally invested in Hart as an *idea* rather than a living, breathing body and thus is readying herself for a Gothic replay, she dreams about her ex-husband:

> I was with my lawful husband again, that we were man and wife, that I was scheming to leave him when he took me in his arms and said that we must never be parted from one another because we would miss one another dreadfully and I agreed. It was ghastly that agreeing of mine because my uppermost wish was to leave him. . . . He was coaxing me and that was intolerable, because I knew that out of weakness, out of helplessness I might stay and to stay was death. I hated my lie, abhorred it, but knew no way, no trick, no speech, with which to undo it, unsay it, unbe it. (119)

This dream offers Nora the possibility of feminist analysis. The particular horrors of her marriage are framed by the fundamental inequality of the institution ("man and wife"). Romantic ideology, with its promises of forever, is exposed as a form of self-destruction ("to stay was death"). Perhaps most important is the tacit acknowledgment that "weakness" might be distinguished from "helplessness," the latter term ignoring the agency embodied in that ghastly act of agreement. However, Nora's reaction to this dream evinces her desire to avoid such a painful confrontation with the complicitous mother she rightly fears is interred in herself:

"Yet the next morning what engrossed me was not my husband, not my employer but Jude" (119). Rather than face the content of her dream and enable consciousness of oppression to work with consciousness of complicity, Nora tries to pinpoint when Jude's feelings changed from love to hate, when his desire to be with her forever waned. Nora can only see herself as a wronged woman: she can more easily continue her litany of sorrow and exploitation at the hands of men than question the ideology of romance or consider that she may bear some responsibility for her own broken heart. Here knowledge of gender oppression puts knowledge of complicity under erasure; thus the line that divides self from other and male victimizers from female victims remains firmly and seemingly irrevocably in place.

Modleski argues that the paranoid plot of the popular Gothic enables women to explore the ambivalence embedded in their primary relationships: mother-daughter, father-daughter, and, as an extension of the latter, husband-wife. However, in order to "fathom" or "piece together" Nora's motive for killing her young lover, "Hart," the reader must attend to one other significant relationship, that of mother and son. Indeed, Freud's optimistic pronouncement on that relationship serves as the epigraph to this novel: "A mother is only brought unlimited satisfaction by her relation to a son; that is altogether the most perfect, the most free from ambivalence of all human relationships." For Freud, the son functions as a third term, a resolution to the tension of sexual antagonism that inheres in the patriarchal family romance. However, through Nora's story, O'Brien suggests that this view of the son as Gothic hero is a form of cultural wish fulfillment. As both part of the mother and a clearly identified other, the figure of the son becomes both symbol and embodiment of the fragmented consciousness of the paranoid female subject. Thus the son exacerbates and exposes the ambivalence that the paranoid process of projection is designed to foreclose even as he is promoted by cultural and psychoanalytic narratives as the Gothic solution.

Nora's son remains unnamed in *I Hardly Knew You*, a sign that he functions as mere figure in her psychosocial drama. Chodorow notes that the mother-son relationship can compensate women for the distant and dissatisfying relationships they often have with their husbands (104). Nora's early history with her son is an extreme example of this. When she and her husband are engaged in a bitter custody battle, the son must decide with which parent he will live. At this crucial juncture, he chooses his mother, thus making him a loyal male, seemingly an oxymoron in Nora's and perhaps O'Brien's world. As he grows older, his mother continues to look to him for solace. Significantly, on the day that the narrator finds that Jude has abandoned her, the son demonstrates his devotion by driving her all over the countryside in pouring rain and by comforting her throughout the night. Repeatedly, the narrator invokes a lover's discourse when she discusses her son. For example, "We lay in bed once and though our walls did not adjoin I knew that he was weeping, slow quiet terse unsatisfying tears" (63). "Though our walls did not adjoin" seems to refer not only to a present in which distance can be bridged, but also to a past of literal connection in the womb. As Chodorow has argued, women reenact their relationship with their own mothers by bearing children; significantly, then, the narrator explains her desire for her son: "It must be the nearest thing to birth, to couple with one's own, to reunite" (17). Nora's complicity with the Gothic family romance extends to her relationship with her son; indeed, she, along with psychoanalysis, invests him with the power to heal the painful split between mother and daughter and between men and women.

Incest taboos notwithstanding, tension in this supposedly idyllic relationship is bound to surface as the maturing male child becomes more autonomous, a member of the victimizing class and the lover of other women. Long after the narrator's relationship with Jude is over, she throws a party on his birthday, half hoping that he will intuit her actions and show up. The night becomes special due to a particularly seductive moment with her son: "He allowed me to caress his bare insteps, and stroke his toes" (99). The verb "allowed" implies that her son has become a more powerful being, one who can accede to or deny the narrator's requests. The potential victimizing power of the son is further suggested by the fact that the long country drive with her son recalls the episode with the taxi driver that culminates in attempted rape. Significantly, a young peasant boy rescues the narrator on that day, and together the taxi driver and that boy seem to reflect the son's possibilities. The narrator's hostility toward the son is most dramatic when he tries to comfort her in jail: "When I see him now I see how he is also living my plight. He is ashen and he puts on a facade of manliness, so as to hide his upset. He almost chokes. Just before he leaves he takes my elbow and says everything will be all right. In those moments I want to hit him" (99). In her son's face, Nora sees a reflection of her own fear and helplessness; her offspring therefore becomes a symbol of vulnerability, a condition that she has dreaded her entire life. However, it is her son's "facade of manliness" that provokes her. The narrator feels most violent when her son acts like other men she has known, when he makes promises that he cannot keep, and when he reminds her how much she has invested in such manly (im)possibilities. As an emblem for a painful cross-generational family romance that is inextricably connected to gender hierarchy, gender oppression, and patterns of complicity, the son cannot help but be an ambivalent figure for the narrator, despite Freudian wishes to the contrary.

Ultimately, this overdetermined ambivalence gets worked out on Hart's body. At one point, the narrator says about her relationship with her son, "We knew each other by heart" (99). The homophonic equivalent of this sentence is equally true: mother and son know each other by Hart, the young man whom Nora has murdered. Hart is her son's best friend; loving, fearing, and killing him is the closest she can come to expressing the range of feelings she has toward her male offspring and toward herself.

In an acerbic review of *I Hardly Knew You*, Anatole Broyard complained that O'Brien does not flesh out Hart's character: "The title of the novel is intended as a rueful irony, addressed to the young man who is its love object; but I'm afraid that I hardly knew him either and I see no reason to regret his demise. I'm more perplexed by the fact that the heroine could get worked up enough to kill him" (12). However, I would argue that the absence of Hart as a multidimensional textual entity is precisely the point. O'Brien uses the narrator's evocation of her affair with Hart not to describe that relationship but to demonstrate how, for Nora, Hart is the bodily screen onto which she projects the gendered warfare that rages within and without.

The Gothic setting in which she and Hart come together foreshadows that this relationship will not be a new beginning but rather a replay of an old script. At this point in the novel, Nora is staying with Hart and her son in an old Scottish castle; the latter two are working with a theatre troupe on an upcoming production. Disgruntled with her small, depressing living quarters, she requests a room change. During the first night in this new room, she hears footsteps and the slamming of a door. Positing the presence of a ghost or a practical jokester, she waits and listens:

> I watched in the dark with every perception on edge, waiting to see who would enter and by what means. . . . The waiting got too much, or rather the waiting without the climax, so all of a sudden I got out of bed, left my room, crossed the stone corridor and returned to my old room. (168)

Neither a spectre nor a joker awaits her; rather, Hart has come to her, bearing salve for the midge bites she had complained about earlier in the day. Significantly, the narrator's description of these bites suggests that they symbolize her psychic scars: "I imagined a pyramid of bites contracted in different places, at different moments, all accruing to make me blotched and itching for life" (160). Hart's ministering actions begin with ointment and end with "wild," "stormy," and "rapacious" lovemaking that brings "roses to . . . [the] limbs" of the narrator. Thus Hart is fatally cast as sexual savior, and Nora's diction underscores the fantasy nature of such a role. Hart promises that their affair will leave out the sorrow of the rosary and will only contain the other two elements, glory and joy. Moreover, according to Hart, he and Nora constitute a formidable "we," capable of overcoming such relational taboos as age difference. Such words seem like paradise; ever since Nora's first husband thrust her back into the familial "them," she has sought to become part of a new, idyllic "we," a social unit that will heal the dis-ease of justified paranoia.

However, like the son for whom he serves as substitute, Hart can only come to embody the disease he is supposed to cure. At one point, Nora looks at Hart in stage makeup and sees a "villainous gypsy"; this phrase recalls the content of Nora's adolescent fantasies and underscores that, for Nora, Hart is more projection than flesh and blood. Hence he is destined to suffer the fate of all other fantasized rescuers and be included in the generic category "men, the stampeders of our dreams" (129). Hart unwittingly hastens this process with his own generalizing about, and participation in, the script of sex antagonism. When Hart confesses that he fears Wynne, a member of the theatre troupe who is also attracted to him, he murmurs "women" and gives "a little shudder." This reaction causes Nora to reappraise Hart and his status as an ideal lover: "For the first time I saw the thin raised thatch of black hairs on the rim of his shoulder and I felt repelled, almost afraid. 'I'm a wolf,' he said" (181). Such an evocation of female fear and male predation suggests that Nora's affair with Hart will reinforce rather than intervene in the paranoid process.

I Hardly Knew You climaxes with the narrator's memory of Hart's murder, and both she and the reader come to understand that while misguided self-defense serves as the impetus for that tragic event, revenge and self-destruction also play a significant role. On that fatal night, Hart purposefully teases Nora about not being uppermost in his mind: Nora's son had told him about her temper, and he wished to see it himself. Then he initiates lovemaking, and Nora notes that "he was beginning to be more knowing and more daring" (197). Hence the prelude to murder includes a young lover who is becoming more like a man and less like a boy, shared information between son and lover and thus a reminder of their relationship, and a recalling of the narrator's emotional vulnerability. In the midst of erotic caresses, Hart suffers an epileptic seizure, which functions here as a Gothic contrivance. Predictably, the narrator responds not to him and his desperate, immediate need, but rather to the past phantoms his tormented body evokes for her:

> "Jesus, he has gone mad," I thought. The thing I dread most, in bed with a madman. Did I not see instantly my mad father with his long shins and his cuttlebone tongue standing over me, frothing. . . . A gyrating grotesque beast of a face stared at me . . . and all the latent ugliness of the wide world was contained in it. Gone the St. John of the Cross and instead the very features of a Lucifer. (197–198)

In this first moment of panic, fear, and misinterpretation, Nora envisions Hart as the repository of all evil; no longer a harbinger of hope, he has become an emblem of the incestuous father, her archetypal male victimizer.

Fear soon gives way to a desire for revenge, and Nora revels in her new-found ability to victimize:

> For the first time I felt the gruesome power of the hand that strikes. Love him—no. Be his companion—no. Grow old in his service? No. I had the breeches now, the upper hand. Gangsters all would get their goriest comeuppance. It is true that I killed them, in killing him. Cruelly, lovelessly I would have ridden him until he snapped and broke except that his poor organ was limp and ragged. (199)

Here Nora acknowledges the symbolic nature of her crime: Hart's body stands for the body of all men, a generalized "them" undeserving of mercy. Sexual difference has become indistinguishable from sexual antagonism; thus the narrator seeks to vent her wrath on the male sex organ. For Nora, the masculine role is inextricably connected to abusive power. At this point, she readily assumes that role ("I had the breeches now"), just as she had in her brief affair with the Swedish woman.

Indeed, as was the case during her pseudolesbian affair, this reversal, this identification with the position of victimizer is the only way she can imagine disidentifying from the position of victim. In Hart's dire need, Nora recognizes her own vulnerability and ultimately cannot bear the sight:

He begged for help, with the worst, the most humiliating, the most craven, the most needful beg and undoubtedly I saw my own begging helpless self reflected in him and I took the pillow from under the bed cover, placed it across his contorted face, pressed with all my might, and held it there until he went as quiet as a baby whose breath is almost inaudible. (199)

In a mad frenzy, Nora seeks to eradicate not only the victimizing father, but also the internalized version of the victimized mother (i.e., her own victim self). The phrase "as quiet as a baby" suggests the other family member who is symbolically annihilated here—Nora's son. Although the narrator does not acknowledge the infanticidal nature of her crime, Hart's helplessness in his final moments closely resembles that of infancy. Through Hart, we know that the narrator felt murderous rage not only for both her parents but also for her beloved son, emblem of her own fragmented consciousness and a social history of gender oppression with which she has been complicit.

Nora's narrative ends at dawn; for the second time in her life, she will make a court appearance: the first time, she fought for custody of her son. Yet the connection between her male child and her murdered young lover is a painful one and thus invites denial, from Nora as well as from some readers. Broyard concluded his review of this novel with dismissal: "The climax of *I Hardly Knew You* is so awesomely silly that I think everyone should read it in order to enjoy for a few moments the uncanny sensation of feeling superior for a few moments to an author as talented and worldly as Miss O'Brien." However, perhaps just as uncanny is an earlier line from the same review: "All too often writers love their mistakes with a fierce, defensive love, *as a parent loves a retarded child*" (my emphasis). Broyard's assumption of unconditional parental love echoes the sentiments contained in the epigraph from Freud and attests to the strength of cultural prohibitions against maternal ambivalence. However, in *I Hardly Knew You*, O'Brien intimates that such prohibitions fuel the paranoid process of projection, a process that propelled Nora into killing Hart and landing herself in jail. As both lover and mother, Nora unwittingly tells a story not only of oppression but also of complicity. Her failure to recognize the latter part of that story need not be normalized, and as *The Shadow Knows* suggests, a paranoid subject can (re)produce more than Gothic prisons.

N., the first-person narrator of Diane Johnson's *The Shadow Knows* (1974), has fallen into the same romantic traps that ensnared O'Brien's Nora. Having idealized marriage and family life, N. finds herself disappointed by the domestic quotidian and her childlike husband; hence she eschews the protections and frustrations of matrimony for the passionate embraces and emotional insecurity provided by a married lover. However, her readiness to demystify motherhood suggests a level of honesty and self-awareness lacking in Nora. At one point in the novel, N. tells her friend Bess that if she had to leave graduate school for the sake of her children, she would hate them. Bess is shocked by such sentiments, and N. responds with canny insight:

> I've noticed that the psychoanalyzed can face some things—sexual feelings, say—with utmost equanimity but have a special inability to face the really nasty shocking things like feeling hostility to your children. It's as though, assaulted by the disease of self-knowledge in its most elementary form, they develop antibodies which keep them from finding out anything really important. (114–15)

N.'s willingness to "face the really nasty shocking things," her desire to seek self-knowledge at an advanced level, sets her apart from Nora. The plot of *The Shadow Knows* takes place within eight action-packed paranoiac days in which N. must contend with repeated malevolent acts directed against her female-headed household, acts that she fears will end in her murder. Playing detective in her own case, she searches her past and present for clues. Her Gothic quest entails not only the identification and analysis of male domination but also a journey into the underworld of female-female relationships across the racial divide. Indeed, N.'s story suggests that consciousness of oppression and consciousness of complicity can coexist, though not without a struggle.

N. has recently divorced her husband, Gavvy, and has relinquished some of the physical and financial security accorded the wife of a prominent attorney. Hence at the outset of the novel, N. resides in a Sacramento housing project with her four young children and Ev, her African American live-in babysitter/domestic. Violence and poverty abound in this housing project, and N. discovers that her status as a white lady and a former middle-class suburban housewife can no longer protect her. Indeed, the plot of the novel revolves around the terror and paranoia caused by a series of premeditated assaults against this newly formed household. There are harassing phone calls, someone smears disgusting substances on her front door and on her car window, a strangled cat appears on her doorstep, her tires are slashed, the crotches of underwear on the laundry line are removed with a knife, and the morning mail contains photos of Vietnam atrocities; significantly, these photos feature the mutilation of a woman and her children. One night, Ev is beaten as she enters the laundry room. The blows Ev suffers from this anonymous attack exacerbate an already existing medical condition; thus Ev dies and leaves N. to identify the perpetrator of such ill-will.

Throughout the novel, Ev and N. are identified with one another: both are small and skinny, both are without husbands, and both are in love with men incapable of making commitments. Ev represents N.'s victim-self, her passivity, her own inclination to "just lie there."[6] N. recognizes this doubling effect, as she makes clear in her description of their first meeting:

> We were like two halves of a mirror. In her was a deep unspoken fear. In me was a deep unspoken fear. How implacable our eyes. We were both struck silent by our fears, but the person worse off has to speak first; that is the rule of desperation, I guess. Ev was the more desperate; like me, her husband had deserted her, but she was also Negro and didn't even have a quarter for the bus ride home. (99)

Through Ev, N. learns about her own vulnerability. As Elyse Blankley puts it, Ev "coaxes N. away from her solipsistic self-scrutiny to consider the larger social forces of which even she, a privileged, educated white female, is a victim" (191). N. clearly remembers the time when she, Ev, and the kids visited her uncle in a retirement home, and a racist caretaker threatened Ev with a pipe. N. first responds by standing up for Ev, who moves to retreat in terror. However, when the caretaker raises his pipe against N., she is shocked at both his action and her reaction: "and I cowered, too, like Ev; I cringed and began to back away like a pitiful cowed animal" (191). Since N. identifies with Ev, indeed, since Ev's dead body stands in place of her own, the search for Ev's assailant becomes a way for N. to understand the forces that have led *her* to this housing project.

Early on, N.'s prime suspect is Gavvy, her ex-husband; thus her present predicament leads her to reflect upon marriage, motherhood, and the social networks of power that surround those institutions. N.'s marital experiences constitute a classic case of the feminine mystique discovered and confronted, and her story represents a whole generation of middle-class white women. Indeed, like Nora, N. discovers that the experiences of marriage and motherhood are radically different from the propaganda that promote them:

> With what feelings of singularity you lend yourself to each thrilling act of girlhood, marriage, to the growing troupe of exquisite babies with their tender fingers, like the beautiful mother in a diaper ad you are, and then it begins to seep away, the picture is torn off the billboard and torn into little bits and these bits washed down a drain, a whirling vortex. (67)

The chaos, fragmentation, and isolation associated with young children, combined with her husband's impatience, dishearten this narrator. Gavvy does not want to hear about N.'s need for intellectual stimulation; rather, he can only complain about the disorder of the house and the incompetence of N. as a wife and mother. Thus N. concludes, "Mine was the ordinary misery of mothers of young children. . . . Men hate to hear about this" (38).[7]

Like Nora, N. is destined to leave the war zone that her marriage has become. With the hiring of Osella, an African American live-in domestic—Ev's predecessor—N. returns to school to pursue a graduate degree in linguistics and discovers sexual pleasure in the form of extramarital affairs. Although N. decides that the existence of such liaisons will paradoxically enable her to maintain family ties, Gavvy cannot accept this coping strategy, and the Hexams divorce. Significantly, the court denies her request for financial support in order to complete her education, and Melvin Briggs, Gavvy's partner and attorney, suggests that she teach elementary school, a job "which would be consistent with her role as a mother of young children" (113); thus N. learns about institutionalized androcentrism: "How I hate Melvin Briggs, first man to illustrate to me— I guess I had been overprotected—the power and malice of the rules by which men help and protect each other and turn on women they have no reason to turn on because men are loyal to one another" (115). Overprotection here is equivalent to ignorance, and, as *The Shadow Knows* consistently argues, only risk produces knowledge. As Cara Chell writes, N.'s "'reckless' behavior puts her both outside her marriage and outside traditional society, a process that then allows her to recognize certain attributes of society that are harder to define when immersed in the structure" (162). By leaving the normative institution of marriage, N. comes to recognize networks of patriarchal power.

N.'s awareness that male privilege and male violence are interconnected and that she incurred Gavvy's resentment by not fulfilling his great need for mothering causes her to view her ex as a viable suspect. Although N. does not make much of the one time in which Gavvy slapped her during an argument, she does consider the significance of a brief altercation between Gavvy and Ev. One weekend when Ev was taking care of the kids, she had a fight with her boyfriend, A. J. Frightened by this disagreement, one of the older children called Gavvy, who came over, slapped Ev, and verbally abused her. According to N., "Gavvy had acted to Ev in a way he had never dared act to me" (189); thus it becomes conceivable that Ev's body affords Gavvy opportunities for the expression of murderous rage that N.'s does not.

Ultimately, N. *wants* Gavvy to be the one who attacked Ev and indirectly caused her death. If he were the perpetrator, then his violence against Ev—and, by extension, against herself—would legitimate the risky path she has taken and ameliorate the guilt she feels for violating the marital contract. In addition, Gavvy as the villain, the one who brings Gothic horrors into the realm of the real, would fit a predictable pattern. N., like Patsy and Willa in *Casualties of Peace*, is alert to news stories that chronicle the murderous rage of husbands against wives, especially ex-wives, and understands that such events are indicators of male-female relations rather than simply the tragedies of aberrant couples. As N. observes, "Husbands killing wives—that's an especially recurrent sort of murder—estranged husband kills wife, children, self. It's *always* husbands. Wives *never* do" (34—my emphasis). Paradoxically, the certainty embodied in "always" and "never" provides a measure of comfort: Gothic certitude is better than none, and scripts of murderous husbands and besieged wives keep the violence of domesticity within the family and at the hands of men.

Yet N. knows that Osella, her former African American domestic who became emotionally unstable while serving the Hexam family in the suburbs, is just as likely a suspect as Gavvy, and this knowledge forces her to consider Osella's motives and confront her own complicity in gendered racism. The hiring of Osella freed N. to a great extent. While Osella cooked meals and tended the children, N. pursued her advanced degree in linguistics and engaged in numerous love affairs. Significantly, however, Osella had little choice in the matter: as a recent and impoverished widow, she had no place to go; thus she became N.'s replacement and assumed control of the Hexam household. The Hexams not only financially exploited Osella but also used her to work out their marital tensions. Frustrated by Osella's domestic imperfections and ambivalent about N.'s newly acquired independence, Gavvy would sometimes want Osella to leave; of course, N. would protest. However, at other times, N. feared that Osella could really replace her and thus wanted to resume her wifely duties; at these moments, Gavvy reminded N. of her domestic incompetence and insisted that Osella stay. Osella's position was fundamentally insecure, since her presence enabled a marital transformation about which both husband and wife were ambivalent.

On one level, Osella and her descent into madness serve to illuminate the dangers of wifedom and confirm N.'s flight from her marriage. The antithetical doubling relationship between Osella and N. recalls that of Bertha Mason Rochester and Jane Eyre; indeed, Janet Todd has commented that Osella is N.'s "madwoman in the attic" (126). Ostensibly, Osella and N. are quite different. One is Black; the other White. Osella is obese; N. is quite slight. While Osella revels in domesticity and child-rearing, N. loses herself in transformational grammar. Yet, in her undertaking of N.'s domestic duties, Osella literally functions as N.'s double. Additionally, N. realizes "an odd thing: Osella and I have the same birthday, May 5; also we are both left-handed" (46–47). Osella's madness, her out-of-control rage that manifests itself in the wielding of a kitchen knife and the burning of a doll dressed in N.'s clothing, affirms that the role of housewife is hazardous to women's health.

Ev is imagined as N.'s victim self, Osella as N.'s mad housewife self. Thus these Black domestics do a lot of dirty work for both N. and Johnson. However, the extent to which White women's complicity in racist oppression is explicitly thematized in *The Shadow Knows* makes this text more than simply a purveyor of problematic racializations.[8] Ultimately, Osella's burning of N. in effigy is not a random act of madness but rather points to N.'s role as oppressor. In chronicling the servitude of the Black female domestic, Angela Davis analyzes the imperviousness of a White feminist toward the plight of her Black female servant: "The servant . . . labored solely for the purpose of satisfying her mistress' needs. Probably viewing her servant as a mere extension of herself, the feminist could hardly be conscious of her own active role as an oppressor" (97). Significantly, in her paranoiac state, N. comes to consciousness of her crimes against Osella. N. remembers witnessing Osella's grief and rage upon visiting the grave of her late husband; with N. as listener, Osella chronicled the losses of her life and expressed her desire never to leave the Hexam children. Yet N. did not recognize Osella as a fellow-sufferer: "Even when she told me as plainly as this, I could not believe Osella to be as hungry and tormented as she was. She looked so well-fed" (45). However, unlike N.'s mother-in-law, who advocates that live-in help develop "a life of their own" because "it helps them to bear it better," N. learns to eschew the indefinite pronoun "it" and not to depend on the connotations of a verb such as "bear" to convey the burdens of being a domestic. Rather, N. painfully but plainly uses such words as "exploitation," "victim" and "slave." Writes N., "It took me much too long to understand she had any needs at all. This is because I was so preoccupied with my own, I am ashamed to say, and also because Osella concealed hers for a long time. . . . Osella *was* a slave, and a slave was what I wanted" (36).[9] Unlike Nora, N. strives to understand the ghastly cultural agreements she has made; indeed, she intuits that her survival is predicated on such understanding.

For N., investigating Ev's death becomes an opportunity to learn from her past complicitous acts and not to repeat them. The detective assigned to Ev's case is anxious to keep the number of unsolved crimes down and believes that reporting homicides increases the murder rate. As Inspector Dyce explains, for the public good "sometimes we don't call murder murder" (178). Thus his inclination is to discount the beating Ev received in the laundry room and deem her death the result of "natural causes." However, N. understands that Dyce's willingness to naturalize Ev's cultural dispossession (a dispossession that N., as a single woman in a housing project, now shares to a certain extent) makes him "a force of darkness disguised as a force of reason" (201). The revelation that Inspector Dyce "was more sympathetic than I to murder" causes N., like many Gothic heroines before her, to take on the role of detective.[10]

N.'s reading has prepared her for her investigative duties; indeed, when her children were infants, N. was an obsessive consumer of conventional whodunits: "For a while I gave up all reading but detective stories, whose sameness comforted me, whose morality assured me of order outside my disorder" (39). However, as detective, N. must learn—along with the reader—that such order is constructed rather than discovered and that knowledge is always already the product of interpretation. Such lessons constitute an epistemological crisis that can easily be deployed to prohibit consciousness of complicity and complex social analysis. At one point, N. is striving to understand her (dis)connections with Ev and the exponential accumulation of privilege:

> Also you can't help but wonder whether people would care more, if there would be less shrugging, if Ev had been white. White or black, if she lived in these units I doubt people would care. So much of it around these days. But if she'd lived up on the hill where I used to live, then people would vigorously investigate, no stones

would be left unturned, the whole world a rubble of stones, from looking for her murderer. Of course, if she'd been white living up on the hill, she would have fewer reasons for drinking her insides away so she would die at a blow. It's hard to assign causes and effects. I had started by saying there is much I understand now, which I mostly would rather not have known, but there is much that can never be known, too. (202)

Here, N.'s analysis that race and class are overlapping but not coinciding analytical categories is short-circuited; significantly, she seeks to lessen the impact of the confession that she would have preferred liberation with her white, middle-class privilege intact and hidden ("would rather not have known") by invoking generalized epistemological limits. Complexity and uncertainty converge here, and N. summons them to resist knowledge of complicity.

The use of the uncertainty principle—summarized by the opening phrase of the book, "you never know"—to evade responsibility is demonstrated most clearly when N. reacts to accumulating evidence against Osella. Ultimately, N. believes that Osella is Ev's attacker, although she hates to admit it; after all, "it's so unfair that Ev, who never hurt Osella, should be lying dead because of—because of what? Unknown causes is maybe the only way of describing it" (193). Of course, there *are* known causes for Osella's hostility toward Ev, most notably the fact that Ev replaced Osella. Ev's access to Osella's babies (N.'s children) reminds Osella that she is dispensable, that she is not a family member, not a loved one, not one with a place of her own. Significantly, N., in an initial interview with Dyce, tells him that Osella might have had reason to resent Ev: "I told [the Inspector] . . . about Osella. I explained that she had been our maid, and that she was mad, with jealousy over the children, and might have hated Ev because they were Ev's babies now" (184). By invoking "unknown causes," a phrase that originates with Inspector Dyce, N. betrays a moment of resistance and denial: while she readily admits her crimes against Osella, she has difficulty acknowledging that those crimes played a part in Ev's demise.

Despite these symptoms of resistance and the temptation of closing the investigation by invoking "unknown" rather than "natural" causes, N. is determined to know as much as she can and to confirm or refute her suspicions regarding Osella. Given that she identifies with Ev, that Ev's dead body stands in place of her own, this commitment becomes an act of survival as well as an act of recognition. The antithesis of Brenda in *The Bottle Factory Outing*, N. will not turn back, will not forget her suspicions and try to find a safe place for herself. According to N., "you must sometimes dare and risk all you have. . . . I mean, if you once admit that your life is wrong and you know why and still fail to change it, then you are doomed forever." Yet, as the conclusion of this thought demonstrates, there is nothing Pollyanna-like about N.: "And what you risk you sometimes lose" (141). Upon inspecting the laundry room where Ev was beaten, N. finds an ashtray from the Zanzibar, a nightclub owned by Osella's boyfriend, Big Raider. Despite her considerable fear, N.'s next stop, then, is the Zanzibar, "where everything was to be made clear" (240). Of course, clarity is associated with the conventional detective stories N. used to read, not the revised version she is living. Thus N.'s discussion with Raider *provisionally* establishes Osella as Ev's attacker.[11] In addition, Osella's presence as the nightclub's main attraction reinforces N.'s sense that the same body can perform simultaneously narratives of oppression and narratives of complicity.

At the Zanzibar, Big Raider markets Osella as the epitome of the "female principle." Indeed, the mythic dimensions of her body are emphasized to the point of parody:

> She wore little trunks of purple satin and nothing else but a gold armlet around the expanse of her upper arm—a brilliant stroke, a rather Egyptian, goddess-like adornment calling to mind one of those frightening and horrifying fertility goddesses with swollen bodies and timeless eyes and the same engulfing infinitely absorbing quality Osella radiated now. She seemed the embodiment of a principle, passive and patient, frightening to men, I guess, absorbing them into her immense proportions. She seemed a sort of superfemale needing only the tiny seed of men and she would grow and grow and grow and keep on growing. (245–46)

Significantly, Osella's purportedly archetypal female power is here exposed as an attempt to embody and contain the threat posed by sexual and racial otherness. As O'Donnell puts it, "Osella is the embodiment of 'otherness,' brought under control and theatricalized for the consumption of the fascinated audience" (203). Indeed, it seems no coincidence that Gavvy, who when overwhelmed with his growing family would have nightmares about fertile women mocking and abusing him, is present and delightedly awestruck at Osella's debut.

Initially, N., too, is taken with Osella's masquerade of femininity and feels diminished by contrast, just as she had when Osella took on the role of housewife. However, she soon views her former maid in a less mythological and more analytical light: as a hungry, needy woman who fattened herself up for a husband who liked "a lot of woman" and has now become a circus performer cum fertility goddess who will line the pockets of both Black and White men. As Big Raider, Osella's boyfriend and promoter, unabashedly puts it to N., "[Osella's] got a good act. . . . She's gonna make a pile" (248). N. recognizes that while Osella has cultivated her bulk and feminine virtues as a defensive strategy, it has only enabled further exploitation. For N., Osella is simultaneously a pathetic and malignant figure, one whose violence and objectification symbolize the high cost of uncritically embracing socially sanctioned forms of racialized female power.

Elaine Showalter has commented that the "Gothic center of the book is the relationship between N. and Osella" (142). However, part of the project of *The Shadow Knows* is to decenter the Gothic; by the time N. provisionally establishes that Osella is Ev's assailant, it seems unlikely that all the acts of terror against N.'s household and all of her guilt refer back to Osella's body. As McCaffery describes the development of the novel, "Instead of clarity being created out of ambiguity and mystery, quite the opposite occurs—the possibilities seem to proliferate as the book goes on" (211).[12] Bess, purportedly N.'s best friend, is the other presumed perpetrator. Toward the end of the novel, N. experiences a spontaneous though desired abortion caused by the insertion of an IUD, and Bess comes over to take care of her. When N. spies a hunting knife—a weapon handy for slashing doors and tires—in Bess's bag, the glimmerings of suspicion she had felt of late intensify. N. then realizes that Bess volunteers at a hospital and thus has ready access to the disgusting bodily fluids that have been smeared on her door and car windshield. That night, Bess, who is staying in Ev's old room, "begin[s] surreptitiously to pace; I could hear the almost silent scuff of her feet on the cold floor walking back and forth or else around and around" (224). Like Bertha Mason Rochester, like Osella, Bess is a figure of rage out of control.

Bess, burdened by a mentally handicapped child and shocked by N.'s admission that she could resent her children, cannot sanction N.'s resistance to the feminine mystique. As Bess hisses to N., "You do nothing but take. Your normal children, having a maid, love affairs, not even appreciating how it is for most women or how you have reason to be grateful. . . . You expect to have your own way. . . . You represent something to me and I think that's why I hate you" (221). Of course, what N. represents to Bess is not only a woman of privilege and luck but also a woman who dares to have and act on desires of her own. Bess is what Millett termed a "virtual forewoman of patriarchal society"[13] and, significantly, is also an externalization of N.'s own guilt-ridden, self-recriminatory voice. Indeed, even when N. extols the virtue of living a liberated life, the spectre of self-blame and imminent disaster appears: "If you are going to have lovers and a life of freedom and intellect, you have to expect unwed pregnancies and divorces and malice and mistakes. There is a safe way to conduct your life and then there is the other way, reckless and riddled with mistakes but I don't care" (204). In the journey that one reviewer has called "the second stage of consciousness-raising" (Haynes 38), Bess represents both an internal and an external force to be reckoned with, a psychological and a sociological phenomenon.

N.'s guilt-ridden narrative voice thus becomes an emblem of the narratives of female complicity that proliferate in *The Shadow Knows*: N. oppresses Osella, who in turn assails Ev; Osella assuages male anxiety by masquerading as a fertile femme; Bess terrorizes N.'s household. Whereas in *I Hardly Knew You*, consciousness of oppression works against consciousness of complicity, in *The Shadow Knows*, the potential exists for a backlash narrative in which complicity displaces oppression. However, the final controversial pages of the novel, in which N. is raped by an unidentified man,[14] foreclose such displacement while working against the ultimate positioning of N. as victim. In other words, the rape does not become a grand narrative act of projection designed to resolve the psychosocial tensions and ambivalences of the paranoid subject.

To be sure, N.'s unconventional reaction to being raped stems in part from the confirmation that her gendered fears are justified:

> I don't know. I felt happy. Anything bad can happen to the unwary, and when life sends you the *coup de grace* you have a way of knowing. So I felt better, then, thinking wee, that was the *coup de grace* and here I still am. There is a badness to things that satisfies your soul, confirming that you were right about what you thought was what. (254)

N.'s use of the French phrase "coup de grace" clashes with the childlike utterance "wee"; indeed, linguistically and otherwise, N.'s relief borders on the perverse.[15] However, her gratitude for rape rather than murder needs to be contextualized not only in relation to the potential crimes against her body but also in relation to her changing life circumstances. Throughout the novel, N. fears that she will be murdered, murder serving as a powerful metaphor for the obliteration of self. Such fears result not only from external malevolent threats but also from the psychological trauma associated with her divorce and her shifting perceptions of her social location. As she embarks on a journey of liberation, she worries that she will be destroyed in the process, that self-knowledge equals self-destruction. Thus rape in lieu of murder confirms that risk and danger attend such journeys; however, the ending suggests that violation rather than annihilation will be the outcome. N. may have affinities with Ev but will not *be* Ev because she is lucky, because she is white, and because she comes to know herself as more than a victim.[16]

Although Johnson has been accused of portraying rape as enjoyable,[17] it seems clear that N. views her sexual violation not as a turn-on but rather as a cathartic and educational experience:

> I feel better. You can change; a person can change. I feel myself different already and to have taken on the thinness and the lightness of a shadow, like a ghost slipping out from his corporeal self and stealing invisibly across the lawn while the body he has left behind meantime smiles stolidly as usual and nobody notices anything different. You can join the spiritually sly, I mean. Well, maybe I'm making too much of this. I mean your eyes get used to the dark, that's all, and also if nothing else you learn to look around you when you get out of your car in a dark garage. (254)

Rubenstein reads this scene and thus the novel as one "that validates the paranoid vision—or, more accurately, compels its redefinition. By insisting that N.'s world is every bit as dangerous as she imagines it to be, Johnson implies that her character's fantasies are not paranoid at all but utterly credible" (147). I wholeheartedly agree with the substance of Rubenstein's comment here; however, I would argue that retaining the term *paranoia* simultaneously emphasizes that paranoid anxiety is a necessary self-defense strategy (indeed, to ignore the very real Gothic violations that too often await female bodies becomes an act of masochism to be avoided) *and* invites feminists to think about the projection that often accompanies complicity.

N.'s final shift from the metaphysical to the pragmatic, from spiritual slyness to looking around in a dark garage, is noteworthy and suggestive of a philosophical critique implicit in this novel. Clearly, the title of this work refers to the Shadow, the fictional crime fighter of the 1930s who boldly claimed to "know what evil lurks in the heart of men." However, as the following passage illustrates, Johnson calls upon not only the shadows of popular culture but also those of Platonic thought: "[N]ow surely there is a flicker of a shadow outside my window. I could imagine my room a cave now, myself a cave dweller forever made to look at the shadows of the real and I would never recognize the real when I saw it; now here was a real shadow" (227). For Plato, the cave and the shadow are the site and image of damaging illusion; however, for N., the world of shadows becomes the last repository of knowledge and self-protection as well as the ultimate threat. Although Western metaphysics would consider the idea of a real shadow oxymoronic, by the end of *The Shadow Knows*, N. has not only seen one but has also taken on its properties ("the thinness and the lightness of a shadow"). Significantly, N. connects the shadow with the paranoid subject who learns to see in darkness and to watch out in the seemingly safe space of one's own garage. Clarity and certainty may be the ultimate values of the conventional detective story, but Johnson intimates that female survival is better served by exploring the shadows of space and psyche and not giving in to the temptation of purifying projection when confronted with complicity.

❧   ❧   ❧

The paranoid subject is marked by perceptions of persecution and patterns of projection. Both Johnson's and O'Brien's narratives suggest that female persecution complexes are justified; indeed, female paranoia seems not only a reasonable but also a necessary survival strategy when one takes into account rapists who emerge from the shadows of garages and taxis, detectives who seek to naturalize femicide, judges who promote economic oppression, as well as family structures and romantic paradigms that reproduce female victimization. However, even as these texts affirm the existence of gender oppression and thus the legitimacy of the paranoid subject, they reveal the problematic of the paranoid process of projection. Striving to resolve psychic tension, the paranoid subject uses this strategy to turn herself into a unified subject, a blameless, besieged Gothic heroine. Thus victim and victimizer, oppressor and oppressed become mutually exclusive terms. Both Nora and N. contend with the frightening possibility that the refusal to embrace one of these identities constitutes the passive acceptance of the other. Nora veers back and forth from one position to the other, unhappy in both, but unwilling to examine the construction of this psychosocial seesaw and her own complicitous agency. Imprisonment and almost certain death seem to be the price of such analytical lack and intolerance for impure suffering. However, N., who mines her paranoid state for an articulation rather than a resolution of her psychosocial contradictions, comes to embody the paradox of being on both sides of the seesaw at once. Ultimately, narratives of oppression and narratives of complicity come to inform rather than compete with one another, and she emerges a survivor.

Perhaps the fear—or desire—that victims and victimizers cannot inhabit the same body explains the tendency of cultural feminism to emphasize and globalize female victimization and male monstrosity. It hardly seems coincidental that cultural feminism seems to be "the product of white feminists" (Alcoff 413) and "reflect[s] the historical conditions of white women in particular" (McCaughey 146). Once multiple and interlocking forms of oppression are taken into account, "white women cannot be all good or all bad; neither can men from oppressed groups" (Alcoff 412). Thus while Black women have a long tradition of regarding Black men as "love and trouble" (Collins 183–84), while Cherríe Moraga, a Latina lesbian feminist, readily asserts that "the enemy is not easy to name" (108), while the Combahee River Collective proclaimed "we struggle together with Black men against racism, while we also struggle with Black men about sexism" (213), while bell hooks writes that "the process by which men act as oppressors and are oppressed is particularly visible in black communities, where men are working class and poor" (*Feminist Theory* 74), while Gloria Anzaldúa argues that the new *mestiza* copes by developing a tolerance for contradictions, a tolerance for ambiguity" (79), white cultural feminists have sometimes used paranoia to quell such ambiguity. At one point in *Gyn/Ecology*, Mary Daly cites David and Vera Mace's scholarship on suttee to illustrate the perils of patriarchal scholarship: "My purpose here is to detect in these perpetuations of murder patterns whose effect is mental murder. This pattern-detecting—the development of a kind of *positive paranoia*—is essential for every feminist Searcher, so that she can resist the sort of mind-poisoning to which she must expose herself in the very process of seeking out necessary information" (125—my emphasis). Thus for Daly, as for Halberstam, paranoia has a protective function. However, it seems crucial to ask from what are Daly's Searchers being protected. Significantly, right before this invocation of positive paranoia, Daly suggests that one of the dangers of the Mace's presentation and prose is that the female reader might be "tempted to feel guilty for not understanding women in 'another culture'" (124). For Daly, female guilt and differences that divide women are symptoms of patriarchal false consciousness. Thus positive paranoia becomes a way of unifying women as a class of subjects, and the possibility that a feeling of guilt might be justified is given short shrift.

Indeed, in *Outercourse*, Daly provides a cursory response to Audre Lorde's suggestion that *Gyn/Ecology*, with its token inclusion of African women as the victims of clitoridectomy, demonstrates that "beyond sisterhood is still racism." Writes Daly in 1992, "I regret any pain that unintended omissions may have caused others, particularly women of color, as well as myself. The writing of *Gyn/Ecology* was for me an act of Biophiliac Bonding with women of all races and classes, under all the varying oppressions of patriarchy" (232). Significantly, Daly has cast herself as a victim of her own exclusions, while asserting a firm line between the "biophiliac bonding" of sisterhood and patriarchy, the originator and progenitor of race and class oppression. For Daly, consciousness of oppression and consciousness of complicity work against one another, as they did for Nora.

However, other such noted cultural feminists as Susan Griffin and Adrienne Rich began in the 1980s to identify and resist feminist patterns of projection and complicity. Griffin's lyrical, fragmentary essay "The Way of All Ideology"[18] distinguishes between dynamic theorizing and the stasis of ideology:

> But when a theory is transformed into ideology, it begins to destroy the self and self-knowledge. . . . It organizes experience according to itself, without touching experience. By virtue of being itself, it is supposed to know. To invoke the name of this ideology is to confer truthfulness. No one can tell it anything new. . . . All that it fails to explain it records as dangerous. All that makes it question, it regards as the enemy. Begun as a theory of liberation, it is threatened by new theories of liberation; *slowly it builds a prison for the mind.* (280—my emphasis)

Throughout this essay, Griffin argues the dangers of paranoid projection; indeed, she posits that the coherent self constructed by "self-denial and projection" (280) is an impoverished self, one without "complexity and subtlety," one whose "imagination grows small" (289). Thus Griffin aligns herself not with Nora's imprisoning certainty but rather with N.'s epistemological openness. As Griffin puts it, "Thus I begin to learn to live with questions. With uncertainty. With an unknowingness" (290).

Likewise, in "Notes Toward a Politics of Location," Rich rebukes herself for starting a sentence "Women have always. . . ." As she explains her own patterns of re-vision, "If we have learned anything in these years of late twentieth-century feminism, it's that that 'always' blots out what we really need to know" (214). Indeed, in that essay, Rich explicitly connects the mindset that "attribut[es] all our problems to an external enemy" to "a form of feminism so focused on male evil and female victimization that it, too, allows for no differences among women, men, places, times, cultures, conditions, class, movements. Living in the climate of an enormous either/or, we absorb some it unless we actively take heed" (221). Interrogating herself, her "whiteness," and cultural feminist thought, Rich implicitly rebukes Nora's formulation "men, the stampeders of our dreams" and, like N., moves beyond the "always" of murderous husbands to include the racialization of womanhood. Thus cultural feminists charted ever more subtle narratives of oppression and complicity; indeed, the integration of particular forms of fragmented subjectivity into their discourses suggests ways in which cultural feminism can be imagined in productive dialogue with poststructuralist thought. However, "a certain paranoia around the perceived threat of essentialism" (Fuss 1) as well as the sometimes related prominence accorded to postfeminist discourses became both symptom and cause of the shifting relationship between feminism and Gothicism.

Chapter 6

The Perils of Postfeminism

Second-wave feminists in general and cultural feminists in particular have chronicled the horrors that women routinely face: economic dependence and vulnerability, sexual victimization, psychological battering from an androcentric culture. Feminist writers such as Susan Brownmiller, Andrea Dworkin, Mary Daly, Susan Griffin, and Dale Spender argue that women are at risk when they roam the streets, when they make love in their bedrooms, when they enter their gynecologists' offices, when they consume or produce culture. Taken together, such accounts of women's lives suggest that the world is a Gothic place for the second sex.

The appearance and continued use of the term *postfeminism* suggests that narratives of the female Gothic provided by the second wave have been superseded. However, whether or not these "new" stories are women-friendly or even all that new remains under debate; indeed, it is this critical controversy that accounts for the often contradictory and ambiguous definitions of postfeminism. Deborah Rosenfelt and Judith Stacey offer the most lucid—and, I think, most accurate—description of this social and critical trend: "[P]ostfeminism demarcates an emerging culture and ideology that simultaneously incorporates, revises, and depoliticizes many of the fundamental issues advanced by Second Wave feminism" (341).[1] Joyce Carol Oates's *Soul/Mate* (published under the pseudonym Rosamond Smith and discussed in this chapter) and Margaret Atwood's *Bodily Harm* (the focus of chapter 7) dramatize the perils of postfeminism via the tropes of the Gothic. Indeed, both texts read postfeminism as a retreat not only from a Gothic quotidian but also from women. As such, postfeminism and its sometime sister, poststructuralism, become no less implicated in the female Gothic than cultural feminism. Put another way, postfeminism, with its tendency to deny the Gothic world, threatens to become anti-Gothic Gothic.[2]

❧ ❧ ❧

The term *postfeminist* appeared early in the twentieth century and marked the beginning of the end of the first-wave of feminism. Caught between the paradoxical discourses of individualism and feminism, the latter increasingly fragmented, a group of Greenwich Village literati in 1919 started the journal *Judy* with the following agenda: that "[W]e're interested in people now—not in men and women"; that guiding principles "should not have anything to do with sex"; that it was necessary to be "pro-woman without being anti-man" (Cott 282). Terming their position "postfeminist," these radicals articulated profound discomfort with sex consciousness, a discomfort Virginia Woolf would echo nine years later in *A Room of One's Own*.

A 1982 *New York Times Magazine* article entitled "Voices from the Post-Feminist Generation" popularized the term *postfeminist*. In that political essay, Susan Bolotin put a name to the already widespread attitude that "feminism had become a dirty word." Without necessarily adopting Bolotin's commitment to an unprefixed movement, journalists and critics have adopted the term, definitional difficulties and variations notwithstanding. Mary Russo begins a conference paper entitled "Notes on 'Postfeminism'" with a frank disclaimer: "It is not my purpose to define 'postfeminism'" (27). Janice Doane and Devon Hodges write, "It is time to investigate the relation between the feminist project to develop an emancipatory maternal rhetoric and conservative, postfeminist narratives of mass culture" (422); thus they, like Rosenfelt and Stacey, seem to view postfeminism itself as a conservative move to "transcend sexual politics" yet believe that it might promulgate a necessary critique of contemporary feminist thought. Tania Modleski, in her book-length study of postfeminist culture, is decidedly pessimistic about this trend, which she sees as "negating the critiques and undermining the goals of feminism—in effect, delivering us back into a prefeminist world" (*Feminism Without Women* 3). Gayle Greene shares Modleski's pessimism and associates postfeminism with retrenchment, dismemberment, and contracted possibilities. A more eccentric, alarming, but popular view of postfeminism comes from Carol Rumens, who uses the term to describe a transhistorical space of sexual freedom: "'Post-feminist' expresses a psychological, rather than political, condition, though its roots are no doubt political. It implies a mental freedom which a few outstanding women in any age have achieved, and which many more, with increasing confidence, are claiming today" (xvi).

Although the definitional variations of postfeminism deserve note, it seems to me that the impulse for a prefixed movement comes from two main directions: social critics who blame second-wave feminists for disrupting traditional female roles without providing workable new ones and theorists who are uneasy with the subject "women" and with the explanatory power of gender as a category of analysis. Although I think it worthwhile to separate—at least provisionally—these postfeminist "camps," I also want to emphasize the ways in which popular and academic discourses echo and reinforce one another. Postfeminism becomes the meeting ground for liberal individualism (the reigning ideology of *Newsweek* as well as Sommers, Patai, Roiphe, and Wolf) and poststructuralism. Significantly, both camps tend to sidestep issues of oppression and complicity, except when feminists are the purported perpetrators. Thus postfeminism often slips into the discourse of Gothic feminism.[3]

Postfeminist social critics often concern themselves with the significant difficulties that plague the lives of contemporary middle-class, heterosexual working women. The plight of working mothers (a.k.a. Superwomen) in particular has become a postfeminist cause célèbre. Many so-called Superwomen understandably find themselves exhausted and torn between their responsibilities at work and those at home; however, they vent their legitimate frustrations on feminists who promoted economic independence as a prerequisite of liberation. Indeed, in her 1986 book *Sequencing*, Arlene Rossen Cardozo argues that worn-out working mothers are the victims of feminist thinkers, who childless themselves, "prescribed one lifestyle for all women" and caused "for the first time in American social history, the haves [to predicate] their lifestyles on those of the have-nots" (8). Cardozo's solution entails women "sequencing" their professional and personal responsibilities:

> Women who elect to sequence first complete their educations and gain career experience, then leave full-time work during the years they bear and mother their young children, and then—as their

children grow—innovate new ways to incorporate professional activities back into their lives, so that mothering and profession don't conflict. (17)[4]

Significantly, Cardozo's plan requires that every woman find her own individual solution to what she presents as a collective problem. Her scheme reinforces the assumption that children are the responsibility of women and that parenting equals mothering. Cardozo assumes a much more flexible marketplace than actually exists, and her "solution" promotes economic inequities between men and women. Moreover, she conveniently erases the plight of the have-nots, those women who cannot afford to leave the workplace during their childbearing years. Noticeably absent from her discussion are demands for daycare, an insistence that fathers share professional sacrifices, and a call for the end of the split between the hierarchically gendered public and private spheres, a split that ultimately puts women and family life at risk. In other words, Cardozo isolates the goal of economic independence from the larger reformist/ revolutionary agendas of second-wave feminism. Remarkably, feminists who share many, if not all, of Cardozo's concerns, have become the bad guys, and a socioeconomic order whose practices belie its profamily rhetoric remains unquestioned. As a representative postfeminist social critic, Cardozo evinces the heightened individualism, the classism, and the retreat from social activism that seems to mark this "emerging culture and ideology."[5]

Theoretical postfeminists, influenced by poststructuralist/ postmodernist thinkers (Lacan, Derrida, Foucault, Lyotard), look beyond feminism because of its putative philosophical naivete. Jane Flax, wary of Enlightenment beliefs in reason and a stable self, posits that "the notion of a feminist standpoint that is truer than previous (male) ones seems to rest upon many problematic and unexamined assumptions" (56). Nancy Fraser and Linda J. Nicholson argue that feminist social theories are "quasi-metanarratives" (27) and thus perpetuate totalizing, universalist truths that enable exclusion and domination. The ultimate goals of theorists (who are social critics of a different order) such as Fraser, Nicholson, and Flax are worthy ones: they seek to address problems they associate with a retrograde cultural feminist essentialism and strive to theorize difference so that white, middle-class women are no longer the privileged subjects of feminist discourse. However, some question whether such theoretical maneuvers disable feminist practice, that is, whether social change can be effected without some sort of sex consciousness, a "quasi-metanarrative." As Christine Di Stefano puts it, "To the extent that feminist politics is bound up with a specific constituency or subject, namely, women, the postmodernist prohibition against subject-centered inquiry and theory undermines the legitimacy of a broad-based organized movement dedicated to articulating and implementing the goals of such a constituency" (76). While Judith Butler argues that the category "women," among others, needs to be invoked *and* contested, such thinkers as Tania Modleski, Susan Bordo, and Chandra Mohanty worry that endless contestation hobbles the political efficacy of such invocations; moreover, Modleski, Mohanty, and bell hooks have all pointed out that anti-essentialist postfeminists are not necessarily or inherently democratically inclusive.[6]

Ultimately, such concerns put into question the narrative of progress that is often assumed to attend the prefix *post*. Eager for the demise of "Woman," postfeminist theorists may unwittingly sell out women.[7] Massé has suggested that the foundational horror of the Gothic is the cultural refusal of female subjectivity. To the extent that postfeminism in its varied forms reneges on viewing women as a gendered category of beings, it becomes part of the female Gothic experience. Oates's thriller *Soul/Mate* performs the Gothic potential of postfeminism through its protagonist, Dorothea Deverell, a successful career woman who strives to contain the Gothic world made manifest by the second wave, particularly cultural feminist thought. Suggesting an uncanny resemblance between post- and prefeminist women, *Soul/Mate* charts the desire for, and ultimate danger of, relegating the Gothic to the past.

In 1987, a minor literary scandal erupted: Joyce Carol Oates, presumably the "property" of E. P. Dutton, was revealed to be the author of *Lives of the Twins*, a mystery/thriller written under the pseudonym Rosamond Smith and published by Simon and Schuster. Unlike Doris Lessing, who had adopted the pen name of Jane Somers in order to test the integrity of the publishing industry, Oates claimed that her reasons for assuming a new literary identity were purely personal: she wanted a temporary escape from "fame's carapace" and assumed that since this "genre work" was so different from her other fiction, she should seek a new publisher.[8] *Soul/Mate* (1989) is a literary thriller that self-consciously recalls *Jane Eyre*, *Middlemarch*, and, to a lesser extent, *Frankenstein* and John Fowles's *The Collector*. In *Soul/Mate*, Oates attempts to escape but ends up uncannily repeating the frightening visions contained in the fiction she writes under her own name.[9] Indeed, written for popular consumption, *Soul/Mate* simultaneously embodies and frustrates a postfeminist retreat from the Gothicism of heterosexual romance.

Dorothea Deverell has led a tragic life. As a young bride, she endured a miscarriage and the death of her husband in quick succession; as a "virginal" widow, she fell in love with a married man, Charles Carpenter. Intelligent, ambitious, but infuriatingly self-deprecating, Dorothea has written several monographs on contemporary artists and holds a position as assistant to the aging director of Brannon Institute, the local arts foundation. She is next in line for the directorship of this same foundation. Dorothea's life is catapulted first into nightmare and then into bliss by the actions of Colin Asch, a murderous psychopath, who, believing that he is Dorothea's soul/mate, takes it upon himself to become her protector. Thus he murders the two people who stand in the way of her happiness: Agnes Carpenter, Charles Carpenter's wife, and Roger Krauss, a member of the foundation's Board of Trustees who objects to Dorothea becoming the next director of the Institute because she is too feminist (i.e., she wanted to sponsor a public lecture on battered women). After Colin exterminates both Krauss and Agnes, he goes to Dorothea with the revelation that he has been her agent; when she responds with horror, he abducts her, and they end up at the appropriately named Land's End, a mock Swiss chalet in upstate New York. After they live in a parody of domesticity for a hundred hours, the police arrive, there's a shoot-out, and Colin gives up his romantic dream that he and Dorothea will die together. Thus he slits his own throat, splashing Dorothea with his arterial blood (*Soul/Mate* is *not* a novel for the squeamish). The epilogue briefly summarizes Dorothea's recovery and shows her and Charles house-hunting in preparation for their normal, conjugal life together.

The resolution of *Soul/Mate* follows the pattern of the traditional Gothic. The repository of violence, Colin Asch, has been eradicated, and the heterosexual couple is reestablished, however fantastically and unconvincingly à la Radcliffe, as an idyllic unit. Dorothea has the man and the job she wants, and thus her life has taken the form of a postfeminist fairytale. The Gothic world represented by Colin Asch's murderous psychopathology is thrust into the past and becomes a world apart. Significantly, Dorothea notices and offers minor resistance to such disconnection: "It's as if Colin stands on the far side of an abyss . . . speaking to me, trying to explain himself, in a normal voice—but a normal voice, under the circumstances, isn't sufficient. *I can't hear*" (247).

Uncannily, Colin's voice is marked by normalcy, while Dorothea, seemingly a paragon of virtue, finds her hearing defective and impaired. Such subtle contradictions point to the underlying tension of *Soul/Mate*, the unconfronted fear that the quotidian cannot be separated from the Gothic.

Indeed, the fundamental connection between Colin and Dorothea puts into question the possibility of such a separation. While the relationship between the Gothic heroine (the emblem of feminine goodness) and the Gothic villain (the emblem of masculine evil) has traditionally been one of antagonism, in *Soul/Mate* it becomes one of unconscious collaboration. Plot, image, and form—as well as the title—converge to establish Colin as Dorothea's double. Colin's life, like Dorothea's, has been marked by a tragic, precipitous expulsion from the nuclear family: his parents drowned after their car veered off a bridge and into a river; Colin alone survived this accident. From their first meeting, Dorothea and Colin uncannily communicate with one another. At a particularly tense moment during that dinner, as Colin's newly adopted vegetarianism and the status of human beings as animals are being debated, Dorothea finds herself simultaneously defending and gently correcting Colin's proclamations: "In the silence Dorothea spoke, in a peculiar slow voice, as if the words were being coaxed from her against her will, 'But animals too eat one another. We, I mean—since we are animals. It is something of which we should be ashamed, but even shame is not enough to defeat hunger'" (26). These odd, almost prophetic words not only establish sympathy between them but also implicate Dorothea in the predatory model Colin enacts.[10]

Moreover, at various points in the novel, Colin responds aloud to Dorothea's thoughts. In discussions of painting and literature, they discover similar aesthetic sensibilities. Significantly, when Dorothea hears from a friend that Colin has been asking about her, the protagonist's initial response is self-reflexive: "the situation was a mirror of sorts in which Dorothea might view herself from a new and unexpected—and possibly advantageous—angle, but she did not want to pursue it" (54). As the novel progresses, such figurative mirrors become literal ones. At one point, as Colin helps Dorothea on with her coat, "their eyes met in the mirror beside the door" (102). In another instance, Dorothea must interrupt a conversation with Colin in order to answer the telephone; while attending to her caller's voice, she is depicted as "absentmindedly watching her visitor through a mirror—in fact, through two mirrors" (135). That Dorothea looks in mirrors and sees Colin underscores their doppelgänger relationship. The bifurcated structure of this novel further reinforces such reflective distortions. As the narrative shifts from

Dorothea's to Colin's point of view, the same events are often chronicled from their respective positions.[11] Thus meaning resides not only within but also between their perspectives.

Writes Creighton, "The double, for Oates, often functions as an alter ego, embodying unfulfilled contexts of the self to which one is both attracted and repelled" (59). As Dorothea's double, Colin enacts her repressed wishes. When Krauss becomes a subject of conversation at the dinner party, Dorothea evinces both her penchant for denial and her wish to eradicate her professional persecutor: "The problem of Roger Krauss and his heartbreaking campaign against her was one Dorothea dealt with by not thinking about it at all: simply blanking the horror out, as a dirtied wall is whitewashed, cruelly and expediently" (16). By cruelly and expediently "garroting" Roger Krauss, Colin establishes himself as Dorothea's active male alter ego. During that same party, Dorothea observes Charles covertly and admiringly and thinks, "A man one might kill for . . . if one were that sort" (14). Being "that sort," Colin kills Agnes, Charles's wife, and enables Dorothea to take her place.

By presenting Agnes as an insuperable impediment and by relieving Charles of any literal responsibility for her death, Oates recalls the plot of *Jane Eyre*. Significantly, Colin's role parallels that of Bertha Mason Rochester.[12] A brief reference to a fire Colin set in an adolescent rage constitutes the first clue to this cross-gender literary lineage. As Gilbert and Gubar argued in their now classic reading of *Jane Eyre*, Bertha "acts *for* Jane" (*Madwoman* 361); in a similar vein, Dorothea's repressed wishes become Colin's command. Moreover, by the end of the novel, Colin himself is seemingly the last impediment to Dorothea and Charles's happiness; thus his bloody act of self-destruction recalls Bertha's leap from the burning battlements of Thornfield. In this postfeminist fantasy, a man doubles for a woman, seemingly a sign of nonessential gender identities. Paradoxically, however, cross-gender doubling here reproduces a gendered status quo. As the repository of violence and aggression, Colin enables Dorothea to retain her facade of femininity.

Yet, as the title indicates, Colin represents not only Dorothea's soul but also her mate. Indeed, this psychopathic murderer symbolically serves as Dorothea's lover, and their relationship takes the form, albeit a distorted one, of courtship and marriage. Anonymously, Colin sends Dorothea a "white lace formal blouse—or was it a little jacket?—exquisitely beautiful, and in her size—size 6—and there was a matching skirt, floor-length, silken wool, dazzlingly white" (89), clearly his version of a wedding gown. At the party Colin gives in Dorothea's honor after she has been named the new director of the Brannon Institute, Dorothea wears that dress and thus symbolically constitutes herself as Colin's bride. Not coincidentally, Colin experiences at this party "the happiness of a man among men" (159); by "marrying" Dorothea, Colin affirms his homosociality and thus his masculinity.[13] Significantly, Colin's plan even includes a postwedding rendezvous. Immediately after the party, while Dorothea remains in a deathlike sleep caused by a drug he had slipped into her tea, Colin breaks into her home, slips into her bedroom, and contents himself with the feel of her slip and that of her bare foot.

While Colin symbolically takes Dorothea as his bride the night of his party, she recognizes him as a demon lover during their cohabitation at Land's End.[14] Colin's parody of postnuptial activity is recalled during their first night at the mock Swiss chalet when Dorothea awakens to find Colin's "face pressed against the calf of her right leg" (228). Indeed, it is only when Colin abducts her that she becomes aware of his masculinity, his sexuality, his otherness. Upon arriving at Land's End, Dorothea views her abduction as "a parody of a honeymoon" (227). As the hours she and Colin spend together accumulate, Dorothea muses, "We are a grotesque parody of domesticity . . . but of what sort of domesticity *is* the parody?" (231). Her question implies a breakdown between the parodic and the straight, the Gothic and the normal.

That breakdown is furthered by the fact that, as Dorothea's Gothic mate, Colin doubles not only for her but also for Charles, the man she wishes to marry. Charles and Colin are often attracted to the same women. When Colin first meets Charles's wife, he feels connected to her; indeed, even as he murders Agnes, he regards her with pity rather than malice. Colin also becomes involved with, and eventually murders, Susannah Hunt, a woman with whom Charles has flirted at social gatherings. And, of course, both are taken with Dorothea. Significantly, when Dorothea first receives the white outfit, she assumes that Charles has sent it and wonders if it signifies a proposal. Although she understands the gift's symbolism, she unwittingly confuses the identity of the giver. Interestingly enough, Colin abducts Dorothea an hour before Charles is expected at her home and thus figuratively supplants her suitor. As Colin orchestrates their departure, he speaks to Dorothea with "husbandly solicitude," the same phrase formerly used to describe Charles's attitude. Colin's last name, *Asch*, is an anagram for *Chas*, a nickname for Charles.[15] The fact that Charles pronounces Colin a "psychopath" long before his crimes become public knowledge serves as further evidence of the uncanny connection between Dorothea's lover and her self-appointed agent.

Rosenfelt has argued that postfeminist novels "relax feminism's political critique of heterosexuality as an institution. Yet they do not abandon it completely" (284). The doubling of Colin and Charles signifies some retention of this critique. While Colin physically kills Agnes, Charles is her metaphorical murderer. Even Dorothea intuits that Charles possesses deadly, albeit figurative, power. The day after Charles comes to Dorothea and announces that he is leaving Agnes, Dorothea insists that he slow down and consider Agnes's welfare: "In time, perhaps—in a few months, gradually—it could all be explained to her, but not so suddenly—so cruelly. It's like *murder!*" (143—my emphasis). On the surface, such melodramatic utterances read like a symptom of Dorothea's oversensitive conscience, a sign of the selflessness she assiduously cultivates. However, they represent much more than that, for Dorothea identifies with Agnes.

Of course, Dorothea's love for Charles entails fantasies about replacing Agnes: "[Dorothea] had the vague hazy warmly comforting conviction that, yes, she and Charles would one day be married, and there would be, in town, a new Mr. and Mrs. Charles Carpenter" (11). Yet, Dorothea and Agnes potentially share more than the same last name. Their mutual emotional dependence upon Charles has already been keenly imprinted on Dorothea's consciousness:

> Once, at a cocktail party, Dorothea had spent an anguished half hour observing, out of the corner of her eye, her beloved Charles Carpenter in a spirited, laughter-punctuated conversation with the glamorous divorcée [Susannah Hunt]; to her mortification she had happened to glance across the room to see Agnes Carpenter similarly observing the couple.... Staring at them with a Gorgon's unwavering eye. How sisterly she'd felt toward poor Agnes in that instant! How united in their mutual helplessness! (135)

Significantly, Dorothea feels "sisterly" toward Agnes and recognizes Charles's potential to hurt them both at the same moment that she compares her to a Gorgon and thus evinces her willingness to accept the story of Agnes's monstrosity. Here, postfeminist consciousness seems to have complicated but not transcended misogynist representations of the other woman. However, when Charles announces his intention of ridding himself of his first wife, Dorothea reluctantly reexperiences a bond with Agnes. Trying to fantasize about being Charles's future bride, Dorothea keeps on returning to the picture of his present wife: "Dorothea lay wakeful, rigid, her eyes starkly open and her brain a storm of thoughts.

. . . [She] kept envisioning Agnes Carpenter, her rival, her sister rival, lying at the same moment sleepless in *her* bed, in *her* bedroom, on the other side of town" (142). That the present and the future Mrs. Carpenter may be related haunts Dorothea and fosters her desire to move more slowly. Even a modicum of feminist consciousness makes Dorothea smarter than the second Mrs. de Winter. Yet the phrase "sister rival," like the Gorgon comparison, underscores the fragility of Dorothea's identification with Agnes. Caught between the scripts of sisterhood and female competition for men, Dorothea embodies the paradoxes of postfeminism.

The presentation of Agnes suggests that Oates as well as Dorothea is ensnared in such paradoxes. Clearly, the old Mrs. Carpenter—"poor Agnes"—is pathetically unhappy and alcoholic. However, the cause for the former's misery remains inchoate:

> [Agnes's] round stolid face was a defiant pug's face, with the liverish cast of a being of action who has for mysterious reasons refused to act, so that her energy, her very life, had backed up in her, choking her. It was not known in Lathrup Farms whether she drank because of chronic ill health or whether her chronic ill health was the result of her drinking; whether she was "difficult" because she drank or drank because she was "difficult," trusting to alcohol to free instincts that social decorum would otherwise have suppressed. (11)

This confusion of cause and effect, the evocation of "mysterious reasons" alongside the inhibiting role of "social decorum" simultaneously points to, and retreats from, an analysis of Agnes's predicament. As we saw in *The Shadow Knows*, epistemological uncertainty can mystify social relations. Apart from accounts of her being "difficult," her drunken rages and vindictive expenditures, we are given little information about Agnes. That a "being of action" lives with a man who "did all the driving" (5) perhaps accounts for her "liverish cast"; the narrative suggests but does not pursue this possibility. Although Charles repeatedly portrays his wife as a willful and stubborn woman, the only outlets she has found for such personality traits involve self-destructive, addictive behavior. An emblem of conspicuous consumption and totally alienated from work, Agnes is reduced to, and dismissed as, a monitory story about an obsolete female role.

Yet while Agnes's role may be outmoded, her struggle with issues of self-expression and self-suppression are not, as Dorothea's story makes clear. A postfeminist woman who desires and expects both romantic and professional fulfillment, Dorothea is nevertheless plagued by an interior voice that is harsh and judgmental. Paradoxically, the goal of such self-policing is a posture of selflessness; Dorothea deliberately deflects attention from herself and her interests. As a latter-day Dorothea Brooke—at one point, her face is likened to the "sculpted face of Saint Theresa" (72)—Dorothea Deverell shares Agnes's stubbornness and willfulness. However, rather than unleash such traits with alcohol, Dorothea strives to balance them with a veneer of femininity. Although Dorothea thinks of and presents herself as one who is devoid of will, her actions suggest that she expresses herself through indirection. When asked unwelcome questions about her past, she shifts attention onto others; in this way, self-effacement becomes an act of self-assertion. Depressed and angered by the stasis of her relationship with Charles, she withdraws into the country during the Christmas season and does not call her beloved, though she had promised she would. When an older man identifies her as a pretty girl who should be married, her superficially sweet response contains a double-edged corrective: "I was, once—when I *was* a girl" (7). Acute self-consciousness becomes a survival strategy for Dorothea, and clearly she is healthier and more successful than Agnes. Nevertheless, *Soul/Mate* demonstrates that such battering self-examination is an exhausting modus operandi.

Dorothea's need to disguise, even to herself, her desire for power and change becomes abundantly clear in her professional context. [16] Roger Krauss's "heartbreaking campaign" against Dorothea is based on his antifeminist fears that, as director, she would "'subvert' the Institute for her own political ends" (15). Significantly, after Colin has murdered Krauss, it becomes clear that the anxieties of her professional antagonist are not as preposterous as they are initially represented. Dorothea has numerous plans for changes, notable among them the inclusion of a female attorney who works with battered women and children in the Institute-sponsored lecture series; formerly, such a speaker was considered too "controversial." Having incorporated second-wave feminist thought into her consciousness to a certain extent, the postfeminist Dorothea *does* represent a threat to the status quo: quietly but insistently, she will chip away at the conservatism of the Brannon Institute. Yet by resisting such knowledge, she undercuts her own agency.

Rather than explore the contradictions that mark her life, Dorothea becomes the mistress of denial. Unable to acknowledge her own aggression, Dorothea likewise rewrites that of others. Thus, once Colin, her murderous alter ego, neutralizes the threat of Roger Krauss, formerly the insuperable impediment to her professional advancement, Dorothea castigates herself for her overactive imagination:

> In time she might even convince herself that Mr. Krauss had merely been baiting her, taking a devil's advocate sort of stand vis-a-vis "feminism," as often, in social situations, meaning no real harm, good-hearted men will do. To think of him as her enemy was surely to exaggerate? "I must guard against that sort of thing." (128)

The feminist reader can't help but note that Dorothea would do better to guard against her own revisionist tendencies. Similarly, when Howard Morland, the current director of the Brannon Institute, announces to Dorothea that she will be his successor, she "suddenly" views him not as a conservative incompetent who would have been swayed by the vicious Krauss, but rather as "a beneficent father, her friend and protector all along" (125). In postfeminist fantasies, the good daddy of the conservative Gothic is now a company man, and backlash is nothing more than an unjustified paranoid fantasy.[17] Here, the invocation of paranoia domesticates and short-circuits rather than sharpens feminist consciousness.

Against such a backdrop of denial and self-delusion, the ending of *Soul/Mate* reads like more of the same, even as it promises an idyllic married life. It seems no coincidence that Dorothea develops selective amnesia and can remember little of the hundred hours she spent with Colin at Land's End. The domesticity parodied during that period may be perilously close to that which she looks forward to with Charles. At a particularly dramatic and dangerous juncture during the Land's End siege, Dorothea imagines the face of Charles, "but it was a face of studied calm, remoteness, he knows nothing of me, she thought. It was all a dream" (237). Although fear and illness frame her perceptions here, they nonetheless seem uncannily accurate as they recall another moment of defamiliarization: when Dorothea gets the directorship and shares her plans with Charles, he, her closest intimate, is shocked by the range of her ideas and the depth of her hunger for change. Similarly, when Dorothea implores Charles to consider Agnes's feelings, she sees her lover from a new and alarming angle: "This side of him, this sense of an impatience, even anger, barely restrained, was new to Dorothea Deverell, and intimidating" (143). Ultimately, Dorothea and Charles do not really know themselves or one another all that well, and one wonders how substantial the differences will be between the new and the old Mr. and Mrs. Carpenter.

By accepting Charles's dictum to "let [Colin] go. The contemptible son of a bitch" (247), Dorothea thrusts the Gothic into the shadowy past and allows Colin to be cast as a monster, an absolute other unrelated to her or to her husband-to-be. Creighton reads this as a "wise" move, a sign that "Dorothea can let go of her dark double" (89).[18] However, I would argue that such rejection of a being who is, at least symbolically, of Dorothea's own making invokes the Frankenstein myth.[19] About that myth, Oates has written, "It is a parable for our time, an enduring prophecy, a remarkably acute diagnosis of the lethal nature of *denial*: denial of responsibility for one's actions, denial of the shadow self locked within consciousness" ("Frankenstein's Fallen Angel" 122). In *Soul/Mate*, Dorothea's final act of denial is to assert that she "can't hear" her alter ego; "won't" would seem more accurate. In her willingness to view the Gothic world as passé and to normalize the passive-aggressive behavior fostered by hegemonic femininity, Dorothea may well represent a generation of postfeminists.

Wesley writes that "this most uncharacteristically unambiguous ending sets the recovery of familial arrangement against the disorder Colin has introduced" (149). The feminist reader—multiformed though she may be—can only view Dorothea's happy ending ironically. Her readiness to deny her relationship with both Agnes and Colin seems like an artificial, conservative, and dangerous containment of the Gothic world. Moreover, those readers attuned to the intertextual echoes of *Middlemarch* and *Jane Eyre* cannot help but notice that Dorothea Deverell's resolution to such vexed issues as heterosexual romance and female self-assertion resembles those of her nineteenth-century counterparts, thus suggesting that the postfeminist woman has not come such a long way. Yet, marketed for mass-consumption, *Soul/Mate* also can and will be read as an endorsement of postfeminism. Dorothea's noncombative attitude combined with her success in love and work is sure to appeal to a "post-feminist generation" that characterizes feminists as "bitter," "unhappy," "tortured," "alone," "people for whom going to the bathroom is a political issue" (Bolotin 30). *Soul/Mate* is an interesting but troubling text because it serves as both an example and a critique of postfeminism.[20] In the character of Dorothea Deverell, Oates delineates the paradoxes of the postfeminist woman. Despite that being's considerable ambition, she self-consciously strives not to appear too aggressive, too willful, too feminist. Even as she evinces interest in "women's issues," she resists the politics of sex consciousness; indeed, the "we" in her vocabulary gener-ally refers to the heterosexual couple. Profoundly individualistic, she relies upon her own professional and personal haven for security and is shocked when the Gothic intrudes upon her charmed life. As Dorothea puts it during the terrifying drive to Land's End, "this can't be happening . . . such things do not happen to people like us" (225). Significantly, the epilogue of *Soul/Mate* reinscribes—albeit with the potential for irony—this fantasy of insularity. Replete with nostalgia[21] for a prefeminist separation of the quotidian and the Gothic, such postfeminist fantasies seem no less likely than an underscrutinized cultural feminist paranoia to engender bodily harm.

Chapter 7

Beyond Postfeminism: Revaluing the Female Body and the Body Politic

As I have argued throughout, Gothic negotiations are the stuff of theory as well as fiction. Many poststructuralist thinkers would seem to argue that gender is a nightmare from which we are trying to awake and that any analytic framework that reifies men and women contributes to, rather than ameliorates, the Gothic horrors of the sex/gender system. Thus feminist Gothic subtly and perniciously shifts into Gothic feminism. However, such theoretical positions can themselves be read as the product of gender privilege; as Elizabeth Grosz so succinctly and audaciously puts it, "The proclamation of a position outside, beyond, sexual difference is a luxury that only male arrogance allows" (191). Teresa de Lauretis has convincingly argued that such male arrogance is remarkably "self-serving to the male-gendered subject" (15). According to de Lauretis, such a theoretical rush to deny gender is an attempt to "contain the trauma of gender—the potential disruption of the social fabric and of white male privilege that could ensue if this feminist critique of gender as ideologico-technological production were to become widespread" (21). In other words, de Lauretis suggests that, for those who consciously or uncon-sciously experience feminists as Gothic transgressors, feminism itself becomes a version of the male Gothic that must be contained. Of course, this strategy of containment entails the denial not only of gender but also of gender hierarchy and gender oppression. Hence postfeminist con-sciousness and prefeminist consciousness look uncannily familiar, and while men wake from their feminist nightmares, women continue to need valium to sleep well.

However, we must also take into account the effects of this "trauma of gender" upon women. As this femicidal strand of the contemporary female Gothic indicates, hegemonic definitions of masculinity and femininity—the rules of gender—can and, in many cases, do constitute trauma for women: they encourage overinvestment in heterosexual institutions that enable female victimization; they foster the construction of female masochists and male sadists; they promote the legitimate fear of the Gothic dimensions of normality. Ultimately, understanding the trauma of gender can, itself, be traumatic. Tania Modleski unwittingly glosses the extent of this trauma when she asserts that the oft-reviled term "women's experience" functions as shorthand for women's oppression. Such an easy equation between womanhood and oppression may well explain why "for many 'women' the very term arouses a visceral, even phobic reaction" (Modleski 16). The specificity of the female body can easily become a locus for this phobia, especially when representations of the female body as a colonized, violated space predominate. Significantly, the theoretical flight from "woman" and from feminisms that identify with her partakes of the somatophobia endemic to Western philosophy. In *Bodily Harm* (1981), Margaret Atwood reads postfeminism as symptomatic of somatophobia, the fear of the body that is projected onto women. For Atwood, the cure for this cultural disease necessitates a return to, rather than an escape from, the female body. This narrative actively works against unitary stories of male vice and female virtue; indeed, it clearly privileges the multiplicity and fragmented subjectivity associated with poststructuralist thought. However, by revaluing what may be among the most undervalued female attributes—the female body—Atwood refuses gender skepticism. Rather than a Gothic prison, the specifically female body becomes here an emblem of personal and political agency.

Like *Soul/Mate*, *Bodily Harm* chronicles a postfeminist's encounter with the Gothic.[1] Rennie Wilford, the protagonist of *Bodily Harm*, is a journalist and the lover of Jake, a successful businessman. Obsessed with her own image, Rennie, like Dorothea, resists acknowledging connections with other women and believes herself immune to horrific happenings. However, while Oates's tale attempts to contain the Gothic world, Atwood's enlarges it mercilessly.

Rennie earns her living as a writer. An expert on lifestyles, Rennie reports on chic vacation spots and the ephemera of fashion. At the outset of *Bodily Harm*, the threat of violation and the ambiguity of rescuers—key Gothic tropes—are introduced: upon returning home one afternoon, Rennie finds two policemen sitting at her kitchen table and a rope left by a "faceless stranger" on her bed. Overwhelmed not only by the tendency of the police to blame her for the rope-bearing pervert but also by recent crises (a partial mastectomy, the departure of her lover, Jake, a less than satisfying affair with her surgeon), Rennie seeks an escape. Thus she sets off on a travel assignment to St. Antoine, a Caribbean island about which she knows nothing.

In this Caribbean locale, the undercurrent of Gothic doom that pervaded Rennie's life in Toronto takes on new and extreme dimensions. Formerly under British control, St. Antoine and her sister island, St. Agathe, prepare for their first independent elections. Three men vie for the office of prime minister: Ellis, the established and corrupt leader favored by the CIA; Prince, whose naive beliefs in communism and "the people" allow him to be manipulated by Marsdon, his campaign manager; and Dr. Minnow, a former veterinarian trained in Canada who apprehends the needs of his motherland. Although Rennie tries to preserve her tourist status, she becomes involved in island politics through meetings with Dr. Minnow; Lora, Prince's lover; and Paul, a handsome and independent drug and gun smuggler. Caught in a staged and quickly aborted revolution, Rennie winds up in an underground prison with Lora as her cellmate. The fate of both women is left ambiguous; however, in this literal prison Rennie must forfeit all illusions of insularity and immunity. Against this backdrop of political unrest in the Caribbean, Rennie experiences fear and dread from which she had deemed herself "exempt" and comes to realize the seamlessness of the normal and the Gothic.

Formally, this seamlessness is underscored by variations of voice and transgressions of time and space. *Bodily Harm* is framed by third-person narration limited to Rennie's point of view. Interspersed within this third-person narration are stories told by Rennie and later by Lora in the first person. Thus distinctions between narrating subject and narrated object, self and other, are diminished by Atwood's narrative strategy. Similarly, past, present, and future appear synchronically in the pages of this text. While Rennie's Caribbean experience is chronicled progressively in the present tense, flashbacks abound. In the final pages of the novel, Rennie's release from prison is partially narrated in the future tense, though

whether this constitutes a genuine flash-forward or is merely a record-
ing of Rennie's fantasy remains unclear.

Significantly, this ambiguous use of the future tense amplifies rather
than clarifies the spatial vagary inscribed in the first sentence of the novel:
"'This is how I got *here*,' says Rennie" (my emphasis). Is "here" Toronto,
the place to which Rennie has returned after her sojourn in prison? Or is
"here" the underground cell which Rennie shares with a battered and,
most probably, deceased Lora? "Here" could also refer to a psychic place,
the measure of growth that Rennie has achieved, "the metaphysical state
of Rennie's regeneration" (Rigney 113). While the above possibilities
assume that this narrative structure is circular (i.e., that the enigmatic first
sentence necessarily relates to the ambiguous futuristic ending and that
this story is told retrospectively), another interpretation also exists: the
referent of "here" could simply be St. Antoine, and thus this first sentence
would merely serve as a prelude to exposition about the man with the rope
and Rennie's need to escape. Ultimately, the lack of clear, consistent
spatial and temporal markers,[2] as well as the complex, achronological
narrative structure, causes the reader to share Rennie's dislocation and
suggests that there is no escape from the Gothic.

Such formal features anticipate that Rennie's attempts to constitute
herself as the consummate "escape artist" (Rigney 104) are doomed to
failure. Long before her Caribbean getaway, Rennie attempts her first
escape from Griswold, her provincial hometown. For Rennie, Griswold
represents misguided morality, the enforcement of standards of decency
that uphold prudish conservatism rather than justice. Indeed, as an adult,
Rennie assiduously works to neutralize the effects of her "background."
Most importantly, she strives to avoid any resemblance to her mother,
who, having been abandoned by her husband, took refuge in martyrdom
as she cared for Rennie's aged grandmother. Growing up, Rennie felt
anger at her father not for abandoning her mother but rather for leaving her
behind in the static, overwhelmingly female world of Griswold. Duty,
responsibility, embittered suffering, entrapment, and femaleness become
hopelessly entangled for Rennie; thus her personal history sets the stage
for her postfeminist flight from women and points to the desperate need
for female-positive narratives.

Grosz argues that "the female body has been constructed not only as
lack or absence but with more complexity, as a leaking, uncontrollable,
seeping liquid; as formless flow; as viscosity, entrapping, secreting; as
lacking not so much simply the phallus but self-containment" (203).
Rennie's desire for that lacking self-containment and her mother and

grandmother's fear of it is, appropriately, performed in her mother's Griswold kitchen. Aged and senile, her grandmother often had the illusion that she had lost her hands; for her, that lack of physical connection with the world caused panic.[3] One day, not wanting "to be touched by those groping hands," Rennie allowed the old woman to lapse into hysteria rather than grasp the latter's hands and show her that they were at the end of her arms and, therefore, that she still had contact with the world. Upon entering the kitchen and surveying this scene, Rennie's mother regarded Rennie with disgust and restored her own mother's hands by "clasping them within her own" (298). Significantly, the state of inviolability that is Rennie's dream equals isolation and powerlessness for her maternal relatives. This scene functions to dramatize the cost of self-containment: determined to distance herself from the groping hands of female need, Rennie ironically denies the power of her own touch. Such metaphors may well describe the postfeminist condition.

Although Rennie, like Dorothea, has a modicum of feminist consciousness, she resists sustained feminist analysis. When the Toronto police investigate the break-in of her apartment, Rennie recognizes that the questions posed by one of the officers—about her living habits, her relationships with men, whether or not she undresses with the curtains open—constitute an interrogation and exemplify his inclination to blame the victim: "He wanted it to be my fault, just a little, some indiscretion, some provocation. Next he would start lecturing me about locks, about living alone, about safety" (15). Yet despite such insights, Rennie chides herself for being afraid after this break-in and decides not to tell anyone about the man with the rope. At this point in her story, legitimizing the fear associated with cultural feminist Gothic is too risky: she might be labeled a "man-hater" and find herself thrust back into the company of women.

Bouson rightly notes that Rennie "is determined not to overvalue love" (123); however, the same cannot be said for men. Whereas Willa (*Casualties of Peace*) and Brenda *(The Bottle Factory Outing)* seek male rescuers to protect them from other men, Rennie looks to men to rescue her from the nature and culture of women, as she understands them. Given that the female body is aligned with lack, with vulnerability, with violability, heterosexual relations with men become overvalued since they offer a respite from femaleness. Rennie's relationship with Jake, a man who designs and packages products for a living, illustrates the paradoxes of expecting those who construct the burden of femaleness to then rescue women from it. Fearful of succumbing to the prudishness of her upbringing, Rennie accepts Jake's penchant for kink, his hanging of lewd photographs on her walls, his fondness for mild S&M, his requests that she pretend she's being raped during lovemaking, his gifts of lingerie that leave her feeling exposed and vulnerable. Although Rennie feels some qualms about such pornographic fantasies, she invokes the spirit of play:

> Jake liked to pin her hands down, he liked to hold her so she couldn't move. He liked that, he liked thinking of sex as something he could win at. Sometimes he really hurt her, once he put his arm across her throat and she really did stop breathing. Danger turns you on, he said. Admit it. It was a game, they both knew that. He would never do it if it was real, if she really were a beautiful stranger or a slave girl or whatever it was he wanted her to pretend. So she didn't have to be afraid of him. (207)

Although Rennie seeks to reassure herself, the language of this passage betrays the extent to which this is Jake's game. The repetition of the phrase "he liked" indicates that such scenes fulfill *his* desire. However, by identifying with that desire, by making it her own, she can vicariously experience the self-containment that she believes is anatomically denied to her. Of course, such identification can never be complete. Moreover, the pornographic mastery that Jake performs is itself a cultural symptom of somatophobia: fear of embodiment and mortality is projected onto the specifically female body and then that body comes under male control. Thus pornographic relations with Jake uncannily recall Rennie to her body; in these performances, she must bear not only her own vulnerability but also his. However, access to his illusion of mastery functions as adequate compensation for a time.[4]

Rennie's postfeminism extends from her bedroom to her byline. As Roberta Rubenstein rightly notes, Rennie has written "more than one article reiterating the traditional role for women in relationship with men" (263). Indeed, her professional trajectory indicates that her allergy to female bonding is a cultural phenomenon and has considerable market value. Her exposé on ex-feminists who had decided that "women were just so difficult to work with" earns Rennie praise from her editor, and a male editor tired of the "heavy," "humorless" antiporn written by feminists commissions Rennie to provide a "light" look at the subject. Rennie accepts this assignment and proceeds with her research. First, she visits an artist who constructs furniture from female body parts. Then she surveys a collection of pornography housed by the police department. Although undaunted by the erotic gadgets and the film clips of "sex-and-death pieces" which had to be "done with ketchup" (210), Rennie finds an image of a rat emerging from a black woman's vagina literally nauseating and vomits on her police escort's shoes. Although her visceral reaction would seem to invite her to connect the latent content of such images with her own female fears, she chooses instead to withdraw from the assignment. Sounding like N. at her least attractive moments, Rennie actively works to resist knowing the gender trouble of pornographic scripts: "There were some things it was better not to know any more about than you had to" (211).

However, Rennie's development of breast cancer and the subsequent mastectomy she undergoes function symbolically to remind Rennie—and the reader—of the body knowledge she seeks to evade. Indeed, the images of violation, fragmentation, and contamination that Rennie associates with femaleness seem confirmed by her illness and its treatment. Her breast, metonym of her sexed body, becomes an agent of betrayal, a site of vulnerability.[5] Moreover, the mastectomy serves as a physical manifestation of the flight from womanhood that has been her life practice. After surgery, Rennie's desire for self-containment is thwarted by nightmares of invasion and seepage. At one point, she tells Daniel, her surgeon, "I feel infested . . . I dream I'm full of white maggots eating away at me from the inside" (83). At another point, feeling her scar, she's "afraid to look down, she's afraid she'll see blood, leakage, her stuffing coming out" (22).

Knowing that Jake shares her horror of these real and imagined transgressions of bodily boundaries, Rennie looks to Daniel as her rescuer. Rennie imagines the man who has plunged into the depths of her body, who has seen and presumably excised her physical malignancy, as her metaphysical savior. Moreover, the thought of coming with Daniel holds out the prospect of a sort of homecoming: with his unswerving belief in duty and "human decency," Daniel embodies the values of Griswold without the attendant threat of femaleness. However, despite the fact that Rennie is in flight from female vulnerability, she cannot imagine herself otherwise. When she and Daniel eventually end up in bed, Rennie feels cheated and resentful: "He had needed something from her, which she could neither believe nor forgive. She'd been counting on him not to: she was supposed to be the needy one, but it was the other way around. . . . She felt raped" (238). By speciously invoking rape, perhaps the paradigmatic form of female victimization, Rennie defines herself as a vessel to be alternatively filled or violated and rewrites Daniel into the fantasy of masculine autonomy which his need has belied. Grosz writes,

"Sexual difference entails the existence of a sexual ethics, an ethics of the ongoing negotiations between beings whose differences, whose alterities are left intact but with whom some kind of exchange is nonetheless possible" (192). However, for Rennie, whose postfeminist sensibilities lead her to believe that her femaleness leaves her nothing to give, such an exchange model is unworkable and even unimaginable. Inter-course can only be rape,[6] and Rennie once again finds herself caught in a Gothic mirror where images of victimized women prevail.

Consistent with her modus operandi, Rennie decides that she needs a "small absence from real life" (16) and flies off to St. Antoine to do a "Fun in the Sun" piece. However, like St. Anthony, for whom this Caribbean island is named, Rennie experiences a magnification of her struggles during her retreat and is forced to deal with her flesh and her female demons.

Ironically, Rennie initially views the enclosed Gothic world of St. Antoine as a haven and embraces her displacement: "She discovers that she's truly no longer at home. She is away, she is out, which is what she wanted. The difference between this and home isn't so much that she knows nobody as that nobody knows her. In a way she's invisible. In a way she's safe" (39). Of course, the qualification "in a way" foreshadows the fact that such safety and invisibility will be short-lived, that at a certain point Rennie will pine for home and will be unable to get there. Just as importantly, the phrase "in a way" indicates the double-edged nature of invisibility as a defense mechanism. For Rennie, being seen equals exposure and vulnerability. However, by defining her status by how and whom she is seen ("nobody knows her") rather than by whom she sees ("she knows nobody"), she objectifies herself and denies the power of her own gaze just as she has denied the power of her own touch.[7]

Although Rennie embarks on her Caribbean getaway in part to escape Daniel, his sense of duty and his implicit demands upon her, Rennie meets his analogue, Dr. Minnow, on the plane to St. Antoine. Ironically, Rennie initially and erroneously fears that Minnow has sexual designs upon her—although she does not choose to identify herself with women, she assumes that she is always seen as one. However, rather than a rake, Minnow is a visionary: he sees the people of his country suffering and can imagine their situation being other than it is. When Rennie asks Minnow why he continues his efforts against all odds, he asserts the power of imagination: "You do it because everyone tell [sic] you it is not possible. They cannot imagine things being different. It is my duty to imagine, and they [the current, corrupt government] know that for even one person to imagine is very dangerous to them" (229). Atwood's 1981 address to Amnesty International indicates the extent to which Minnow's political strategy mirrors her own artistic credo:

> [I]t is the human mind also that can summon up the power to resist, that can imagine a better world than the one before it, that can retain memory and courage in the face of unspeakable suffering.
> . . . If the imagination were a negligible thing and the act of writing a mere frill, as many in this society would like to believe, regimes all over the world would not be at such pains to exterminate them.
> . . . The writer, unless he [sic] is a mere word processor, retains three attributes that power-mad regimes cannot tolerate: a human imagination, in the many forms it may take; the power to communicate; and hope. (397)

Echoing Atwood, Minnow speaks of his "duty" and exhorts Rennie to realize hers. Fully aware that "nothing is inconceivable" on St. Antoine and that Ellis, the current leader, can only be controlled by his reputation abroad (which equals his ability to get foreign aid), Minnow views Rennie's journalistic presence as potentially stabilizing, a way to avoid "excess." Thus this good man[8]—an embodiment of male virtue—takes it upon himself to become Rennie's tour guide. Although Rennie's real interests lie in tennis courts and exclusive restaurants, Minnow wants to show her his beleaguered country. Hence he introduces her to some of the survivors of the latest hurricane and explains to her that while these unfortunates live in squalor, the rations donated by wealthier, charitable societies (e.g., Canada) are served at banquets for the government's corrupt elite. Similarly, he tries to impress upon her the havoc that colonial rule and neglect have wrought upon this island society. Leading her through the women's prison, symbolic both of her future fate and the range of crimes that the "fairer sex" is capable of committing, Minnow points out a recently constructed gallows. Predictably, Rennie does not initially understand what she's seeing and cannot make the connection between this structure and human rights violations.

Dr. Minnow's emphasis on duty causes him to become too connected with Griswold; thus, he, like Daniel, must be rejected. When the former explains island politics to Rennie, she "tunes out": "It's too much like small-town politics, the tiny feuds in Griswold, the grudges, the stupid rivalries. Who cares?" (129). Apathy is also Rennie's response to Minnow's chronicling of abuses of power and to his plea that she write about them: "Rennie knows she's supposed to feel outrage. . . . At the moment though all she feels is imposed upon. Outrage is out of date" (135). Using the cloak of postfeminist fashion, Rennie evades the responsibilities that come with her privilege; although the time she spends with Dr. Minnow makes her self-conscious about being a "tourist, a spectator, a voyeur" (125), she refuses to acknowledge the visionary power that might inhere in her gaze. As a woman and a "sweet Canadian," Rennie can only imagine herself as a colonized body and thus manages not to see her implication in bodily harm on the international scene.

Repetition with a difference marks the narrative of *Bodily Harm*; hence, Rennie's disregard for the impoverishment and corruption that plague St. Antoine closely resembles her reaction to the streets of Mexico, where she traveled with Jake a year earlier. During that trip, she gloried in their insularity: "She felt she was walking inside a charmed circle: nothing could touch her, nothing could touch them. . . . Rennie refused to feel guilty about anything, not even the beggars" (72). However, such refusal of guilt becomes harder during her Caribbean sojourn when Dr. Minnow is murdered by political opponents. Only at his wake does Rennie begin to understand the meaning of "excess" and the role that she could have played in preventing it: "Now she knows why he wanted her to write about this place: so there would be less chance of this happening, to him" (251). Minnow's death brings Rennie insight that his life could not; indeed, bearing the name of a small fish, Minnow functions as a Christ figure (Rigney 110; Jones 92–93). In Toronto, Rennie looked to Daniel and heterosexual romance to save her; yet his martyred political double on St. Antoine is the one who partially fulfills that mission. In Atwood's world, the work of love is not the only kind available to women.

In the figure of Elva, Prince's grandmother, Rennie encounters the female analogue to Daniel and Dr. Minnow. Elva's healing hands ease the pain of a tourist whose foot has encountered a poisonous sea urchin. During this public spectacle of female healing, Elva credits her matrilineage for her powers: "It in the hands . . . It a gift, I have it from my grandmother, she give that when I small" (193). Significantly, Rennie encounters this female healer who celebrates the power of touch on St. Agathe, St. Antoine's sister island "named after the patron saint of breast cancer" (Hansen 12). Elva's appearance anticipates that femaleness may provide the cure for, rather than the spread of, Rennie's malignancy, the gender trauma metaphorized as breast cancer.

Rennie's affair with Paul, an American expatriate who lives on St. Agathe and smuggles guns and dope for a living, underscores the limits of male touch and thus the need for revaluing specifically female hands.

Paul functions as an emblem of detachment and thus as Rennie's double.[9] During their first meeting, Rennie notes Paul's familiarity: "She recognizes something about him, a deliberate neutrality. He's doing what she does, he's holding back, and now she's really curious" (46). Later, as he explains his lifestyle to her, he explicitly compares them: "I'm an independent operator. Freelance, same as you" (241). Like Rennie, Paul has deliberately displaced himself. As a former agronomist for the U.S. Department of Agriculture and later as an "adviser" in Vietnam and Cambodia, he has taught himself to ignore corruption and destruction. Aware of, but untouched by, the suffering that surrounds him in St. Antoine, Paul strives for personal gain rather than social change. Not surprisingly, then, his judgment of Dr. Minnow—"Good men can be a pain in the ass" (247)—is a cruder form of Rennie's own assessment.

Paradoxically, Paul's secure investment in detachment enables him to bring Rennie back to her sexual body. In a dream that dramatically represents the profound mind-body split that has only been exacerbated by the mastectomy, Rennie experiences herself hovering near the ceiling as she watches masked figures operate upon her body.[10] Distrustful of these beings who seek her heart, she strives unsuccessfully to rejoin her own flesh. Paul's touch, his disregard for her disfigurement, invokes and resolves the tensions of this dream: "[S]he's being drawn back down, she enters her body again. . . . He's touching her, she can still be touched" (204). Paul lacks Daniel's need and Jake's fear; thus intercourse with Paul allows Rennie to glimpse the pleasures of flesh seemingly without traces of vulnerability.

Ultimately, however, this erotic resolution to the body problem can only work in bed. Paul's alienation from the female world—symbolized by his disaffection from a wife and two kids—mirrors Rennie's own and thus thrusts her back into a self-conscious awareness of female lack. Good-humored disdain and condescension often mark his attitude toward her, and his geopolitical experience serves as a foil for her touristic naivete. Significantly, Rennie acquiesces to Paul's tendency to lump her innocence (i.e., ignorance) with her nonmale body. At one point, when she and Paul are walking down the street, they witness a police officer beating an old mute man who had chased Rennie earlier that day. Disturbed by this scene, Rennie stops; Paul urges her onward and later responds to her concern with snide indulgence:

> "That was horrible," says Rennie.
> "Up north they lock them up, down here they just beat them up

> a little. I know which I'd choose," says Paul.
> "That wasn't a little," says Rennie.
> Paul looks over at her and smiles. "Depends what you think a lot is," he says.
> Rennie shuts up. She's led a sheltered life, he's telling her. Now she's annoyed with herself for acting so shocked. Squealing at mice, standing on a chair with your skirts hitched up, that's the category. *Girl.* (147)

Ever attentive to the dangers and diminishment seemingly inherent in associating herself with women, Rennie turns her attention away from the beaten man, away from male embodiment and back to her own image. Thus Atwood points both to the solipsistic self-policing of the postfeminist flight from femaleness and to the need to revalue such feminine qualities as human empathy and a recoiling from abusive violence.

Rennie's need to remove herself from the category of "girl" is characteristic of the first victim position that Atwood outlines in *Survival.*[11] That position, denial of victimization, is "usually taken by those in a group who are a little better off than the others in that group" (36). As Atwood explains it, "fear of losing the privileges they possess" motivates such denial. Significantly, "if anger is felt by victims in position one, it is likely to be against one's fellow victims, particularly those who try to talk about their victimization" (36). The latter tendency becomes manifest throughout Rennie's relationship with Lora, a fellow Canadian whom Rennie derisively decides the women's movement would "have given . . . ten out of ten for openness" (93). Like Paul, Lora functions as a double for Rennie[12]; although originally cast as a nuisance and a potential rival for Paul's attention, Lora becomes the connection between Rennie and her matrilineage. While Oates relegates Agnes, Dorothea's "sister rival," to the role of mere figure, Atwood uses Lora to explore the intricacies and necessity of female-female relationships. Indeed, the fact that, after the first hundred pages or so, Lora's first-person stories stand alongside Rennie's serves as formal evidence of her previously unrecognized value. As Bouson puts it, "If the dominant culture denies women like Lora a speaking voice, one of the narrative's goals is to invert common social and literary practices by telling Lora's story side by side with Rennie's" (126).

Rennie's initial encounters with both Paul and Lora reflect her gendered double standard.[13] When it becomes obvious that Paul is involved in questionable activities, Rennie tries to be cool and sympathetic: "Ten years ago she would have felt entitled to moral outrage, but it's no skin off her nose. People get trapped in things that are beyond their control, she ought to know that by now" (47). However, she does not extend such understanding to Lora; in fact, Rennie makes no effort to check her bitchy, judgmental Griswold voice as she sizes up her smoking, nail-biting companion:

> Lora, she's decided, is one of those women you meet in bars in foreign countries who seem not to have chosen anything but merely ended up wherever they happen to be, and it's too much effort for them to go home. Rennie can't imagine why Lora has been so insistent about coming with her. They have nothing in common. (91)

Yet, of course, the last statement is more wish fulfillment than fact, since they are both Canadian escape artists who have made love with Paul.

Moreover, Lora's stance toward politics closely resembles Rennie's. To the subject of social change, Lora responds with a sneer of self-interest and disenchantment:

> Change the system. . . . Why would I want to do that? I said. It's working just fine for me. Stuff politics, I'd tell him. . . . But [the freedom-fighters] seemed to think it was enough for them to be right. Getting rid of Ellis [the current, corrupt leader], that was the point. Nobody's denying it would of been nice, but there's real life, you know. I mean, I used to think I'd like to fly like a bird but I never jumped off any roofs. (265–66)

Thus Lora evinces a profoundly fatalistic world view. Human agency has no effect upon "real life," and resignation necessarily accompanies desire. Less privileged than Rennie, Lora is well schooled in privation and making do. She grew up in cellars and learned to accept sexual exploitation as a fact of life and a means of survival.[14] Bereft of choices, she comforts herself with mindlessness: "at least when you don't have a choice you don't have to think, you know" (194). Lora exemplifies the second victim position, defined by Atwood as "acknowledg[ing] the fact that you are a victim, but . . . explain[ing] this as an act of fate . . . or any other large general powerful idea" (37). Significantly, although Rennie and Lora inhabit two different victim positions (denial and resignation), they both assume that their vulnerable female bodies can have no effect on the body politic.

Unnerved by Lora's crude honesty, Rennie seeks to distinguish herself from Paul's ex-lover but mires herself further in hypocrisy and self-deception. Prior to her proclamation that she and Lora have "nothing in common," Rennie's thoughts not only mirror Lora's speech but also reveal Rennie's self-serving need to dismiss Lora as the victim only of her own aimlessness. Over drinks, Lora alludes to Rennie's economic privilege by saying, "people like you"; such linguistic pigeonholing elicits Rennie's resentment:

> Rennie dislikes having these kinds of assumptions made about her, she dislikes being lumped in with a fictitious group labeled people like you. She can't stand the self-righteousness of *people like Lora*, who think that because they had deprived childhoods or not as much money as everybody else they are in some ways superior. (90—my emphasis)

As Bouson rightly notes, "by bringing Lora's speech into dialogue with Rennie's, Atwood . . . focuses attention on the importance of social class in women's experiences of social and sexual oppression" (126). Rennie's defensiveness here, her unwillingness to confront the material differences between her life and that of Lora, her denial of the privilege she indeed possesses, enables her to continue her flight from duty and responsibility. Furthermore, since Rennie's unconfronted fears about men and sexual violence are actualized in Lora's life—Lora has been raped as well as exploited—Rennie must either trivialize her female doppelgänger or explore the range of gender traumas associated with the category "girl." Ultimately, Lora embodies patterns of victimization and complicity that the postfeminist Rennie has assiduously ignored. As such, Lora constitutes a considerable threat to Rennie, but also, as Atwood subsequently shows, perhaps the only path to salvation.

Suspected of revolutionary activity, Rennie is imprisoned in the place that she had previously visited with Dr. Minnow and is transformed from the North American tourist to the subversive reporter, from one who looks to one who sees and touches. Appropriately, this imprisonment not only recalls the recent past with Minnow, but also the distant past of Griswold when her grandmother used to lock her in the cellar as punishment for childish crimes. The past and present uncannily converge during an altercation with Lora, her cellmate. Forced to live under barbarous conditions and anxious for information about Prince, her revolutionary lover, Lora uses the only currency available to her in prison: her body. When Rennie realizes that Lora has bought cigarettes, gum, and a hairbrush with sex, the former responds with puritanical judgment and disgust. Lora mirrors that response as she snarls, "Women like you make me sick. . . . Tightass. You wouldn't put out to save your granny, would you?" (285).

Lora's words contain an unintentional double entendre, for the figure of her grandmother haunts Rennie precisely because the latter was unable to "put out" (her hands) at a crucial moment. In prison, the present repeats the past, and Rennie demonstrates that she has not changed much from that girl in Griswold who insisted upon her separateness from other women. Shortly after Rennie rebukes Lora for her indecent behavior, the latter expresses her anger, anxiety, and degradation in a flood of tears, while the former seems stuck in time: "Rennie is embarrassed. She looks down at her hands, which ought to contain comfort. Compassion. She ought to go over to Lora and put her arms around her and pat her on the back, but she can't" (286). For Rennie, relatedness equals duty, something one "ought" to do and thus an imposition. Enclosed in the self, perhaps the ultimate Gothic structure, Rennie repeats the crimes of her past and fosters her own helplessness. Indeed, unable to use her hands, Rennie simultaneously inhabits the position of her younger self and that of her needy grandmother.

In prison, Rennie is reminded yet again that the boundaries of her body are permeable and that her desire for physical and psychic inviolability, for self-containment, cannot be fulfilled. Just as Rennie's breast was infiltrated by cancerous cells in Toronto, so does bacteria invade Rennie's intestines in St. Antoine. However, this illness, infectious diarrhea—locally and appropriately known as *turistas*—suggests that this corporeal permeability is *not* a function of femaleness and that the flight from sexual difference paradoxically overestimates it. In the tormenting dreams that accompany her illness, the man with the rope reappears, and Rennie discovers that his very facelessness is hauntingly familiar: "The face keeps changing, eluding her, he might as well be invisible, she can't see him, this is what is so terrifying, he isn't really there, he's only a shadow, anonymous, familiar, with silvery eyes that twin and reflect her own" (287). Thus Rennie recognizes the man with the rope as a "shadow," a double, a constituent part of her identity. In part, "he" represents her desire for invisibility and her lack of vision, both of which ultimately endanger her very being since a fully human subject must see and be seen. Moreover, this internalized rope man becomes an emblem of the threat that lies within Rennie, her own capacity to aid and abet the bodily harm of others.[15]

However, the psychological epiphany realized in this dream does not tell the whole story, for the man with the rope—along with the police—has really been in her Toronto apartment, and his kind appears in St. Antoine as an entity of the state. At one point, Rennie looks out of her prison window and sees pornographic scenes of torture being enacted in the courtyard. A group of policemen stand over kneeling male prisoners. With bayonets in hand, the uniformed men yank back the heads of the male captives; however, rather than slit throats, the guards cut the long, womanly hair of the prisoners. One of the prisoners, who turns out to be the mute man Rennie has encountered before, is wounded in this show of abusive power. When the mute man howls with pain, the officers brutally respond with a cattle prod.

As Rennie views this scene, she intuits both the connections and the disconnections between these images and those that she saw on display in the Toronto police station:

> It's indecent, it's not done with ketchup, nothing is inconceivable here, no rats in the vagina but only because they haven't thought of it yet, they're still amateurs. She's afraid of men and it's simple, it's rational, she's afraid of men because men are frightening. She's seen the man with the rope, now she knows what he looks like. She has been turned inside out, there's no longer a *here* and a *there*. Rennie understands for the first time that this is not necessarily a place she will get out of, ever. She is not exempt. Nobody is exempt from anything. (290)

The allusion to the "rats in the vagina" demonstrates that Rennie connects the sickening script of pornography with the atrocities she is witnessing; yet, she also distinguishes between ketchup and blood, images and bodies.[16] Moreover, Rennie finally admits rather than denies her fear of men and thus moves beyond the first victim position. However, along with recognizing the legitimacy and necessity of the fear she tried to quell in Toronto, she also sees the embodiment of men, the fact that a male body is no guarantee of exemption from the inconceivable. Decency, formerly the buzzword of female Griswold, takes on a new and positive meaning here; concomitantly, Rennie now can incorporate the vision and the language of Dr. Minnow—"nothing is inconceivable here"—into her own discourse. No longer a tourist, no longer in postfeminist flight from femaleness, Rennie understands that denying the Gothic world only magnifies its power.

Rennie's acknowledgment that the man with the rope is both within and without alters her posture toward Lora. Subsequent to Rennie's viewing of the bayonet scene, she urges her cellmate to eat and thus assumes, albeit in a minor way, a caretaking role. After the guards beat Lora mercilessly and leave her for dead, Rennie commits what for her is a heroic act and demonstrates that the past need not be repeated and that she *can* use her mother as a model:

> She's holding Lora's left hand, between both of her own, perfectly still, nothing is moving, and yet she knows she is pulling on the hand, as hard as she can, there's an invisible hole in the air, Lora is on the other side of it and she has to pull her through, she's gritting her teeth with the effort, she can hear herself, a moaning, it must be her own voice, this is a gift, this is the hardest thing she's ever done.
>
> She holds the hand, perfectly still, with all her strength. Surely, if she can only try hard enough, something will move and live again, something will get born. (299)

Significantly, when Rennie first met Lora, the latter's hands disgusted her: "She wouldn't want to touch this gnarled hand, or have it touch her. She doesn't like the sight of ravage, damage, the edge between inside and outside blurred like that" (86). However, the Rennie who is now "inside out" herself desires connection rather than separation; she attempts to cross the barrier that divides her from Lora and in the process revises the Gothic scene of her childhood by emulating the bond that existed between her mother and her grandmother. Appropriately, such emulation is textualized via the imagery of birth.[17]

By using her hands to touch another woman in need, by figuratively participating in the female process of birthing, Rennie apprehends new possibilities for the female body. Previously, the female body had been only a negative site, a space associated with lack, vulnerability, pain, seepage. Yet via her newly forged connection with Lora—and, by extension, with her mother, grandmother, and Elva—Rennie apprehends that a body marked female also has potential to be life sustaining, empowering, and active. Atwood does not nullify or trivialize the horrors of the female Gothic; yet she refuses to subscribe to a myth of female powerlessness just as she refuses the idea that the Gothic is only and always female.

Neither does she offer guarantees that female bonding will necessarily save the world or even individual women. The text does not definitively establish whether or not Lora survives; indeed, critical opinion is divided on this issue, and Hansen reads this ambiguity as Atwood's refusal to engage in feminist mythologizing (18). However, if Rennie's dreams are any clue, then Lora's death seems likely. Earlier in the novel, Rennie dreams that she puts out her hands to touch her grandmother but to no avail: her grandmother is dead, and Rennie's outstretched hands go right through the old woman's body. If we accept a correspondence between Lora and Rennie's grandmother as well as the dream logic that permeates *Bodily Harm*, the most plausible interpretation is that Lora dies in the underground prison that resembles the cellars of her childhood. Bouson follows Hansen in suggesting that "Lora is sacrificed so that Rennie's character may be redeemed" (131). However, to ultimately view Lora's likely demise in terms of Rennie's raised consciousness undercuts the value the text has given to Lora as a subject in her own right. I tend to read their potentially different fates as Atwood's further commentary on class privilege or the lack thereof and the possibilities such privilege affords.

Of course, neither Rennie's privilege nor her newly acquired feminist consciousness guarantees her survival. However, if she gets out of this prison alive—and that remains a substantial "if"—she intends to use rather than deny her privilege. In the section of the novel framed by the future tense, Rennie proclaims herself "a subversive. She was not one once but now she is. A reporter. She will pick her time; then she will report. For the first time in her life, she can't think of a title" (301). Thus Rennie, short for "Renata" (meaning "reborn"),[18] lives up to her name. Ironically, her imprisonment has caused her to realize the agency that her jailors always assumed she had and of which they were so afraid. Rennie envisions, perhaps too late, the responsibilities and the power that accompany a woman's access to the written and spoken word.[19]

Rennie's futuristic encounter with a Canadian official who subtly urges her *not* to write about what she's seen underscores the idea that nations as well as individuals have a responsibility to forgo the solipsistic illusion of self-containment. Atwood habitually establishes parallels between Canada and women, and it is no coincidence that Minnow labels Rennie a "sweet Canadian." The contradictions of Rennie's life represent not only those of the privileged North American woman but also those of the privileged "colony"; thus her transformation has national as well as sexual implications.[20] Throughout *Bodily Harm*, Canada's complicity with, and condescension toward, St. Antoine's corrupt regime are manifest; thus Atwood fictionally mines the paradox of the colony as colonizer.[21] Furthermore, the fact that Toronto and St. Antoine become doubles for one another suggests that the "nobody is exempt from anything" rule applies to Canada in particular and to Western democracies in general. Atwood makes this point explicitly in her address to Amnesty International: "We should not overlook the fact that Canada's record on civil rights issues is less than pristine.... Worse things have not happened not because we are genetically exempt but because we lead pampered lives" (395).

For Atwood, the Gothicism of the world is relative but inescapable. However, she places a high premium on how one positions oneself in relation to such multiformed malignancy. Acutely aware that women have historically been among the dispossessed, she nevertheless refuses to fall into the cultural feminist trap of endorsing their moral superiority and innocence. The epigraph to *Bodily Harm*, from John Berger's *Ways of Seeing*, underscores the defensive posture that women have traditionally assumed: "A man's presence suggests what he is capable of doing to you or for you. By contrast, a woman's presence ... defines what can and cannot be done to her." In his multimedia study, Berger argues that women are constructed to be seen; such a construction combined with the fact that women, as human subjects, *do* see tends to make the female stance self-reflexive. Indeed, the clause of Berger that Atwood ellipses stresses this self-reflexiveness: "a woman's presence expresses her own attitude to herself" (46). Thus Berger implicitly identifies the constructed feminine attitude as narcissistic and solipsistic.[22] Significantly, Atwood believes that some strands of American feminism have unwittingly replicated this attitude: "If I have anything to say to the American feminist, it's that they've been too parochial. America is very big, you can get lost in it, but they haven't looked enough outside" (184).[23] By having Rennie's consciousness raised in an/other culture, Atwood envisions a repudiation of postfeminism that does not entail getting lost in a Gothic mirror composed only of images of victimized women. For Atwood, the Gothic begins at home but doesn't end there.

In her final, futuristic vision, Rennie foresees the need to make compromises, but she will make those knowingly, shrewdly, and temporarily. As a subversive, Rennie challenges the boundaries that separate the public from the private, the social from the psychological, thus suggesting that transgression may be the means of engaging with, rather than the cause of, the Gothic. Atwood uses the Gothic to demonstrate that havens—be they domestic idylls or touristic get-aways—are actually microcosms of the world at large. Such a characterization of Gothic space precludes the possibility of transcendence and self-containment, and thus perhaps sets the stage for the assumption of personal and social responsibility. In *Bodily Harm*, Atwood extends the script of the female Gothic so that it includes not only sexual relations but also (trans)national relations. Here, the female body, with its permeable boundaries, is revalued as an emblem of the transgressions necessary to reinvigorate the body politic and feminist thought.

Epilogue:

Toward Feminisms without Demons

From 1975 through 1981, women of Northern England were terrorized by "The Yorkshire Ripper," a serial killer who was not a mythic being but rather a man named Peter Sutcliffe. As the police investigated this case, they categorized Sutcliffe's victims into two groups: prostitutes or other women of "loose morals" and "innocent" victims. Police encouraged women to rely on men for their security; however, the police also asked women to consider whether the men in their lives might be the "Ripper." Peter Sutcliffe himself served as a male escort for a woman with whom he worked; he also was part of a local group organized to catch the "Ripper." When the police received what turned out to be a bogus tape of the killer's voice, they played it at soccer games, hoping that someone might be able to identify the killer. At one game, after Sutcliffe had murdered twelve women, fans chanted, "You'll never catch the Ripper. 12 nil! 12 nil!" At a later game, the chant became "Ripper 13, Police 0." Some feminist activists found pornographic and violent cinematic imagery intolerable during this period of terror; over fifty women were arrested for acts of civil disobedience and property damage. Both the media and the police characterized these activists as irrational and dangerous.[1]

The response to Peter Sutcliffe's murder of thirteen women suggests the difficulties and complexities of refusing victimization in a femicidal culture. Institutionalized heterosexuality means that officials advise women to rely upon potential victimizers for protection. Only "innocent" women are culturally legible as undeserving of victimization. A vast array of class and social antagonisms are worked out by identifying with the Ripper rather than the police. Perhaps most importantly, those who read the Ripper and the police as sharing similar gender ideologies, those who are justifiably afraid and enraged by violence against women, are seen as transgressing the boundaries of good taste, rational discourse, and civil order.

The strand of the contemporary female Gothic that constitutes *Femicidal Fears* takes seriously such difficulties of refusing victimization. However, taken together, the texts discussed here insist not only on the difficulty of refusing victimization but also on the necessity and the possibility of such refusals. By devoting the final chapter to Margaret Atwood, by making her into the heroine of my critical story, I risk falling back into the valorization of the usual suspects, the explicitly and self-consciously feminist writers. However, I chose to end this book with *Bodily Harm* because it seems to me that that text echoes and extends the thematics of a Gothic tradition that is profoundly useful for feminist theorists still struggling with the spectres of the essentialist debate.

Rennie's frustrated desire for male rescuers reminds us that although heterosexual romance can provide much pleasure for some women, as an institution, it is a blueprint for gender hierarchy, gender oppression, and sadomasochism. Plots such as *The Bottle Factory Outing, Casualties of Peace, The Driver's Seat, Honeybuzzard, I Hardly Knew You, The Shadow Knows*, and, to a lesser extent, *Soul/Mate* denaturalize and demythologize heterosexual relations. If, like cultural feminism, these texts do not do enough to reconstruct heterosexuality, that work can be done elsewhere; however, we should not underestimate the importance of debunking the myth that Mr. Right can save women from male violence and provide easy answers to the question of what it means to be a specifically female embodied human subject.

Atwood extends the pornographic plot beyond the erotic zone of Jake and Rennie's bedroom, beyond the gendered identities of Morris and Lise, into the human rights abuses of antidemocratic regimes. Rennie's fear of men—which she struggles to deny—proves justified; however, such justification, supported by O'Brien and Johnson as well, is accompanied by a sharpened awareness of privilege, of complicity, of the power to aid and abet bodily harm, and of the agency to act on behalf of oneself and others who were not born to be victims. To a greater or lesser extent, all of these femicidal plots suggest that oppression and agency can—and do—coexist in bodies, systems, and narratives. Thus victimization can be recognized as such without attendant claims of powerlessness, virtuousness, innocence, or purity.

Perhaps most significant for the contemporary moment, Rennie's fear of female identification and of being too feminist is revealed as that which reproduces rather than ameliorates her vulnerability. Indeed, only when she embraces the agency, fear, and complicity that attend a body marked female can she imagine impacting the world and being truly subversive. Ultimately, both my readings of these texts and my life in the world suggest that denying the feminist Gothic is a much greater threat than any so-called Gothic feminism.

As I have argued throughout, I think that both cultural feminism and poststructuralist thought are implicated in female Gothic scripts; the former tends to underestimate female agency (which necessarily includes complicity), while the latter overestimates it. However, I take seriously Judith Butler's observation that "[t]o be *implicated* in the relations of power . . . is not . . . to be reducible to their existing forms" (123). Thus while cultural feminists and poststructuralists all swim in Gothic waters, they neither cause nor are reducible to a femicidal plot. It seems to me that critical discourses that assume and demonize an oxymoronic "victim feminism" or "Gothic feminism" miss this critical point. Bell hooks has argued that "while it is useful for everyone to critique excesses in feminist movement, as well as mistakes and bad strategies, it is important for the future of feminism that those critiques reflect a genuine will to advance feminist politics . . . and to be clear that our interests are not . . . articulated in shallow ways that mirror and perpetuate antifeminist sentiments" (*Outlaw*, 108). I can't help but think that such glib and increasingly automatic phrases as *essentialist, victim feminist,* and *Gothic feminist* make it harder for women to refuse victimization, in part because such terms seem to deny that gendered patterns of victimization exist as anything other than a pose, a masquerade, a feminist fantasy. In contrast to such shortcuts through the labyrinths of feminist consciousness and feminist theory, the femicidal plots analyzed here affirm that refusing victimization is not a simple story but nevertheless is one worth telling. Perhaps by restaging and embodying familiar feminist debates, this strand of the contemporary female Gothic can help us to imagine feminist movement without the accompanying construction of feminist demons.

Notes

Critical Femicide: A Polemical Preface

1. For a provocative and useful discussion of the move to gender studies, see Tania Modleski's *Feminism without Women*, esp. 5–12.

2. See *Changing the Story*, 25.

3. The phrase "male vice and female virtue" is often used in discussions of cultural feminism; see Walkowitz, "Male Vice and Female Virtue: Feminism and the Politics of Prostitution in Nineteenth-Century Britain." The phrase "gender skepticism" is Susan Bordo's; see her essay "Feminism, Postmodernism, and Gender Skepticism" in *Unbearable Weight*.

Chapter 1

Introduction: Feminist Gothic/Gothic Feminism

1. For a useful, nonliterary introduction to femicidal cultural tendencies, see Radford and Russell's anthology, *Femicide: The Politics of Woman Killing*.

2. Information on the Montreal massacre and responses to it have been culled from the following sources: *The Montreal Massacre*, eds. Louise Malette and Marie Chalouh; Dufresne, "Focus on the Gynocide in Montreal"; Pitt, "Canada Unnerved by Slayings of 14"; Stone, "Trigger Happy"; Malmsten, "Report for Metro Men against Violence"; unsigned editorials from the Thunder Bay *Chronicle-Journal* titled "Overreacting" and "For

Women Only"; Lester and Nesdoly, "'Propaganda' Blamed"; an unsigned article in the *Toronto Star* titled "59% Call Massacre Only Random Act, Poll Finds."

3. See Patrice McDermott, "On Cultural Authority: Women's Studies, Feminist Politics, and the Popular Press," for a compelling discussion of the ways in which critics of feminism and the popular press share investments in, and make strategic use of, "the liberal idea of value-free knowledge" (672).

4. Mark Edmundson is among the most recent advocates of Gothic feminism. Feminism is cited as one among several examples of Gothic theory: "[A]n analytic method that might have as its objective a critique of Gothic culture, with all of its facile pessimism, un-self-consciously repro- duces Gothic assumptions" (43). There are only passing references to feminism in this piece of "public criticism" (xvii); thus it is unclear whether Edmundson discounts, or is unaware of, the hyper-self-consciousness of academic feminism. Although his third of three chapters is devoted to S & M culture, he does not cite Massé's major study of masochism in the Gothic; thus it is unclear whether he would count her work as an example of, or a counter to, Gothic theory.

Even more recently, Diane Long Hoeveler has used the term "Gothic feminism" as both title and frame for her argument that early female Gothic writers are the progenitors of contemporary "victim feminism." According to Hoeveler, female Gothic writers construct a code of "professional femi- ninity" whereby women derive power from "carefully cultivating the ap- pearance of their very powerlessness" (7). In a telling footnote, Hoeveler distinguishes her work from Massé's: "Whereas Massé sees women in the gothic novel as actually victimized and internalizing that victimization. . . I have taken a poststructuralist position and instead see women as parodically playing with or masquerading in a pose of victimization: miming the mime" (13, n. 13). Hoeveler's basic assumptions—her acceptance of the term "victim feminism" and her belief that in a poststructuralist universe, female victimization is a "pose" and a dis- course constructed primarily by and for women—are precisely those that I seek to problematize here.

5. In literary studies, Toril Moi's influential but reductive reading of "Anglo-American" feminist literary criticism as well as the critical industry's even more reductive appropriation of Moi's critique of feminism fomented this line of thinking.

6. See Donovan, *Feminist Theory*, 31–63; Judith Walkowitz, "Male Vice and Female Virtue: Feminism and the Politics of Prostitution in

Nineteenth Century Britain"; Alice Echols, "The New Feminism of Yin and Yang."

7. See, for example, Alcoff 413–14; Freccero 310; Taylor and Rupp 41–42.

8. In "The New Feminism of Yin and Yang," Echols reads cultural feminism as a strategy for healing the split between lesbians and heterosexual women. See esp. 445–46.

9. Daly's writing style is deliberately playful; while terms such as *Hag* and *Crone* are usually pejoratives, Daly invests them with positive, subversive meaning. Thus she enacts the principle of reversal both theoretically and linguistically.

10. Common themes of cultural feminism are pornography, witch burning, and Chinese foot binding. In addition to *Gyn/Ecology*, see Dworkin, *Woman-Hating*, and Susan Griffin, *Pornography and Silence*.

11. Although I disagree with Dworkin on many points, I think she is a brilliant and impassioned writer. With that said, I must add that this argument not only is theoretically questionable but also constitutes an affront to those women who have been "occupied" by men who choose to use their penises as weapons.

12. See also her commentary on the dangers of the "utopia of historical reversal" (161).

13. See "Choreographies," Derrida's interview with Christie McDonald. Also see Fuss 12–14.

14. Taylor and Rupp have argued that the attack on cultural feminism is a "disguised attack on lesbian feminism"; they note that the sins of cultural feminism—essentialism, separatism, and prioritizing alternative culture—are associated with lesbian feminist communities.

15. In her more general discussion of the connections between a postmodern sensibility and the Gothic, Maggie Kilgour worries that "we will repudiate all power, authority, even action, for its Gothic potential" (223). Such worries strike me as particularly relevant to a feminist climate in which fears of essentialism have become both philosophically and professionally overdetermined.

16. This is Bordo's term. See "Feminism, Postmodernism and Gender Skepticism" in *Unbearable Weight*.

17. In *Bodies That Matter*, Butler astutely notes, "To be *implicated* in the relations of power, indeed, enabled by the relations of power that the 'I' opposes is not, as a consequence, to be reducible to their existing forms" (123). Thus the term "implication" suggests that while we necessarily work within [Gothic] systems that cannot be transcended, we are not destined to merely reproduce those systems in exactly the same form and with identical power configurations. Implication leaves room for repetition with a difference making a difference. I view complicity as a *form* of implication in which the agency afforded by relations of power is mobilized to bolster or reproduce *elements* of a [Gothic] system. In "The Technology of Gender," de Lauretis wisely distinguishes between "complicity" and "full adherence": "[I]t is obvious that feminism and a full adherence to the ideology of gender, in male-centered societies, are mutually exclusive" (11). Thus feminists are implicated in, and may be complicit with (support elements of), patriarchal power systems; however, feminists are neither identical with, nor do they create, patriarchal power systems.

18. Joan Scott and Judith Butler co-edited the anthology *Feminists Theorize the Political* as a response to such charges.

19. De Lauretis defines "upping the anti" as follows: "[B]y analyzing the undecidability, conceptual as well as pragmatic, of the alternative as *given*, such critical works release its terms from the fixity of meaning into which polarization has locked them, and reintroduce them into a larger contextual and conceptual frame of reference; the tension of positivity and negativity that marks feminist discourse in its engagement with the social can then displace the impasse of mere 'internal' opposition to a more complex level of analysis" (336).

20. For a discussion of the relationship between Gothicism and Romanticism, see Williams, esp. 3–6, 175–238.

21. In "Female Gothic Writing: 'Under Cover to Alice,'" Frances Restuccia argues that "the woman Gothicist sees in her own terror before the monstrous injustices of patriarchy only the commonplace" (247). Showalter comments that the "Female Gothic looks more and more like a realist mode" (144).

22. As Williams notes, "Most—perhaps all—Gothic conventions express some anxiety about 'meaning'" (67).

23. See also Day's discussion of the instability and fragmentation of the self in the Gothic, 21–23.

24. Hoeveler reads the desperation of heroines as involving faux

struggles, which they relish: "[G]othic feminists love nothing more than a struggle against vicious predators, particularly when the heroine knows she is going to win" (206).

25. For a discussion of violence against women as a continuum, see Liz Kelly, *Surviving Sexual Violence*, chaps. 4 & 5.

26. This is, of course, de Lauretis's term.

27. Thus I disagree with Massé that the "final step in escaping Gothic masochism is the move to other genres . . . genres such as the detective novel and science fiction" (273) and with Williams who writes that "the Gothic no longer speaks a language compelling to those trying to reimagine culture"; Williams, like Massé, suggests science fiction as the contemporary alternative (240).

28. Barbara Christian has argued that "our [people of color] theorizing (and I intentionally use the verb rather than the noun) is often in narrative forms" (336). Foucault has stated that for him forays into literature "made permeable—therefore in the end derisory—the frontier between the philosophical and the non-philosphical" (313).

29. For a brilliant discussion of the definitional difficulties that plague Gothic studies, see Williams 12–24. See also Massé's discussion of restricting the Gothic arena in order to "localiz[e] anxiety" (11). Maggie Kilgour suggests that "[t]he form is thus itself a Frankenstein's monster, assembled out of the bits and pieces of the past" (4).

30. For a good discussion of transgression, its limits, and its ambiguous effects, see Botting 7–9 and Kilgour 8.

31. In "Experience," Scott defines that concept as "that which we seek to explain, that about which knowledge is produced. To think about experience in this way is to historicize it as well as to historicize the identities it produces" (26).

32. As Gilbert and Gubar argue in *The War of the Words*, vol. 1 of *No Man's Land*, femicidal sexual fantasies had already become a normative part of the male literary tradition: "Indeed, if anything, a Kowalskiesque impulse to use the penis and other implements as battering rams with which to assault or destroy women intensified in the 1950s and 1960s" (52).

33. Massé indicates that Dinesen's *Angelic Avengers* is "unusual because of its use of double protagonists, a use that emphasizes the necessary

union between women and the fact that only at her peril can the Gothic heroine believe herself exceptional and her plight unique" (269). The use of double protagonists is not unusual in the contemporary female Gothic tradition I am charting here.

34. Thus I disagree with Edmundson, who argues that the "Gothic, dark as it is, offers epistemological certainty; it allows us to believe that we've found the truth" (68).

35. Modleski also notes the relationship between the Gothic heroine and the reader: "In Gothics . . . the reader shares some of the heroine's uncertainty about what is going on and what the lover/husband is up to. The reader is nearly as powerless in her understanding as the heroine" (*Loving* 60).

36. In *Bodies That Matter*, Butler argues for "establish[ing] a kind of political contestation that is not . . . 'transcendence' of contemporary relations of power, but a difficult labor of forging a future from resources inevitably impure" (241). Halberstam writes that "postmodern Gothic warns us to be suspicious of . . . above all, discourses invested in purity and innocence" (27).

Chapter 2

Gothic Traditions

1. For an extended discussion of Fiedler's masculinization of the genre, see Frances Restuccia's "Female Gothic Writing: 'Under Cover to Alice,'" 245–47.

2. See Moers, *Literary Women*, esp. chapters 5 & 7; Gilbert and Gubar, *The Madwoman in the Attic*, esp. chapters 7 & 10; Radway, "The Utopian Impulse in Popular Literature: Gothic Romances and 'Feminist' Protest"; and Modleski, *Loving with a Vengeance*, esp. chapter 3.

3. For complementary commentary on general shifts in literary studies and their impact on Gothic studies, see Botting 17 and Kilgour 221.

4. In sharp contrast to the approach I take here, see Howard's commentary on what she calls the "theoretical negativity" of feminist Gothic studies (66–67) and Hoeveler's reading of female victimization as "a new discourse system" by which middle-class women "empower themselves. They spoke a new language, and it was not a language marked by anything other than crocodile tears" (102).

5. Botting's assessment is relevant here: "If *Udolpho* restores domesticity, virtue and reason to their proper place in the eighteenth-century order of things, it does so only at a price. . . . Like the unnatural or overly imaginative evils the novel tries to cast beyond the pale of good society, the moral and domestic values *that it would like to naturalise* are glimpsed as part of the fiction" (70; my emphasis).

6. Steven Bruhm astutely notes Emily's disidentification with Madame Montoni, Laurentini, and the Marchioness de Villeroi: they all "die horribly, and so Emily must disassociate herself from them in order to protect herself from sharing their fate." Bruhm reads this series of disidentifications as exemplifying the idea that "it is at the moment of physical sentience that the body's communal possibilities are destroyed" (42). Significantly, in Margaret Atwood's *Bodily Harm*, which I discuss in detail in chapter 7, Lora's beaten female body facilitates rather than disrupts Rennie's embrasure of communal possibilities and responsibilities.

7. Day comments that Emily's "victimization is, not the test of her virtue, but actually the indicator of it" (105).

8. For a more optimistic reading of *Udolpho* in particular and of marriage as a conventional Gothic ending in general, see Williams 159–172 and esp. 150.

9. Howard writes, "We need to remember that Gothic fiction, like any other genre, carries much that is culturally specific—ideological, aesthetic, and literary norms, which are received and interpreted or 'rewritten' by readers on the basis of their own interests, their own cultural and institutional, as well as personal, history" (15). Thus Radcliffe's case is no doubt least convincing to those who accept the credibility of feminist Gothic narratives.

10. This comparison between marriage and prostitution becomes a theme in some cultural feminist writing. See for example, Kathleen Barry, *Female Sexual Slavery*, esp. 271.

11. Heller notes that Jemima's story "inserts a narrative about class foreign to the Radcliffean Gothic, where the heroines are elite women and their servants usually only a form of comic relief" (27).

12. See, for example, Emily W. Sunstein's biography of Mary Wollstonecraft, *A Different Face*, 12, 40, and 82.

13. Hoeveler reads Rochester not as a reformed partner but rather as a "punished patriarch." Indeed, for her, Rochester is "the ultimate embodi-

ment of the masculine victim in the female gothic fantasy" (204).

14. Gilbert and Gubar make this argument in *Madwoman* (369). More recently, Massé has suggested that the felicitous events that proliferate in the latter part of *Jane Eyre* "work together as a form of nineteenth-century 'magic realism' to envision a new social order, one in which love and independence coexist and no woman is beaten" (232).

15. Williams reads this line as exemplifying "that the conventional comic marriage of Female Gothic should be understood as affirmation rather than obliteration" (157).

16. For a discussion of *Jane Eyre* as a product of imperialism, see Gayatri Spivak's "Three Women's Texts and a Critique of Imperialism." Massé argues that in her dealings with other women, Jane's modus operandi is "neutrality" rather than complicity and that she does not "replicate oppression" (195, 236). That view strikes me as an idealized one of Jane and certainly of Brontë.

17. As it was in the case of the Marchioness de Villeroi in *Udolpho*.

18. Horner and Zlosnik suggest that Mrs. Danvers acts as Jack Favell's agent when she sets the fire and thus that Rebecca and her death mediate the class war between Maxim and Favell (108). Massé also reads Mrs. Danvers as a less powerful figure than I do; at one point, she describes Danvers as "Maxim's surrogate"; at another, as "a perfectly stereotypical wife" to Rebecca (175). At stake in this critical disagreement are Mrs. Danvers's identifications. I read Mrs. Danvers as consistently identifying with, and loving, Rebecca, a woman who excels at mimicry and who subverts the patriarchal marriage and love plot. Reading Danvers as Favell's agent, as Maxim's agent, or as Rebecca's "wife" undercuts Mrs. Danvers's preservation and reproduction of Rebecca's subversive tendencies. Indeed, when Favell insists that Rebecca loved him and that's why Maxim killed her, Mrs. Danvers refuses to let Rebecca be positioned between men and within patriarchal romantic arrangements: "'Well,' said Mrs. Danvers, with sudden passion, ' . . .Lovemaking was a game with her, only a game. . . .She did it because it made her laugh'" (340).

19. Both Horner and Zlosnik (106) and Massé (182–84) comment on this relational shift.

20. Thus I disagree with Horner and Zlosnik's conclusion that "in assimilating aspects of Rebecca, the narrator implicitly rejects the social categorizations which separate the 'bad' from the 'good' woman" (126).

Chapter 3

Love Kills

1. Information about the Stuart case has been culled from the following sources: Barnicle, "Behind the Killing That Shook Boston"; Barnicle, "Chuck Stuart's Family Talked of the Murder"; Hays, "Husband of Slain Boston Woman Becomes a Suspect, Then a Suicide"; Sedgwick, "A Case of Wife Murder."

2. Caputi reports that in cases of serial sexual murders, female family members often "come to the police, expressing hesitant but grave doubts about the men with whom they are intimately involved. Actually, this is one of the ways that Ted Bundy was initially listed as a suspect in the 'Ted Murders.' His girlfriend of six years had reported her misgivings about him to the Seattle police" (114).

3. It is important to note that Williams uses the term "female Gothic" to identify a particular strand of the Gothic. As she puts it, "the 'Male' and 'Female' traditions employ two distinct sets of literary conventions" (100). Thus for Williams, the "female Gothic" refers to a Gothic formula and to plots culturally coded female; as such, for her, the "female Gothic" is not necessarily or definitionally the product of a female author.

4. For further discussion of the relationship between Gothic conventions and true crime, see Cameron and Frazer, *The Lust to Kill: A Feminist Investigation of Sexual Murder*, esp. 51–54.

5. Eckley also notes this movement (34); however, I see it as less of a "counterpoint" and more of a cause-and-effect relationship.

6. Eckley points out the connection between Auro's "inheritance" and his vulnerability (49).

7. In an interview with Philip Roth, O'Brien refers to Joyce as "a blinding light and father of us all" (39). Like Joyce, O'Brien was received badly in her native Ireland. Indeed, even O'Brien's mother, to whom O'Brien dedicated her first novel, *The Country Girls*, was outraged by the explicitness of her prose. As O'Brien tells it, "After my mother died five or six years ago, I was cleaning her house and I found the book [*The Country Girls*] buried under a mound of pillows and bolsters. The dedication page had been pulled out. She had gone through the book with black ink and a pen. She had effaced every outspoken word" (Woodward 50).

8. O'Brien clearly is a product of that mythology. In the Nell Dunn interview, O'Brien states, "I don't think I have any pleasure in any part of my body, because my first and initial body thoughts were blackened by the fear of sin and therefore I think of my body as a sort of vehicle for sin, a sort of tabernacle of sin" (105).

9. These letters are also reminiscent of Joyce, specifically Molly Bloom's monologue. For example, "Would I live with you, not half. What do you think I brought the green nightdress along for. That policeman doesn't know what he missed. If he saw you, if I saw it myself. Bring mirrors. I'm only joking. Do what you want. I'm not blocking you (not half)" (103–4).

10. Barbara C. Millard describes this sketch in more detail: "The photograph on the dust jacket of the British edition is a tongue-in-cheek illustration by Austin Davies of Bainbridge as Brenda, her friend who inspired the character as Freda, and Bainbridge's publisher and accountant as Italians—all grouped for the outing" (42).

11. In the May interview, Bainbridge reports that this textual detail is also derived from her experience—her mother-in-law really did try to kill her.

12. In the May interview, Bainbridge insists somewhat peevishly on the primacy of plot: "I love plots. Sometimes people tell me there are no plots. That makes me quite cross because I think I plot very thoroughly, everything is linked to everything else" (49); stylistically, Bainbridge has been influenced by Dickens (Millard 40).

13. In the now classic essay "Compulsory Heterosexuality and Lesbian Existence," Adrienne Rich specifically states that heterosexuality "needs to be recognized and studied as a political institution" (637). Rich also discusses the ways in which men control and deny female sexuality (638–39). Of course, contemporary queer theorists such as Judith Butler and Eve Kosofsky Sedgwick have demonstrated the extent to which the "heterosexual matrix" is a force of culture.

14. For a discussion of the ways in which even some deployments of queer theory are reinforcing heterosexuality, see my "To Queer or Not to Queer: That's Not the Question."

15. For a provocative incitement to reimagine heterosexuality, see Marilyn Frye, "Willful Virgin or Do You Have to Be a Lesbian to Be a Feminist." Also see Lynne Segal, *Straight Sex: The Politics of Pleasure.*

16. See Judith Butler's *Gender Trouble* for a compelling discussion of

the relationship between compulsory heterosexuality and a binary gender system.

17. I discuss paranoia in much greater detail in chapter 5.

Chapter 4

The Construction of the Sadomasochistic Couple

1. Although the relationships between the Gothic and pornography that I will discuss shortly will only put me on the margins of the feminist "sex wars," I want to acknowledge that these wars have been and will continue to be waged, and I want to set forth some of my basic assumptions. I oppose censorship, and I sincerely doubt that antipornography ordinances could be drafted that would protect all the cultural documents that *need* protection in a culture that has strong puritanical roots. This point is relevant to the study at hand; I shudder to think how a conservative court might rule on the literary and theoretical voices at issue in this book. I also think antipornography ordinances put representations of gay and lesbian sexuality especially at risk. I certainly do not trust legislators who oppose including gays and lesbians in an employment nondiscrimination act and who rally for a homophobic defense of marriage act to write more laws that will affect how, whether, and which representations of queer sexuality are disseminated. Moreover, I do not believe that all pornography or representations of sadomasochism are equal or mean the same thing.

2. Hoeveler reads Dworkin as being at the end of a long line of Gothic feminists who "suggest in their writings that they hate their flesh" (246); this is an example of the conflation of those who are designated as "Gothic feminists" with that which they expose/analyze (in this case, the hatred of female flesh). Even if one buys this reading of Dworkin (which I do not), it seems imperative to put it into dialogue with Dworkin's emphasis on masculine culture's power over, and abuse of, female bodies.

3. Moers is responsible for coining the term "female Gothic." Later feminist critics of the Gothic have built upon Moers' throwaway line. Michelle Massé's, *In the Name of Love: Women, Masochism and the Gothic* devotes a chapter to *Story of O.* As Massé puts it, "The depiction of explicitly genital sexual practice which is pornography's metier can be simply a difference in degree, not in kind, from the Gothic's more genteel abuse" (108). In *Art of Darkness: A Poetics of Gothic*, Anne Williams argues that the "line between Male Gothic and pornography is not easy to draw" (106).

In *Gothic Feminism,* Hoeveler comments, "At many points *Udolpho* reads like sanitized pornography, as if Radcliffe had traced over all the monotonous sex in the Marquis de Sade and substituted extended descriptions of the landscape or the chase around the castle as more exciting" (100).

4. William Patrick Day, too, notes that "the pattern of all relationships in the Gothic fantasy . . . operates on the dynamic of sadomasochism" (19).

5. There is now, of course, a compelling body of scholarship that reads sadomasochism as a sexual play with power rather than a crystallization of gender hierarchy. Tania Modleski has sagely noted that the meaning of sadomasochism cannot be divorced from its context and participants. See her discussion in *Feminism without Women,* esp. 148–57.

6. My discussion of Helene Deutsch and Marie Bonaparte is indebted in great part to Kate Millett's work in *Sexual Politics.* For a related discussion of Freud and Deutsch, see Lynn Chancer, *Sadomasochism in Everyday Life,* 127–28.

7. See Spark's *Curriculum Vitae,* 138–39, for discussion of her relationship with Bonaparte. Most pertinent here is Spark's remembrance that "[w]e discussed literature, which she, having been a prominent pupil of Sigmund Freud, approached from a psychological point of view—something quite new to me. I was intrigued, but I felt it left too much unsaid" (138).

8. For other views on the relationship between psychoanalysis and the Gothic, see Williams, esp. 239–248; Judith Halberstam, *Skin Shows: Gothic Horror and the Technology of Monsters,* 8; William Patrick Day, *In the Circles of Fear and Desire,* esp. 177–190; Mark Edmundson, *Nightmare on Main Street,* esp. 32–36, 125–29; and Jerrold E. Hogle, "The Gothic and the 'Otherings' of Ascendant Culture: The Original *Phantom of the Opera,*" esp. 822–26. Massé uses the structure of Freud's beating fantasy to organize her study of the Gothic, *In the Name of Love.*

9. As Marc O'Day points out, "The title switch between the British and American editions, from *Shadow Dance* to *Honeybuzzard,* reflects a shift of attention from the supporting cast to the monster himself" (27). My reading of this novel refocuses attention on one member of the "supporting cast," Morris.

10. Dworkin, *Pornography: Men Possessing Women,* 84. Dworkin situates Carter in a long line of Sadeian apologists.

11. Keenan reads *The Sadeian Woman* as a "reaction to the mythicization

of female virtue" (139). Obviously, I think that argument—as well as the one about intervening in nascent critical debates—holds for *Honeybuzzard* as well. Perhaps significantly, although Keenan notes Carter's use of sexual violence in several texts, she does not mention *Honeybuzzard*. That omission may be due to the assumption, discussed in the next paragraph, that Carter's pre-'68 work is not of feminist interest.

12. In "The Dangers of Angela Carter," Jordan reviews and counters the critical history that reads Carter as a reproducer of patriarchal consciousness.

13. For a provocative theoretical challenge to the concept of male identification, see Judith Butler, *Gender Trouble*, esp. 30.

14. For a fascinating story of the vanquishing rather than the taming of a male sadist, see Carter's "Bloody Chamber."

15. See Susan Griffin, *Pornography and Silence: Culture's Revenge against Nature,* and Jessica Benjamin, "Master and Slave: The Fantasy of Erotic Domination."

16. In *Pornography and Silence*, Griffin argues that "the sadomasochistic ritual demands the invulnerability of the sadist and the vulnerability of the masochist" (48).

17. See Claire Kahane, "The Gothic Mirror." Lorna Sage, in her introduction to *Flesh and the Mirror*, writes that Carter reported in interviews that "houses stood in for mothers" (6).

18. For a discussion of the matricidal tendencies of Western culture, see Luce Irigaray, "Body against Body: In Relation to the Mother."

19. See Robin Ann Sheets, "Pornography, Fairy Tales, and Feminism," esp. 653–54, for a discussion of "the mother as sexual subject" in Carter's "The Bloody Chamber." Like Sage, Aidan Day reads Emily as "the new order that displaces the old reality" (20). In contrast, Linden Peach finds nothing redemptive about Emily, "who manifests her failure to develop the imaginary" (39). Peach reads Carter's work, especially her early work, as in dialogue with the "Euro-American Gothic" tradition (which he unselfconsciously charts as a wholly male tradition) and with Fiedler's *Love and Death in the American Novel*. Such literary and critical frames may help to explain his assessment of Emily.

20. Gamble continues, "but the elaborate mythology which is built up

around Ghislaine tends to obscure the fact that she has done very little, if anything at all, to deserve it. . . ." (55). This statement is consistent with Gamble's view of this novel as exemplifying Carter's pre-'68 "patriarchal bias." I tend to agree with Lee's assessment that, from the start of her career, Carter positions her reader to be an active and responsible interpreter: "Reading Carter's works is always an active process, and this equal exchange between reader and text finally allows new formulations to arise from the old" (11).

21. In *The Sadeian Woman*, Carter foregrounds the cultural equation of the female body with the wounded body: "The whippings, the beatings, the gougings, the stabbings of erotic violence reawaken the memory of the social fiction of the female wound, the bleeding scar left by her castration, which is a psychic fiction as deeply at the heart of Western culture as the myth of Oedipus, to which it is related in the complex dialectic of imagination and reality that produces culture. Female castration is an imaginary fact that pervades the whole of men's attitudes toward women and our attitude to ourselves, that transforms women from human beings into wounded creatures who were born to bleed" (23).

22. As Griffin provocatively puts it, "All the elements of sadomasochistic ritual are present in the crucifixion of Christ." See Griffin, *Pornography and Silence*, 68–69.

23. Aidan Day makes a similar point: Honeybuzzard's "cast of mind has been formed by a culture oppressive to women which is shot through with the attitudes of religious patriarchy" (16).

24. See the afterword to Carter's *Fireworks: Nine Profane Pieces*, 122.

25. *The Ballad of Peckham Rye* (1960) and *Not to Disturb* (1971) are among the violent plots authored by Spark. Many of her early short stories also end in violence; a particularly interesting example is "The Portobello Road."

26. Lise's masochistic contriving of her murder should be distinguished from Rebecca's purported desire for death at Maxim's hands. If Maxim was correct in surmising that "Rebecca wanted me to kill her" (374), we need to remember that she would have been trying to preserve and reinforce her carefully constructed subversive identity in anticipation of the ravages of terminal cancer. Unlike Lise, Rebecca's primary mode of seeking recognition as a subject is not through victimization.

27. Ruth Whittaker uses this term in her discussion of the novel.

28. Spark lived in Rhodesia from 1937 through 1944. This reference may well be a commentary on Southern African white women.

29. Spark has a flair for creating wonderful old women. *Memento Mori* is full of such characters; Lady Edwina in *Loitering with Intent* is another marvelous example.

30. Judy Sproxton comments that Lise "repudiates Bill's advances, implying that she has no interest in sex. Since Bill professes to be merely concerned that he should keep up with his regime of a daily orgasm, his warmth towards her is hardly likely to change her attitude" (141). Thus Sproxton implies that Mr. Right might. Although Sproxton includes her discussion of *The Driver's Seat* in a chapter titled "Women as Victims," she reads Lise's story as an individual case history and concludes that "Lise's morbidity demonstrates the horror of the negative use of free will" (144). Such critical framing seems to reflect her view that "Spark is not a feminist in the sense that she asserts specific rights for women, nor is she interested in decrying a society which might seek to repress women" (18).

31. In the Frankel interview, Spark asserts, "That's the most difficult part of a novel: finding the tone, deciding who the unseen, invisible narrator is, and what role he's going to play for this particular book. You've got to consider then the theme, and what type of narration will best fit that theme and technique. I've got to think about this quite a lot before I begin" (454).

32. Relevant here is Massé's point that "by producing the script of the beating fantasy or a Gothic plot, the script writer works to assure her own agency" (47).

33. I use the word "stigmata" purposefully here. Although I would not want to overemphasize this idea, Lise does strike me as a false Christ figure.

34. Joanna Russ notes that popular Gothics feature detailed descriptions of women's clothing. She sees this convention as inextricably connected to the readership of these Gothics—housewives, who, among many other things, "shop for clothing for themselves and their children" (39). Here women's fashion represents masochistic norms of femininity and emphasizes the importance of (female) appearance. The issue of confused identity that results in Willa's death in *Casualties of Peace* is also effected through clothing, in that case a fur coat, a fetishized object of female consumption obtained through hunting for prey.

35. Lise's view constitutes an interesting though extremely problematic defensive strategy—by asserting that women who get killed actively pursue

that fate, Lise refuses to recognize the ways in which female victimization compromises female autonomy. Thus Spark posits an extremely sophisticated rationale for *women* believing in female masochism.

36. I suspect that Spark has some fun with these seating arrangements. Richard on the right and Bill on the left suggests the thieves that flank Christ at Calvary. Of course, the man on the right would be Lise's "type."

37. Alan Bold points out Spark's subtle depiction of rape: "Readers aware of Spark's meticulous attention to language will realize that her pun on 'plunges' makes it plain that the murderer ignores Lise's request to desist from sexual penetration" (94). Margaret Moan Rowe, in her *Dictionary of Literary Biography* article on Spark, also mentions "the rape-murder" of Lise.

38. Thus I disagree with Lee when she writes that "the tragedy is offset only slightly by Emily's saving herself" (11).

Chapter 5

Paranoia Will Destroy You, or Will It?

1. The mid- to late '80s saw the rise of the "rough sex" defense in cases where men had killed intimate partners. According to Alan Dershowitz, "The she-asked-for-it defense doesn't work anymore. . . . So now we're hearing she demanded it" (qtd. in Lacayo and Goldberg 55).

2. I would argue that those who talk about "victim feminism" (an oxymoron if ever there were one) miss this crucial distinction.

3. In Philip Roth's 1984 interview, O'Brien makes it clear that Joyce has been a significant force on her literary imagination: "In the constellation of geniuses, he is a blinding light and father of us all. . . I came to read *Ulysses*, but as a young girl I balked because it was really too much for me, it was too inaccessible and too masculine, apart from the famous Molly Bloom section. I now think *Ulysses* is the most diverting, brilliant, intricate and unboring book that I have ever read. I can pick it up at any time, read a few pages and feel that I have just had a brain transfusion" (39). O'Brien's novel *Night* (1972) is generally regarded as a monologue indebted to Joyce's Molly.

4. Such threats echo the plight of Wollstonecraft's Maria.

5. Although Russ describes the popular Gothics she studies as "a kind

of justified paranoia," she suggests that such texts dissuade women readers from any sort of feminist systemic analysis: "*Something* is trying to hurt me or tear me down—but I don't know what it is. I suspect it's my man, or men in general, but that's an unthinkable thought" (52).

6. It seems to me that Johnson's accomplishment in this novel is to acknowledge the double jeopardy (racism and sexism) that Black women have historically endured; Johnson also demonstrates the complicity of white, middle-class women in racist systems of exploitation. In the early to mid '70s, such race consciousness on the part of a white author seems exemplary. However, from the vantage point of the '90s and in the wake of Paula Gidding's brilliant work on the ways in which Black women have redefined femininity [see *When and Where I Enter: The Impact of Black Women on Race and Sex in America* (1984)], Johnson's limited, tragic view of the Black woman should be noted and problematized.

7. In an interview, Johnson legitimizes N.'s view of the world by echoing her own creation: "Men don't want to hear about maternal despera- tion" (Bell interview 127). Ironically, a review of this novel by Karyl Roosevelt demonstrates that such resistance to the demystification of moth- erhood is widespread and not necessarily gender-specific. Writes Roosevelt, "We are not told, for instance, why she was incapable of taking care of her children during her marriage. Her husband points out that she couldn't even keep house, let alone take care of the children" (7). Johnson is well aware of this review. "I was very interested in the fact that the things [Roosevelt] most objected to were in fact the most literal depictions of what I take to be very common aspects of female life" (Bell interview 132). One can only wish four children or a course in women's studies for Ms. Roosevelt.

8. Both Rubenstein and Melley, who discuss this novel in terms of paranoia and normative gender relations, have nothing to say about dis- courses of race in the text. This is perhaps a sign that *The Shadow Knows*— with all of its acknowledged limitations--still has much to teach feminist criticism about racialized womanhood.

9. The autobiographical nature of such material should be noted: in an interview with Larry McCaffery, Johnson asserts that the characters of both Ev and Osella are based on real women who worked for her and that Osella's prototype did go mad during the time she worked for Johnson's household (213).

10. Joanna Russ, in her study of popular Gothics, finds that "the heroine does nothing except worry; any necessary detective work is done by other persons" (35). Obviously, this trend contrasts sharply with the strand of the

contemporary female Gothic highlighted here.

11. Chell, too, subscribes to this view. According to her, N. "solves the crime, at least to her own satisfaction" (167). However, Joan Henley, author of "Re-forming the Detective Story: Diane Johnson's *The Shadow Knows*" would seem to disagree. According to her, N. finds "nothing tangible" (91) from playing detective. Of course, this critical disagreement is inextricably connected with the question of N.'s reliability. Johnson comments in the Bell interview that "The narrator in *The Shadow Knows* was intended as an exact and trustworthy reporter of what was happening to her" (127). Significantly, Johnson believes that readers and reviewers often erroneously stereotype female narrators of childbearing age as unreliable.

12. Similarly, Henley comments, "In fact, where the traditional detective story moves toward a resolution of all of the problems and relationships explored, *The Shadow Knows* ends in a mystification and complication of events and characters" (91).

13. Millett uses this term to describe Madame Beck in Charlotte Brontë's *Villette* (201).

14. As Melley points out, "there might be a theoretical advantage to being unable to pin one's persecution on an individual—since the problem may stem not from a single, deviant individual, but from a larger set of social institutions, narratives and conditions" (83). Thus Melley reads N.'s rape at the end by an anonymous man as performing this "theoretical advantage" (see 95–96).

15. Rubenstein reads N.'s response to being raped as representative: "It is generally true of the novels of female paranoia that the characters anticipate and imagine the worst and are thus grateful when only somewhat less terrible events befall them: N. perversely finds her assault almost a relief, having expected to be murdered, not 'merely' raped" ("Bodily Harm" 143).

16. For a much more pessimistic reading of N.'s position at the end, see O'Donnell. According to him, "N's shadowy transformation in the novel's concluding pages is only the obverse of Osella's presence on the stage. Theatricalized or underground, star or paranoid, these strange women are precisely placed" (204). See also his comments on 201–2. Chell, on the other hand, reads the ending as further evidence that N. engages in "active refusal to be a victim" (167).

17. While Johnson asserts that she wrote this scene "lightly" before she

understood the politics of rape, she also notes in her interview with McCaffery that she wanted to put into play the possibility that Inspector Dyce was the rapist (212). Reading the ending through Johnson's comments on her lack of feminist consciousness about rape, Showalter suggests that "the rape is N's punishment for breaking the rules, for protesting and making trouble, for going to graduate school instead of working for the telephone company" (143).

18. This essay served as the epilogue to the 1981 volume *Feminist Theory: A Critique of Ideology*.

Chapter 6

The Perils of Postfeminism

1. In a later essay entitled "Feminism, Postfeminism, and Contemporary Women's Fiction," Rosenfelt offers the following, slightly revised definition: postfeminism is a word used to "connote not the death of feminism but its uneven incorporation and revision inside the social and cultural texts of a more conservative era. The term, read analogously to terms like *postmodernist* or *postrevolutionary*, acknowledges the existence of a world and a discourse that have been fundamentally altered by feminism" (269).

2. Edmundson uses the term "anti-Gothic Gothic" affirmatively. According to him, "we stop being victims, Gothic victims, when we say that everything that has happened to us was for the best, and that we wouldn't have had it any other way. Once you've told that lie, and it is a lie, you put yourself in a position to reveal new truths, in that what you do in the present and future is unchained from the past. You're not trying to undo past traumas anymore" (153–54). Thus Edmundson's anti-Gothic Gothic is, to my mind, exemplary of the dangerous denial tendencies that I analyze here in relation to postfeminism.

3. Indeed, Deborah Siegel as well as the editors of *Third Wave Agenda* use the label "postfeminist" to describe Denfeld, Roiphe, and Wolf, writers whom I discuss in my introduction as part of the Gothic feminism phenomenon.

4. Rosenfelt indicates that postfeminist texts evince little clarity about what can be done to counter gendered inequities. My focus on Cardozo as a representative postfeminist social critic indicates my disagreement with Rosenfelt on this point. Postfeminists *do* have solutions; however, their

strategies tend to be neither collective nor sensitive to racial and class inequities.

5. Greene also discusses the individualist tendencies of postfeminism (194).

6. See Judith Butler, *Bodies that Matter*, esp. 221–22; Tania Modleski, *Feminism Without Women*; Susan Bordo, *Unbearable Weight*, esp. "Feminism, Postmodernism and Gender Skepticism" and "Postmodern Subjects, Postmodern Bodies, Postmodern Resistance"; Mohanty and Alexander, "Introduction: Genealogies, Legacies, Movements," esp. xvii; hooks, "Postmodern Blackness," in *Yearning*.

7. "Unwittingly" is a key word here, as it indicates why I think postfeminism merits serious scholarly attention. Susan Faludi argues that "the backlash is not a conspiracy, nor are the people who serve its ends often aware of their role; some even consider themselves feminists" (xxi–xxii). As if echoing Faludi, Modleski writes that postfeminism is distinct from other types of backlash in that it "has been carried out not against feminism but in its very name" (*Feminism Without Women* x). Thus postfeminists can and should be distinguished from antifeminists by intention if not by the ends they serve. Rosi Braidotti neatly distinguishes between the myth of "Woman" and embodied female subjects in her formulation that "feminists are the post-Woman women" (169).

8. For a full discussion of this scandal, see "A Sad Joyce Carol Oates Forswears Pseudonyms" (*New York Times*, 2 February 1987, rptd. in *Conversations with Joyce Carol Oates*). Oates also discusses this debacle and her desire for a "new identity" in a 1988 interview with David Germain. See also her literary essay "Pseudonymous Selves" [*New York Times Book Review*, December 1987, rptd. in *(Woman) Writer: Occasions and Opportunities*]; Oates discusses the burdens of "fame's carapace" in this essay. Interestingly enough, this pseudonym connects her to her husband, Raymond Smith, without whom she would "be a little disturbed," or so she says (Weldon interview 163).

9. In 1989, Oates also published *American Appetites*, a work that explicitly explores the violence contained in, and unleashed by, the institution of marriage. It should also be noted that Oates's literary appropriation of popular genres does *not* begin with her debut as Rosamond Smith. Indeed, in writing *Bellefleur* (1980), *A Bloodsmoor Romance* (1982), and *Mysteries of Winterthurn* (1984), Oates consciously attempted to view America "through the prismatic lens of its most popular genres" ("Five Prefaces" 373).

10. Thus I disagree with Creighton who finds it "rather odd" that Dorothea identifies with Colin and who reads the psychopath's dark energy as that "which contrasts starkly with [Dorothea's] own genuine 'purity of conscience or soul'" (87).

11. This feature of the text recalls John Fowles's *The Collector* (1963). *Soul/Mate*'s shift from Dorothea's point of view to Colin's parallels *The Collector*'s alternating between Clegg's thoughts and Miranda's. Furthermore, Colin shares with Clegg obsessions about social exclusion as well as passive-aggressive patterns of thought and behavior. As one reviewer points out, the acute respiratory difficulties that Dorothea suffers during her stay at Land's End suggest Miranda's demise.

12. The astute reader will no doubt note that Agnes, too, vies for the role of Bertha. Although, as I argue a few pages from now, Agnes does double for Dorothea, Colin's criminal activity on Dorothea's behalf more closely resembles Bertha's actions (e.g., the attack on Mason, the rending of the veil, etc.).

13. For a discussion of the homosocial continuum and the relationship between homosociality and homosexuality, see Eve Kosofsky Sedgwick, *Between Men: English Literature and Male Homosocial Desire,* esp. 1–5.

14. Land's End is perhaps a parodic allusion to Marsh End, the place where Jane Eyre finds her family, economic independence, and a very modest proposal from St. John Rivers.

15. I am indebted to Mimi Czarnik for this observation.

16. Thus, in contrast to Diane Hoeveler, I see "professional femininity" as a response to—and a strategy to deal with—the very real double bind (with often material consequences) that attends female/feminist assertiveness.

17. Susan Faludi argues, "A backlash against women's rights succeeds to the degree that it appears *not* to be political, that it appears not to be a struggle at all. It is most powerful when it goes private, when it lodges inside a woman's mind and turns her vision inward, until she imagines the pressure is all in her head, until she begins to enforce the backlash, too—on herself" (xxii).

18. Although Creighton notes that the romantic plot of Charles and Dorothea "work[s] out, after all, rather conveniently," she is quick to point out that "neither of them is implicated in Colin's madness" (89). Obviously, my reading is fundamentally at odds with that view.

19. At one point, Dorothea looks at Colin and identifies him with the son she miscarried. Thus the creator-created relationship so central to the Frankenstein myth is superficially put into play. Like Frankenstein's monster, Colin blames his destructive behavior on being excluded from society and forced to live alone. Additionally, variants of "angel boy" serve as epithets for Colin; like Colin, the monster is cast as a fallen angel.

20. Such double-voicedness is related to the pronounced critical disagreement about Oates's feminism. Creighton indicates that while early in her career, Oates resisted identification as a "woman writer," her later work is concerned with "exploring with incisive scrutiny her heritage as a woman and as a woman writer" (57). Following Showalter's charge that Oates has not had the feminist attention she deserves, Wesley contends that "Oates' domestic fiction does not . . . render the effects of gender ideology external to itself, or fully 'visible'; what her literary treatment does instead is to express rather than repress the questions that challenge its limits" (151).

21. Both Greene and Rosenfelt discuss the nostalgic dimensions of postfeminism.

Chapter 7

Beyond Postfeminism: Revaluing the Female Body and the Body Politic

1. As the title of her article indicates, Elaine Tuttle Hansen's "Fiction and (Post)Feminism in Atwood's *Bodily Harm*" also discusses the postfeminist thematics of this novel. Hansen seems to define postfeminism as the attitude that feminism is passé. Although she criticizes that attitude, she suggests that even as the novel validates a feminist conversion experience, it challenges the "durability" of a vision of female "identification" and "solidarity"; thus there may be a double edge to her use of postfeminism. Hansen does not read *Bodily Harm* in the context of the Gothic, and while privileging the doctor-patient script, she is not concerned with the politics of St. Antoine and Rennie's national identity.

2. For a reading of *Bodily Harm* that emphasizes "spatial and temporal alienation," see Lorna Irvine, "The Here and Now of *Bodily Harm*."

3. Bouson reads the grandmother's plight here less sympathetically than I do: "Plotting against the grandmother who victimized Rennie, the novel finds an appropriate punishment for this unfeeling woman" (121).

4. See Massé, 88–93, for a discussion of the concept of overvaluation and a critique of Freud's work on that concept. Of particular relevance here is Massé's comment that "the reverse possibility—that the subordinated may ascribe strengths to the dominant that the latter don't have, or may even define the dominant through their fealty—is hardly considered as a possibility, particularly within a heterosexual frame" (89). It is only at the end of the novel that Rennie recognizes that men's bodies are no less permeable than women's.

5. Bouson argues similarly: "Intensely cathected, the contaminated, fragmented body part—the fetishized breast—is equated not only with female mutilation and narcissistic wounding by the phallic knife of the 'probers' and 'cutters,' but also with the sexually contaminated and contaminating female body which is censored and punished by phallocentric culture" (119).

6. Hansen reads Rennie's response here not as a lack of imagination but as the beginning of feminist consciousness: "Her ostensibly unfair response . . . signals her emerging recognition that power and violence underlie sexuality in our culture and are only barely disguised by the romantic myths of masculine and feminine, rescuer and victim, doctor and patient" (14–15).

7. Of course, the question of the female spectator has been a theoretical snafu in film theory since Laura Mulvey's 1975 essay "Visual Pleasure and Narrative Cinema." By including an epigraph from John Berger, *Ways of Seeing*, a precursor to Mulvey's work, Atwood implicitly engages with such issues. Indeed, *Bodily Harm* stresses not only the possibility of, but also the necessity for, women constituting themselves as active, seeing subjects. For a poetic look at the type of gaze Atwood deems desirable, see her prose poem "Instructions for the Third Eye" in *Murder in the Dark*. I will return to Atwood's use of Berger later in this chapter.

8. In "Writing the Male Character," Atwood, referring to Minnow, asserts that "the good man [in *Bodily Harm*] is black" and thus has been overlooked by male critics who claim she is unfair in her portrayal of men.

9. For a related discussion of Paul, see Rubenstein 129–30. Rubenstein, too, is attentive to Paul's doubling function; however, she sees him and Rennie's attachment to him in a much more positive light than I do: "[T]he very fact that he accepts the 'missing place' naturally allows her to begin to accept herself and allow the severed parts of herself to come together again" (130).

10. Such imagery seems indebted to that which Rankin employs in her

collection *Mud Hut*. For additional information on the connection between Rankin and Atwood, see Judith Rodriguez's introduction in Rankin's *Collected Poems*.

11. *Survival* is Atwood's introduction to Canadian literature. Although the victim positions she outlines there are nationalist ones, she as well as others readily applies this schema to women. See, for example, Atwood's comments in the Davidson interview, esp. 94, as well as "Mathews and Misrepresentation," 145.

12. Rubenstein also attends to this doubling relationship. However, she focuses on Lora's embodiment of victimization (see esp. 268, 273) and does not, as I do, read her also as a double for Rennie's complicity.

13. Such a gendered double standard is echoed in poststructuralist critiques of essentialism. Writes Roland Martin, "[I]n this chilly climate we came to judge women's scholarship by a harsher standard than the one we applied to men's" (631).

14. Significantly, although Lora cannot imagine life without sexual abuse, she refuses to play pornographic games; says she, "I once knew this guy who wanted to tie me to the bedpost. No way, I said. You want to tie somebody up, I've got a few suggestions, but you're not starting with me" (270).

15. Rubenstein makes a similar argument about this faceless entity: "When she looks into the face of evil she sees that everyone is a complicitor; there is no escape. . . . [S]he is condemned by the fact of being alive, guilty of being human, despite her protestations of innocence (272). Obviously, I emphasize here Rennie's denial and squandering of her privilege.

16. Atwood emphasizes the necessity of such distinctions in the Lyons interview: ". . . sexual kink and violence. For us, it's just that, underground sexual kink. In other countries it is a political instrument, an instrument of control. It's not something weird sadists and porn fanciers do; it's something governments do to keep them under control" (227). Also relevant here is that in *The Handmaid's Tale*, the demise of the pornomarts signals the beginning of the theocratic Republic of Gilead. Aware that pornography is fundamentally a script of domination and submission, Atwood nevertheless would object to any position approaching censorship.

17. Several critics comment on this birth imagery; see, for example, Rigney 112–13, Hansen 17, and Irvine 98.

18. I am indebted to Jones (93) for this point.

19. Atwood explicitly makes this point in "Amnesty International: An Address": "We in this country should use our privileged position not as a shelter from the world's realities but as a platform from which to speak. Many are denied their voices; we are not. A voice is a gift; it should be cherished and used" (396).

20. In *Survival*, the preferred victim position is "to acknowledge the fact that you are a victim but to refuse to accept the assumption that the role is inevitable" (37). In *Bodily Harm*, it seems to me that Atwood fictionally revises her understanding of this position to admit the paradox that members of victimized groups are often simultaneously members of an oppressor class—that is, that the identity of victim is dynamic and relative rather than essential and fixed.

21. In the introduction to part 3 of *Second Words*, Atwood raises this issue: "We sometimes forget, in our obsession with colonialism and imperialism, that Canada itself has been guilty of these stances toward others, both inside the country and outside it" (282).

22. For a discussion of narcissism in Atwood's work in general and in *Bodily Harm* in particular, see Bouson, esp. 10–11 and 118–19.

23. Atwood reductively uses the term "American feminists" to describe those "white middle-class American women who say they are all women" (Gerald and Crabbe interview 139). Significantly, Atwood finds that such feminists are antagonistic to her nationalist concerns.

Epilogue:

Toward Feminisms without Demons

1. Material on the "Yorkshire Ripper" has been culled from the following sources: Lucy Bland, "The Case of the Yorkshire Ripper: Mad, Bad, Beast, or Male?" in Radford and Russell, 233–52; Joan Smith, "There's Only One Yorkshire Ripper" in *Misogynies*, 163–205; Judith Walkowitz, *City of Dreadful Delight*, 229–45.

Works Cited

Alcoff, Linda. "Cultural Feminism versus Post–Structuralism: The Identity Crisis in Feminist Theory." *Signs* 13.3 (1988): 405–36.

Alexander, M. Jacqui, and Chandra Talpade Mohanty. "Introduction: Genealogies, Legacies, Movements." *Feminist Genealogies, Colonial Legacies, Democratic Futures*. Ed. Alexander and Mohanty. New York: Routledge, 1997. xiii-xlii.

Anzaldúa, Gloria. *Borderlands: La Frontera*. San Francisco: Aunt Lute, 1987.

Atwood, Margaret. "Amnesty International: An Address." *Second Words* 393–97.

———. *Bodily Harm*. 1982. Toronto: Bantam, 1983.

———. "Defying Distinctions." Interview with Karla Hammond. Ingersoll 99–108.

———. "An End to Audience?" *Second Words* 334–57.

———. "Evading the Pigeonholers." Interview with Gregory Fitz Gerald and Kathryn Crabbe. Ingersoll 131–39.

———. "Mathews and Misrepresentation." *Second Words* 129–50.

———. "On Being a 'Woman Writer': Paradoxes and Dilemmas." *Second Words* 190–204.

———. "Playing Around." Interview with J. R. (Tim) Struthers. Ingersoll 58–68.

———. "A Question of Metamorphosis." Interview with Linda Sandler. Ingersoll 40–57.

———. *Second Words: Selected Critical Prose.* Boston: Beacon, 1984.

———. *Survival: A Thematic Guide to Canadian Literature.* Toronto: Anansi, 1972.

———. "Travels Back." *Second Words* 107–13.

———. "Using Other People's Dreadful Childhoods." Interview with Bonnie Lyons. Ingersoll 221–33.

———. "Where Were You When I Really Needed You." Interview with Jim Davidson. Ingersoll 86–98.

———. "Witness Is What You Must Bear." Interview with Beatrice Mendez–Egle. Ingersoll 162–70.

———. "Writing the Male Character." *Second Words* 412–30.

———. Interview. With Jan Garden Castro. *Margaret Atwood: Visions and Forms.* VanSpanckeren 215–32.

Bainbridge, Beryl. *The Bottle Factory Outing.* 1974. New York: Signet, 1976.

———. Interview. With Barbara A. Bannon. *Publishers Weekly* 209.11 (1976): 6–7. Rpt. in *The Author Speaks: Selected PW Interviews 1967–1976.* New York: Bowker, 1977. 11–12.

———. Interview. With Yolanta May. *New Review* 3.33 (1976): 48–52.

Barnicle, Mike. "Behind the Killing that Shook Boston." *San Francisco Examiner* 11 Jan. 1990: A1+.

———. "Chuck Stuart's Family Talked of the Murder." *San Francisco Examiner* 11 Jan. 1990: A20.

Belsey, Catherine. "Constructing the Subject: Deconstructing the Text." Warhol and Herndl 657–73.

Benjamin, Jessica. "Master and Slave: The Fantasy of Erotic Domination." Snitow 280–99.

Berger, John. *Ways of Seeing*. London: BBC, 1972.

Bersani, Leo. "Pynchon, Paranoia, and Literature." *Representations* 25 (1989): 99–118.

Bland, Lucy. "The Case of the Yorkshire Ripper: Mad, Bad, Beast, or Male?" Radford and Russell 233–52.

Bold, Alan. *Muriel Spark*. London: Methuen, 1986.

Bolotin, Susan. "Voices from the Post–Feminist Generation." *New York Times Magazine* 17 Oct. 1982: 28.

Bonaparte, Marie. *Female Sexuality*. New York: International UP, 1953.

Bordo, Susan. *Unbearable Weight: Feminism, Western Culture and the Body*. Berkeley: U of California P, 1993.

Botting, Fred. *Gothic*. New York: Routledge, 1996.

Bouson, J. Brooks. *Brutal Choreographies: Oppositional Strategies and Narrative Design in the Novels of Margaret Atwood*. Amherst: U of Massachusetts P, 1993.

Braidotti, Rosi. *Nomadic Subjects: Embodiment and Sexual Difference in Contemporary Feminist Theory*. New York: Columbia UP, 1994.

Brontë, Charlotte. *Jane Eyre*. Ed. Jane Jack and Margaret Smith. Oxford: Oxford UP, 1969.

Brownmiller, Susan. *Against Our Will: Men, Women and Rape*. 1975. Toronto: Bantam, 1976.

Broyard, Anatole. Rev. of *I Hardly Knew You*, by Edna O'Brien. *New York Times Book Review* 1 Jan. 1978: 12.

Bruhm, Steven. *Gothic Bodies: The Politics of Pain in Romantic Fiction*. Philadelphia: U of Pennsylvania P, 1994.

Butler, Judith. *Bodies that Matter: On the Discursive Limits of "Sex."* New York: Routledge, 1993.

———. *Gender Trouble: Feminism and the Subversion of Identity*. New York: Routledge, 1990.

Cameron, Deborah, and Elizabeth Frazer. *The Lust to Kill: A Feminist Investigation of Sexual Murder.* New York: New York UP, 1987.

Caputi, Jane. *The Age of Sex Crime.* London: The Women's Press, 1988.

Cardozo, Arlene Rossen. *Sequencing.* New York: Atheneum, 1986.

Carter, Angela. Afterword. *Fireworks: Nine Profane Pieces.* By Carter. London: Quartet, 1974. 121–22.

———. *The Bloody Chamber and Other Stories.* New York: Penguin, 1979.

———. *Honeybuzzard.* New York: Simon, 1966.

———. "Notes from the Front Line." *On Gender and Writing.* Ed. Michelene Wandor. London: Pandora, 1983. 69–77.

———. *The Sadeian Woman and the Ideology of Pornography.* New York: Pantheon, 1978.

Chancer, Lynn S. *Sadomasochism in Everyday Life: The Dynamics of Power and Powerlessness.* New Brunswick: Rutgers UP, 1992.

Chell, Cara. "Marriage as Metaphor: The Novels of Diane Johnson." *Portraits of Marriage in Literature.* Ed. Anne Hargrove and Maurine Magliocco. Macomb: Essays in Lit., 1984. 159–69.

Chodorow, Nancy. *The Reproduction of Mothering: Psychoanalysis and the Sociology of Gender.* 1978. Berkeley: U of California P, 1979.

Christian, Barbara. "The Highs and Lows of Black Feminist Criticism." Warhol and Herndl 51–56.

———. "The Race for Theory." *Making Face, Making Soul: Haciendo Caras.* Ed. Gloria Anzaldúa. San Francisco: Aunt Lute, 1990. 335–45.

Collins, Patricia Hill. *Black Feminist Thought: Knowledge, Consciousness, and the Politics of Empowerment.* New York: Routledge, 1991.

Combahee River Collective. "A Black Feminist Statement." *This Bridge Called My Back: Writings by Radical Women of Color.* Ed. Cherríe Moraga and Gloria Anzaldúa. Watertown, MA: Persephone Press, 1981. 210–18.

Cott, Nancy F. *The Grounding of Modern Feminism*. New Haven: Yale UP, 1987.

Creighton, Joanne V. *Joyce Carol Oates: Novels of the Middle Years*. New York: Twayne, 1992.

Daly, Mary. *Gyn/Ecology: The Metaethics of Radical Feminism*. Boston: Beacon, 1978.

———. *Outercourse: The Be-Dazzling Journey*. San Francisco: Harper, 1992.

Davis, Angela Y. *Women, Race & Class*. 1981. New York: Vintage, 1983.

Day, Aidan. *Angela Carter: The Rational Glass*. New York: Manchester UP, 1998.

Day, William Patrick. *In the Circles of Fear and Desire: A Study of Gothic Fantasy*. Chicago: U of Chicago P, 1985.

de Beauvoir, Simone. *The Second Sex*. 1953. Trans. and ed. H. M. Parshley. New York: Vintage, 1974.

DeLamotte, Eugenia C. *Perils of the Night: A Feminist Study of Nineteenth–Century Gothic*. Oxford: Oxford UP, 1990.

de Lauretis, Teresa. "The Technology of Gender." *Technologies of Gender*. Bloomington: Indiana UP, 1987.

———. "Upping the Anti (Sic) in Feminist Theory." Warhol and Herndl 326–39.

Denfeld, Rene. *The New Victorians: A Young Woman's Challenge to the Old Feminist Order*. New York: Warner, 1995.

Derrida, Jacques. "Choreographies." With Christie V. McDonald. *Diacritics* 12 (1982): 66–76.

———. "The Law of Genre." *Acts of Literature*. Ed. Derek Attridge. New York: Routledge, 1992. 221–52.

———. *Positions*. Trans. Alan Bass. Chicago: U of Chicago P, 1981.

Deutsch, Helene. *The Psychology of Women: A Psychoanalytic Interpretation*. New York: Grune, 1944. Vol. 1.

Di Stefano, Christine. "Dilemmas of Difference: Feminism, Modernity, and Postmodernism." Nicholson 63–82.

Doane, Janice, and Devon Hodges. "Undoing Feminism: From the Preoedipal to Postfeminism in Anne Rice's Vampire Chronicles." *American Literary History* 2.3 (1990): 422–42.

Donovan, Josephine. *Feminist Theory: The Intellectual Traditions of American Feminism*. New York: Ungar, 1987.

Dufresne, Martin. "Focus on the Gynocide in Montreal." *Between the Lines*. 18–31 Jan. 1990: 10–11.

du Maurier, Daphne. *Rebecca*. 1938. New York: Avon, 1971.

Durant, David. "Ann Radcliffe and the Conservative Gothic." *SEL* 22 (1982): 519–30.

Dworkin, Andrea. *Intercourse*. New York: Free, 1987.

———. *Pornography: Men Possessing Women*. New York: Perigee, 1981.

———. *Woman Hating*. New York: Dutton, 1974.

Echols, Alice. *Daring to Be Bad: Radical Feminism in America 1967–1975*. Minneapolis: U of Minnesota P, 1989.

———. "The New Feminism of Yin and Yang." Snitow 439–59.

Eckley, Grace. *Edna O'Brien*. Lewisburg: Bucknell UP, 1974.

Edmundson, Mark. *Nightmare on Elm Street: Angels, Sadomasochism, and the Culture of the Gothic*. Cambridge: Harvard UP, 1997.

Eisenstein, Hester. *Contemporary Feminist Thought*. Boston: Hall, 1983.

Ellis, Kate Ferguson. *The Contested Castle: Gothic Novels and the Subversion of Domestic Ideology*. Urbana: U of Illinois P, 1989.

Faludi, Susan. *Backlash: The Undeclared War against American Women*. New York: Crown, 1991.

Felski, Rita. *Beyond Feminist Aesthetics: Feminist Literature and Social Change*. Cambridge: Harvard UP, 1989.

Fiedler, Leslie A. *Love and Death in the American Novel*. New York: Criterion, 1960.

"59% Call Massacre Only Random Act, Poll Finds." *Toronto Star* 29 Dec. 1989: A4.

Flax, Jane. "Postmodernism and Gender Relations in Feminist Theory." Nicholson 39–62.

"For Women Only." *Chronicle–Journal* 9 Dec. 1989: 16.

Foucault, Michel. "The Functions of Literature." *Politics, Philosophy and Culture: Interviews and Other Writings 1977–84*. Ed. Lawrence D. Kritzman. Trans. Alan Sheridan. New York: Routledge, 1988. 307–13.

Fraser, Nancy, and Linda J. Nicholson. "Social Criticism without Philosophy: An Encounter between Feminism and Postmodernism." Nicholson 19–38.

Freccero, Carla. "Notes of a Post–Sex Wars Theorizer." Hirsch and Keller 305–25.

Freud, Sigmund. "The Economic Problem in Masochism (1924)." *Collected Papers*. Vol. 2. London: Hogarth, 1949. 255–68.

Frye, Marilyn. "Willful Virgin or Do You Have to Be a Lesbian to Be a Feminist." *Willful Virgin*. Freedom, CA: Crossing P. 124–37.

Fuss, Diana. *Essentially Speaking: Feminism, Nature and Difference*. New York: Routledge, 1989.

Gallop, Jane, Marianne Hirsch, and Nancy K. Miller. "Criticizing Feminist Criticism." Hirsch and Keller 349–69.

Gamble, Sarah. *Angela Carter: Writing from the Front Line*. Edinburgh: Edinburgh UP, 1997.

Giddings, Paula. *When and Where I Enter: The Impact of Black Women on Race and Sex in America*. 1984. Toronto: Bantam, 1985.

Gilbert, Sandra M, and Susan Gubar. *The Madwoman in the Attic: The Woman Writer and the Nineteenth–Century Literary Imagination*. New Haven: Yale UP, 1979.

————. *The War of the Words.* Vol. 1 of *No Man's Land: The Place of the Woman Writer in the Twentieth Century.* New Haven: Yale UP, 1988.

Gordon, Margaret T., and Stephanie Riger. *The Female Fear.* New York: Free, 1989.

Grant, Judith. *Fundamental Feminism: Contesting the Core Concepts of Feminist Theory.* New York: Routledge, 1993.

Greene, Gayle. *Changing the Story: Feminist Fiction and the Tradition.* Bloomington: Indiana UP, 1991.

Griffin, Susan. *Pornography and Silence: Culture's Revenge against Nature.* New York: Harper, 1981.

————. "The Way of All Ideology." *Feminist Theory: A Critique of Ideology.* Ed. Nannerl Keohane, Michelle Z. Rosaldo, and Barbara C. Gelpi. Chicago: U of Chicago P, 1982. 273–92.

Grosz, Elizabeth. *Volatile Bodies: Toward a Corporeal Feminism.* Bloomington: Indiana UP, 1994.

Gubar, Susan. "Representing Pornography: Feminism, Criticism, and Depictions of Female Violation." *For Adult Users Only: The Dilemma of Violent Pornography.* Ed. Susan Gubar and Joan Hoff. Bloomington: Indiana UP, 1989.

Halberstam, Judith. *Skin Shows: Gothic Horror and the Technology of Monsters.* Durham: Duke UP, 1995.

Hansen, Elaine Tuttle. "Fiction and (Post)Feminism in Atwood's *Bodily Harm.*" *Novel* 19 (1985): 5–21.

Haynes, Muriel. "What Evil Lurks. . . ." Rev. of *The Shadow Knows,* by Diane Johnson. *Ms.* Nov. 1974: 37+.

Hays, Constance L. "Husband of Slain Boston Woman Becomes a Suspect, Then a Suicide." *New York Times* 5 Jan. 1990: 1+.

Heller, Tamar. *Dead Secrets: Wilkie Collins and the Female Gothic.* New Haven: Yale UP, 1992.

Henley, Joan. "Re–forming the Detective Story: Diane Johnson's *The Shadow Knows.*" *Clues* 9.1 (1988): 87–93.

Heywood, Leslie, and Jennifer Drake. Introduction. *Third Wave Agenda: Being Feminist, Doing Feminism*. Ed. Leslie Heywood and Jennifer Drake. Minneapolis: U of Minnesota P, 1997. 1–20.

Hirsch, Marianne, and Evelyn Fox Keller, eds. *Conflicts in Feminism*. New York: Routledge, 1990.

Hoeveler, Diane Long. *Gothic Feminism: The Professionalization of Gender from Charlotte Smith to the Brontës*. University Park: Pennsylvania UP, 1998.

Hogle, Jerrold E. "The Gothic and the 'Otherings' of Ascendant Culture: The Original *Phantom of the Opera*." *South Atlantic Quarterly* 95 (1996): 821–46.

Homans, Margaret. "'Women of Color' Writers and Feminist Theory." Warhol and Herndl 406–21.

hooks, bell. *Feminist Theory: From Margin to Center*. Boston: South End Press, 1984.

———. *Outlaw Culture: Resisting Representations*. New York: Routledge, 1994.

———. "Postmodern Blackness." *Yearning: Race, Gender, and Cultural Politics*. Boston: South End P., 1990. 23–31.

Horner, Avril, and Sue Zlosnik. *Daphne du Maurier and the Gothic Imagination*. New York: St. Martins P. 1998.

Horney, Karen. "The Problem of Feminine Masochism." *Feminine Psychology*. New York: Norton, 1967. 215–33.

Howard, Jacqueline. *Reading Gothic Fiction: A Bakhtinian Approach*. New York: Oxford, 1994.

Ingersoll, Earl G., ed. *Margaret Atwood: Conversations*. Princeton: Ontario Review, 1990.

Irigaray, Luce. "Body against Body: In Relation to the Mother." *Sexes and Genealogies*. Trans. Gillian C. Gill. New York: Columbia UP, 1993. 7-21.

———. *This Sex Which Is Not One*. Trans. Catherine Porter. Ithaca: Cornell UP, 1985.

Irvine, Lorna. "The Here and Now of *Bodily Harm*." VanSpanckeren 85–100.

Johnson, Diane. *The Shadow Knows*. 1974. New York: Fawcett Crest, 1988.

———. Interview. With Susan Groag Bell. *Women Writers of the West Coast: Speaking of Their Lives and Careers*. Ed. Marilyn Yalom. Santa Barbara: Capra, 1983. 123–37.

———. Interview. With Larry McCaffery. *Anything Can Happen: Interviews with Contemporary American Novelists*. Ed. Thomas LeClair and Larry McCaffery. Champaign: U of Illinois P, 1983.

———. Interview. With Janet Todd. *Women Writers Talking*. Ed. Janet Todd. New York: Holmes & Meier, 1983. 121–32.

Jones, Dorothy. "'Waiting for the Rescue': A Discussion of Margaret Atwood's *Bodily Harm*." *Kunapipi* 6 (1984): 86–100.

Jordan, Elaine. "The Dangers of Angela Carter." *New Feminist Discourses*. Isobel Armstrong. New York: Routledge, 1992. 119–31.

Kahane, Claire. "The Gothic Mirror." *The (M)other Tongue: Essays in Feminist Psychoanalytic Interpretation*. Ed. Shirley Nelson Garner, Claire Kahane, and Madelon Sprengnether. Ithaca: Cornell UP, 1985. 334–51.

Kaminer, Wendy. "Feminism's Identity Crisis." *Atlantic Monthly* Oct. 1993. 51–68.

Keenan, Sally. "Angela Carter's *The Sadeian Woman*: Feminism as Treason." *The Infernal Desires of Angela Carter: Fiction, Femininity, Feminism*. Ed. Joseph Bristow and Trev Lynn Broughton. New York: Longman, 1997.

Kelly, Liz. *Surviving Sexual Violence*. Minneapolis: U of Minnesota P, 1988.

Kiely, Robert. *The Romantic Novel in England*. Cambridge: Harvard UP, 1972.

Kilgour, Maggie. *The Rise of the Gothic Novel*. New York: Routledge, 1995.

Lacayo, Richard, and Barbara Goldberg. "The Rough–Sex Defense." *Time* 23 May 1988: 55.

Lee, Alison. *Angela Carter*. New York: Twayne, 1997.

Lester, Lee, and Tracy Nesdoly. "'Propaganda' Blamed." *Toronto Sun* 8 Dec. 1989: 99.

Lorde, Audre. "Man Child: A Black Lesbian Feminist's Response." *Sister Outsider* 72-80.

———. "An Open Letter to Mary Daly." *Sister Outsider* 66-71.

———. *Sister Outsider*. Freedom, CA: The Crossing Press Feminist Series, 1984.

Malette, Louise, and Marie Chalouh, eds. *The Montreal Massacre*. Trans. Marlene Wildeman. Charlottetown, Prince Edward Island: Gynergy Books, 1991.

Malmsten, Eric, ed. "Aftermath of the Montreal Tragedy: Quotes in Newspapers about Feminism and Men." A Report for Metro Men against Violence. n.d.

Martin, Jane Roland. "Methodological Essentialism, False Difference, and Other Dangerous Traps." *Signs* 19 (1994): 630–57.

Massé, Michelle A. *In the Name of Love: Women, Masochism and the Gothic*. Ithaca: Cornell UP, 1992.

McCaughey, Martha. *Real Knockouts: The Physical Feminism of Women's Self Defense*. New York: New York UP, 1997.

McDermott, Patrice. "On Cultural Authority: Women's Studies, Feminist Politics, and the Popular Press." *Signs* 20 (1995): 668–84.

McDowell, Edwin. "A Sad Joyce Carol Oates Forswears Pseudonyms." Milazzo 147–48.

McMillan, Ann. "The Transforming Eye: *Lady Oracle* and Gothic Tradition." VanSpanckeren 48–64.

Melley, Timothy. "Stalked by Love: Female Paranoia and the Stalker Novel." *Differences* 8.2 (1996): 68–100.

Meyers, Helene. "To Queer or Not to Queer: That's Not the Question." *College Literature* 24.1 (1997): 171–82.

Milazzo, Lee, ed. *Conversations with Joyce Carol Oates*. Jackson: UP of Mississippi, 1989.

Millard, Barbara C. "Beryl Bainbridge." *Dictionary of Literary Biography*. Ed. Jay Lottalio. Detroit: Gale, 1983. Vol. 14, pt. 1.

Miller, Nancy, et al. "Criticizing Feminist Criticism." *Conflicts in Feminism* 349-69.

Millett, Kate. *Sexual Politics*. 1970. New York: Ballantine, 1978.

Mitchell, Juliet. *Psychoanalysis and Feminism*. New York: Pantheon, 1974.

Modleski, Tania. *Feminism Without Women: Culture and Criticism in a "Postfeminist" Age*. London: Routledge, 1991.

———. *Loving with a Vengeance*. Hamden: Archon, 1982.

Moers, Ellen. *Literary Women*. 1976. New York: Oxford UP, 1985.

Moi, Toril. *Sexual/Textual Politics: Feminist Literary Theory*. London: Methuen, 1985.

Moraga, Cherríe. "A Long Line of Vendidas." *Loving in the War Years*. Boston: South End Press, 1983. 91–142.

Nicholson, Linda J, ed. *Feminism/Postmodernism*. New York: Routledge, 1990.

O'Brien, Edna. *Casualties of Peace*. London: Cape, 1966.

———. "A Conversation with Edna O'Brien: 'The Body Contains the Life Story.'" With Philip Roth. *New York Times Book Review* 18 Nov. 1984: 38+.

———. *I Hardly Knew You*. Garden City: Doubleday, 1978.

———. Interview with Nell Dunn. *Talking to Women*. Ed. Nell Dunn. Bristol: MacGibbon, 1965. 69–107.

O'Brien, Peggy. "The Silly and the Serious: An Assessment of Edna O'Brien." *Massachusetts Review* 28 (1987): 474–88.

Oates, Joyce Carol. "Author Tells Where She's Been, Where She's Going." Interview with David Germain. Milazzo 173–80.

———. "Five Prefaces." Oates, *(Woman) Writer* 365–82.

———. "Frankenstein's Fallen Angel." Oates, *(Woman) Writer* 106–22.

———. "*Jane Eyre*: An Introduction." Oates, *(Woman) Writer* 123–37.

———. "Making Readers Want Novels Is Writer's Hardest Job." Interview with Michele Weldon. Milazzo 161–63.

———. "Pseudonymous Selves." Oates, *(Woman) Writer* 383–97.

——— [Rosamund Smith]. *Soul/Mate*. New York: Dutton, 1989.

———. *(Woman) Writer: Occasions and Opportunities*. New York: Dutton, 1989.

O'Day, Mark. "'Mutability Is Having a Field Day': The Sixties Aura of Angela Carter's Bristol Trilogy." *Flesh and the Mirror: Essays on the Art of Angela Carter*. Ed. Lorna Sage. London: Virago P, 1994. 24–58.

O'Donnell, Patrick. "Engendering Paranoia in Contemporary Narrative." *Boundary 2* 19.1 (1992): 181–204.

"Overreacting." *Chronicle–Journal* 8 Dec. 1989: A4.

Paglia, Camille. *Sexual Personae: Art and Decadence from Nefertiti to Emily Dickinson*. New Haven: Yale UP, 1990.

Patai, Daphne, and Noretta Koertge. *Professing Feminism: Cautionary Tales from the Strange World of Women's Studies*. New York: Basic Books, 1994.

Peach, Linden. *Angela Carter*. London: MacMillan, 1998.

Pitt, David E. "Canada Unnerved by Slayings of 14." *New York Times* 9 Dec. 1989: A5.

Radcliffe, Ann. *The Mysteries of Udolpho*. 1794. Oxford: Oxford UP, 1966.

Radford, Jill, and Diana E. H. Russell. *Femicide: The Politics of Woman Killing*. New York: Twayne, 1992.

Radway, Janice. "The Utopian Impulse in Popular Literature: Gothic Romances and 'Feminist' Protest." *American Quarterly* 33 (1981): 140–62.

Rankin, Ian. "Surface and Structure: Reading Muriel Spark's *The Driver's Seat*." *Journal of Narrative Technique* 15 (1985): 146–55.

Restuccia, Frances L. "Female Gothic Writing: 'Under Cover to Alice.'" *Genre* 18 (1986): 245–66.

Rich, Adrienne. "Compulsory Heterosexuality and Lesbian Existence." Snitow 177–205.

———. "Notes toward a Politics of Location (1984)." *Blood, Bread, and Poetry: Selected Prose, 1979-1985*. New York: Norton, 1986. 210-31.

Rigney, Barbara Hill. *Margaret Atwood*. London: MacMillan Education, 1987.

Robinson, Lillian R. "Killing Patriarchy: Charlotte Perkins Gilman, the Murder Mystery, and Post–Feminist Propaganda." *Tulsa Studies in Women's Literature*. 10 (1991): 273–85.

Rodriguez, Judith. Introduction. *Collected Poems*. By Jennifer Rankin. Ed. Judith Rodriguez. Queensland, Australia.: U of Queensland P, 1990. xi–xxxi.

Roiphe, Katie. *The Morning After: Sex, Fear and Feminism on Campus*. Boston: Little, Brown, 1993.

Roosevelt, Karyl. Rev. of *The Shadow Knows*, by Diane Johnson. *New York Times Book Review* 22 Dec. 1974: 6–7.

Rosenfelt, Deborah. "Feminism, 'Postfeminism,' and Contemporary Women's Fiction." *Tradition and the Talents of Women*. Ed. Florence Howe. Urbana: U. of Illinois P, 1991. 268–91.

Rosenfelt, Deborah, and Judith Stacey. "Second Thoughts on the Second Wave." *Feminist Studies* 13.2 (1987): 341–61.

Rowe, Margaret Moan. "Muriel Spark." *Dictionary of Literary Biography*. Ed. Jay Lottalio. Detroit: Gale, 1983. Vol. 15, pt. 2.

———. "Muriel Spark and the Angel of the Body." *Critique: Studies in Modern Fiction* 28 (1987): 167–76.

Rubenstein, Roberta. "Bodily Harm: Paranoid Vision in Contemporary Fiction by Women." *LIT* 1 (1989): 137–49.

———. "Pandora's Box and Female Survival: Margaret Atwood's *Bodily Harm*." *Critical Essays on Margaret Atwood*. Ed. Judith McCombs. Boston: Hall, 1988. 259–75.

Rumens, Carol. Introduction. *Making for the Open: The Chatto Book of Post–Feminist Poetry 1964–1984*. Ed. Rumens. London: Hogarth, 1985. xv–xviii.

Russ, Joanna. "Somebody's Trying to Kill Me and I Think It's My Husband: The Modern Gothic." *The Female Gothic*. Ed. Juliann Fleenor. Montreal: Eden, 1983.

Russo, Mary. "Notes on 'Post–Feminism.'" *The Politics of Theory*. Proceedings of the Essex Conference on the Sociology of Literature. July 1982. Ed. Francis Barker, et al. Colchester: University of Essex, 1983. 27–37.

Sage, Lorna. *Angela Carter*. Plymouth, UK: Northcote House, 1994.

———. Introduction. *Flesh and the Mirror: Essays on the Art of Angela Carter*. Ed. Lorna Sage. London: Virago, 1994.

Scott, Joan W. "Experience." *Feminists Theorize the Political*. Ed. Judith Butler and Joan W. Scott. 22–40.

Sedgwick, Eve Kosofsky. *Between Men: English Literature and Male Homosocial Desire*. New York: Columbia UP, 1985.

———. *The Coherence of Gothic Fictions*. 1980. New York: Methuen, 1986.

Sedgwick, John. "A Case of Wife Murder." *Esquire* June 1990: 199–205.

Segal, Lynne. *Is the Future Female? Troubled Thoughts on Contemporary Feminism*. New York: Peter Bedrick, 1988.

———. *Straight Sex: The Politics of Pleasure*. London: Virago, 1994.

Sheets, Robin Ann. "Pornography, Fairy Tales and Feminism." *Journal of the History of Sexuality* 1.4 (1991): 633–57.

Showalter, Elaine. *Sister's Choice: Tradition and Change in American Women's Writing*. New York: Oxford UP, 1991.

Siegel, Deborah L. "Reading between the Waves: Feminist Historiography in a 'Postfeminist' Moment." *Third Wave Agenda: Being Feminist, Doing Feminism*. Ed. Leslie Heywood and Jennifer Drake. Minneapolis: U of Minnesota P, 1997. 55–82.

Smith, Joan. "There's Only One Yorkshire Ripper." *Misogynies: Reflections on Myths and Malice*. New York: Fawcett Columbine, 1992. 163–209.

Smith, Valerie. "Black Feminist Theory and the Representation of the 'Other.'" Warhol and Herndl 311–25.

Snitow, Ann. "A Gender Diary." Hirsch and Keller 9–43.

Snitow, Ann, Christine Stansell, and Sharon Thompson, eds. *Powers of Desire: The Politics of Sexuality.* New York: Monthly Review, 1983.

Sommers, Christina Hoff. *Who Stole Feminism? How Women Have Betrayed Women.* New York: Simon and Schuster, 1994.

Spark, Muriel. *Curriculum Vitae: Autobiography.* Boston: Houghton Mifflin, 1993.

———. *The Driver's Seat.* 1970. New York: Perigee, 1984.

———. "An Interview with Muriel Spark." With Sarah Frankel. *Partisan Review* 54.3 (1987): 443–57.

Spivak, Gayatri Chakravorty. "Three Women's Texts and a Critique of Imperialism." *Critical Inquiry* 12 (1985): 243–61.

Sproxton, Judy. *The Women of Muriel Spark.* London: Constable, 1992.

Stone, Laurie. "Trigger–Happy." *Village Voice* 26 Dec. 1989: 23.

Sunstein, Emily W. *A Different Face: The Life of Mary Wollstonecraft.* Boston: Little, 1975.

Taylor, Verta, and Leila J. Rupp. "Women's Culture and Lesbian Feminist Activism: A Reconsideration of Cultural Feminism." *Signs* 19 (1993): 32–61.

Todorov, Tzvetan. *The Fantastic.* Ithaca: Cornell UP, 1975.

VanSpanckeren, Kathryn, and Jan Garden Castro, eds. *Margaret Atwood: Visions and Forms.* Carbondale: Southern Illinois UP, 1988.

Walkowitz, Judith R. *City of Dreadful Delight: Narratives of Sexual Danger in Late–Victorian London.* Chicago: U of Chicago P, 1992.

———. "Male Vice and Female Virtue: Feminism and the Politics of Prostitution in Nineteenth–Century Britain." Snitow 419–38.

Warhol, Robyn R., and Diane Price Herndl, eds. *Feminisms: An Anthology of*

Literary Theory and Criticism. Rev. Ed. New Brunswick: Rutgers UP, 1997.

Wesley, Marilyn C. *Refusal and Transgression in Joyce Carol Oates' Fiction*. Westport, CT: Greenwood, 1993.

Whittaker, Ruth. *The Faith and Fiction of Muriel Spark*. New York: St. Martin's, 1982.

Will, George. "Gothic Feminism Creates Victims." *Austin–American Statesman* 24 Oct. 1993.

Williams, Anne. *Art of Darkness: A Poetics of Gothic*. Chicago: U of Chicago P, 1995.

Wolf, Naomi. *Fire With Fire: The New Female Power and How It Will Change the 21st Century*. New York: Random House, 1993.

Wollstonecraft, Mary. *Maria or The Wrongs of Woman*. 1798. New York: Norton, 1975.

Woodward, Richard B. "Edna O'Brien: Reveling in Heartbreak." *New York Times Magazine* 12 March 1989: 42+.

Index

agency, 50, 84, 94, 128, 145, 150, 154

agency, female, xii, 6, 14, 23, 87, 88, 134, 155; and masochism, 81, 171n. 32

aggression, 87

Alcoff, Linda, 8, 10, 113, 159n. 7

Alexander, Jacqui, 22, 176n. 6

ambivalence, 56; maternal, 68, 100; *See also* Gothic, ambivalence in

antifeminism, xi, 85, 128, 155, 176n. 7; *See also* Gothic feminism

Antiromantic narratives, 57

Atwood, Margaret, 141; *Bodily Harm*, 1, 19, 21, 22, 23, 117–18, 134–52, 154–55, 163n. 6; *Survival*, 180n. 11, 181n. 20

backlash, 63, 89, 110, 129, 176n. 7, 177n. 17; *See also* postfeminism, and back-lash

Bainbridge, Beryl, xii, 20, 47, 56, 81; *The Bottle Factory Outing*, 19, 20, 23, 40, 47–57, 60, 73, 76, 107, 137, 154

Barry, Kathleen, 163n. 10

Benjamin, Jessica, 68, 169n. 15

Berger, John, 151

Bersani, Leo, 89, 90

binary oppositions, 8, 12, 89; reversals of, 11

Blankley, Elyse, 102

Bold, Alan, 76, 172n. 37

Bolotin, Susan, 118

Bonaparte, Marie, 61, 62–63, 80, 84, 168nn. 6, 7

Bordo, Susan, 7, 13, 121, 157n. 3, 159n. 16, 176n. 6

Botting, Fred, 17, 161n. 30, 162n. 3, 163n. 5

Bouson, J. Brooks, 137, 144, 146, 150, 178n. 3, 179n. 5, 181n. 22

Braidotti, Rosi, 176n. 7

Brontë, Charlotte; *Jane Eyre*, 18, 32–34, 105, 121, 124, 130

Brownmiller, Susan, 117

Broyard, Anatole, 97, 100

Bruhm, Steven, 163n. 6

Butler, Judith, xi, 87, 121, 155, 160n. 17, 162n. 36, 166n.